SIX BATTLES FOR INDIA

The Anglo-Sikh Wars: 1845-6, 1848-9

GEORGE BRUCE

SAPERE BOOKS

SIX BATTLES
FOR INDIA

Published by Sapere Books.
20 Windermere Drive, Leeds, England, LS17 7UZ,
United Kingdom

saperebooks.com

Copyright © The Estate of George Bruce, 1969.
First published by Arthur Barker Limited, 1969.
The Estate of George Bruce has asserted their right to be identified as the author of this work.
All rights reserved.

No part of this publication may be reproduced, stored in any retrieval system, or transmitted, in any form, or by any means, electronic, mechanical, photocopying, recording, or otherwise, without the prior written permission of the publishers.

ISBN: 978-1-80055-043-8.

Table of Contents

Part One: The First Anglo-Sikh War, 1845-6	7
1: Farewell	8
2: Sikhism	12
3: Ranjit Singh	29
4: Militarization	48
5: Murder	68
6: War	85
7: Mudki	114
8: Ferozeshur	137
9: Treason	170
10: Aliwal	183
11: Sobraon	201
12: Victory	214
Part Two: The Second Anglo-Sikh War, 1848-9	231
13: Rebellion	232
14: Edwardes	258
15: Dalhousie	275
16: Failure	293
17: Multan	310
18: Chillianwalla	330
19: Gujerat and The Seizure	350

Note on Wounds	375
Author's Note	378
Selected Bibliography	379
Acknowledgement	383

Part One: The First Anglo-Sikh War, 1845-6

1: Farewell

General Sir Hugh Gough gave a ball at the military outpost of Ambala, northern India, on the night of the tenth of December, 1845. As usual, the officers' scarlet and blue uniforms laced with silver and gold, outshone the ladies' sombre crinolines, as they danced to waltzes played with more vigour than melody by the band of the 3rd Light Dragoons. The music, the ritual and the pleasure of such gatherings inevitably awoke memories of England, but perhaps never more poignantly than on this particular night, when tension and excitement among the men, regret and fear among the women, would have been so much felt.

The British Empire was rising, the 'forward' policy ruled again in India after its temporary eclipse, and though nobody, in those days of the stiff upper lip, would have dreamed of saying so, it was a farewell ball. They danced on the brink of war, for the men were to march at dawn and it was an open secret that the move heralded the long-expected clash with the warlike Sikhs. General Gough, the commander-in-chief in India, had been methodically preparing for more than a year.

Experienced, but oft-criticised was Sir Hugh Gough. This warm-hearted, white-haired Irishman aged sixty-six, with the stamina of a cavalry charger, had fought in more battles than any other British officer living, except the Duke of Wellington. And Gough still loved fighting, invariably taking his place in the thick of the battle, conspicuous in his white 'fighting coat'. His detractors said that he was always too eager to get at and destroy the 'inimy'. And that the smell of gunpowder drove him to such a pitch of excitement that all his strategy and tactics were forgotten in the urge for cold steel and the irresistible infantry charge. If it was true, his bold tactics had succeeded in the past — at Talavera, where Wellington had promoted him on the field to Lieutenant-Colonel, when he was only twenty-eight; at Barossa, at Nivelle, and, more recently, as commander-in-chief of the expeditionary force in China. So Gough brought an aura of success with him to this war looming with the Sikhs.

Nevertheless, the strength and size of the Sikh forces in relation to his own readiness had for long worried him and for months he had tried to reinforce his forward troops at the outpost of Ferozepore. But Sir Henry Hardinge, the Governor-General of India, unwilling to add to the East India Company's financial troubles, had refused to pass Gough's plans. Ineffectually trying to avoid war, he had stubbornly thwarted him, once countermanding his movement orders that would even the balance with the Sikh forces near the frontier. 'I have ample to cut the Sikhs in pieces, but they are not in hand, as they should be,' Gough confessed in an anxious letter to his son.

Only too well justified were Gough's suspicions of the Sikhs. For unknown to him, this very night, while he and his officers were dancing at Ambala, the Sikh army had burst out of the Punjab and was crossing the river Sutlej to cut off General Sir John Littler's small force at Ferozepore. No doubt, the 3rd Light Dragoons would have sounded more peremptory tunes than waltzes on their trumpets had Gough heard of this invasion while dispensing the hospitality he loved.

War between British and Sikh had threatened once before. It had been averted at the last moment by their former leader, Maharajah Ranjit Singh. This ruler of genius with one dark glittering eye, an insatiable lust for women and a passion for raw spirit laced with meat-juice and opium, had tried in 1809 to push his dominions across the Sutlej as far south as Ambala. The British had moved up an army from Delhi and, under this threat, Ranjit had withdrawn, signing a treaty stipulating that neither power would henceforward move an army across the river. Friendship between the two countries had thereafter held good for thirty-six years, until Ranjit — Lion of the Punjab, as both friends and enemies called him — died aged fifty-nine.

The smoke from his funeral pyre was the signal for anarchy. During the six years after his death, murder ended the lives of all who sat the throne except the boy maharajah, Prince Duleep Singh. From the boy's nymphomaniac mother, the Maharani Jindan, the unruly Sikh army, the Khalsa, then seized power and clamoured for war with the British. The sword was a symbol of the Sikh religion and for years the more far-sighted British had predicted trouble with this nation whose urge to expand was equalled only by their own. And now the moment had come. The Khalsa, the strongest army raised in Asia, had crossed the Sutlej to challenge British rule in India.

So it was that wives and sweethearts in the cold early morning at Ambala said last farewells to menfolk they might never see alive again. With red and white plumes streaming from their tall shakoes, the 3rd Light Dragoons, in dark blue tunics, rode off along the first of the one hundred and forty miles of sandy track that passed for the road to Ferozepore. The advance party of the division that expected to reinforce this outpost already cut off, they were followed by the 4th and 5th regiments of Native Cavalry, a sea of brown faces, brilliant turbans and heavy black moustaches.

General Gough was still unaware that the Sikhs had embarked on war. Not until next day did he set off with the rest of the division's three British and five Indian infantry regiments, with three troops of Horse Artillery, the troopers' great brass helmets gleaming in the sun, their gun carriages rattling.

Thus the British went to war, five thousand miles from their homeland. Many of them would never see its green fields again, but they went with an extraordinary light-heartedness. 'At daybreak reveille sounded, and we all formed up in front of the barracks, gave three cheers… and then set out on our march, the band playing of course, "The Girls We Left Behind Us",' wrote Lieutenant Sandford to his sisters in England.

Their light-heartedness stemmed from faith in themselves, in their army and in their Almighty God. God was on the side of Right, and that meant England. The Sikhs were strong, but the Redcoats believed themselves invincible, when led by good officers. Colours flying, drums beating, the invincible army marched westwards over the sandy plains. They knew that ex-officers of Napoleon's Grand Army and a remarkable American soldier of fortune, Colonel Alexander Gardner, had drilled and trained the Sikh army to make it a match for the British or any other. But probably no one, from Gough to the humblest foot soldier doubted that they would crush 'those Sikh rascals' or 'them Saikhs', as officers and men each liked to call them.

2: Sikhism

The Punjab, called Land of the Five Rivers, is a geographical entity often described as shaped like a triangle formed by the Indus flowing first from south-east to north-west and then, changing course suddenly, from north-east to south-west to form two sides. The Sutlej, flowing almost from east to west forms the base. In the north-east the Punjab contains Kashmir and is separated from Tibet by the Himalayas. Beyond the Indus to the north-west it is bounded by the rugged Sulaiman and Hindu Kush mountain ranges, cleft by the Kyber, Bolan and Gomal passes through which from time to time during the centuries have poured the invaders from Persia and Afghanistan.

Five great rivers — the Jhelum, Chenab, Ravi, Beas and Sutlej — rise in the Himalayas and flow in a south-westerly direction nine hundred miles across a great flat plain, until finally, one by one all unite with the Indus. The stretches of land between these rivers are called *doabs* — 'beggars' mantles fringed with gold'. Modern irrigation has since changed the land's character, but in 1845, where the precious water lapped the rich alluvial soil, the peasant harvested sugar, maize and cotton, yet beyond, the sparse soil nourished only thornbush and tamarisk, from which the goat and the camel eked a little nourishment.

Fed in summer by the melting snows, the five rivers poured their great swirling masses of water into the hungry Indus. During June, July and August, when they were in flood, steep banks made them formidable obstacles to an army on the march. Bitter cold in winter, scorching heat in summer is the main climate of the Punjab plains, creating sharply contrasting seasons and a landscape that changes dramatically. Spring, in February, mild and temperate, brings the first harvests, but the heat increases day by day until by the end of April onwards:

> The temperature rises to a fever heat. The parched earth becomes an unending stretch of khaki with dust devils spiralling across the wastes. Even the stolid *pipal* and the tamarisk are shorn of their leaves and the only green that meets the eye are bushes of camel-thorns, prickly cactus and the *ak* ... The succession of hot days and shimmering mirages is occasionally broken by fierce storms which spread layers of dust over everything... On moonlit nights one can see the wavering arrow-head formations of geese honking their way northwards to the snowy Himalayas.[1]

In the rainy season, from July to September, the heat is still great, though slowly lessening and cooled somewhat by the incessant torrents. Rivers become great rolling avalanches of water and the land almost a swamp.

Rain and rivers give life to the Punjab, but the Sutlej runs like a central thread of silver through the tapestry of the First Anglo-Sikh War. Throughout the whole violent epic it is a recurrent theme. It dominated the policies of the British rulers in London and Calcutta who steered the course of relations between the Sikhs and British India, it ruled the strategy and tactics of the military commanders, it was for both sides the rubicon, the very cause of war. It shone between clumps of bamboo and acacia during the cavalry charges and the artillery duels. Within sight of it both armies slept at night. From it, morning and evening, they watered thousands of horses,

---

[1] *A History of the Sikhs*: Kushwant Singh.

elephants and camels. For many officers and men, British and Sikh, it was the grave.

The Punjab, of which it forms the southern border, was densely forested up to the end of the sixteenth century. Before and during the nineteenth century it was inhabited by three main races, Jats, Rajputs and Afghans, or Pathans. The Jats, who were the backbone of the peasantry, traditionally warriors who wore their swords while they ploughed their lands, were of Aryan descent, mark of one of the earliest invasions of the Punjab, about 1500 BC. The main access route to India for invaders from the north-west, the country became unendingly a battlefield and a new home for successive conquerors. The Persians led by Darius occupied the northern Punjab around 500 BC, until in 326 BC, Alexander the Great's Greek forces subdued them and marched on to the banks of the Beas, to be subdued in their turn by the Mauryans, who were overcome by the Bactrians and these by the Scythians. Chandragupta, a Hindu raja, then established the Gupta Empire in central and northern India, held the passes against invaders and enabled his descendants to rule peacefully for several centuries, only to be subdued in AD 500 by the flood of White Huns from Central Asia. A White Hun chief, Toramana, ruled the Punjab in the year 465, until his forces were finally driven out by Vardhana, raja of Thanesar, around 600. Vardhana's son Harsha, last great Indian ruler of the Punjab, succeeded him and extended his empire throughout the whole of northern India. Shortly after his death his forces were defeated by Tibetan armies, his empire disintegrated, the north-west passes became the terror of the Punjab and Muslim invaders swept in from the north-west.

The Afghan, Mahmud of Ghazni, tore down into the Punjab in AD 1001 and ruled it from afar until his death in 1030. The

Punjab and India were free from foreign invasion for nearly fifty years, but then followed the long, battering succession of Afghan, Mongol and Turkish invasions, culminating in 1398 in the merciless onrush of Timur, whose dynasty ruled until it was succeeded by the Afghans in 1451, leading to the arrival of the Emperor Babul from Kabul in 1526, and the eventual creation of the Mughal Empire throughout India in the mid-sixteenth century by the great Akbar Khan.

Thus had the land of the five rivers been an invaders' playground. Carefree, land-hungry warriors sacked villages and temples, looted granaries, drove off herds, raped women, and when powerful enough stayed to settle. The land became a home for successive waves of invading Turks, Afghans and Mongols, whose blood intermingled through the centuries with that of the older Jat peasantry and the Rajputs. Such a savage tide was bound to have its effects. Old and new languages and social customs interacted, creating the beginnings of both a new tongue, a new consciousness and a new people, the Punjabi.

Only the amalgam of a new liberating religious movement was needed to cause these often disparate elements to combine. It came with Sikhism.

Baba Nanak, the founder of the Sikh religion, was born in 1469, some twenty-one years after the first Europeans, the Portuguese, led by Vasco da Gama, first set foot in India. At this time, the conflicting religious beliefs of Muslim, Hindu, Buddhist and Jain still retarded the growth of Punjabi nationalism and the military urge that culminated in the rule of the Maharajah Ranjit Singh. But the pain and terror of the savage Muslim repression of Sikhism would in time change the nature of Nanak's gentle creed.

Seemingly a precocious boy, Nanak is said to have sought the company of holy men when aged only five. Following local custom, he was married when twelve, began living with his wife when nineteen and eventually had two sons. Soon, he turned aside from worldly things and became a disciple of the poet and mystic Kabir (1440-1518), who preached the new monotheistic doctrine of *bhakti*, based on the challenging teachings of the eleventh-century Hindu saint Ramanuja, that God was One and that the way to him was by meditation under the guidance of a guru or teacher. *Bhakti* was greatly influenced by the Sufi Islamic mystics and their preaching of religious toleration, human brotherhood and social equality, as well as fasting and meditation with the aim of mystical union with God.

Profoundly affected by these earlier teachers, and by Kabir, Nanak himself had mystical experiences during meditation and believed himself called upon by God to teach in his name the fundamental truth of all religions — social equality, good conduct and an end to religious conflict and idolatry. The brotherhood he formed, named Sikhs, or disciples, was based simply on two fundamental principles: the unity of God and the brotherhood of man, without distinction of race, class or creed.

Nanak added a new way of life: the then challenging ritual of communal eating in the house of the guru, with the followers taking turns to help in the kitchen — prayers, and the singing of hymns that he wrote in Punjabi, the mother tongue, instead of in Sanskrit or Arabic, the languages of Hinduism and Islam — a new form of greeting that ignored the traditional ones of the two old religions. In the social and religious context of fifteenth century India these liberating rituals and beliefs were in effect revolutionary, especially in the ears of low caste

Hindus of the Jat peasantry. They brought in a flood of followers.

Great reformer and teacher though he was, when the old faiths were jealously defended, Nanak yet caused little hostility, and when he died in 1539 there arose a dispute among Muslims and Hindus about whose rites should be administered at his funeral. Largely, this acceptance was the outcome of his own character — gentleness, goodness, lack of austerity — his preference for the good example instead of moral denunciations or attacks as a means of influencing others. The burden of his teaching was not strife, but peace among men. What a paradox that it led to the growth of the most soldierly race in India. How did this happen?

Nanak's torch was handed on — not without petty strife and discord — to one guru and another, all of whom contributed as they were able to the movement's growth. The fourth, Arjun (1563-1606), a fine poet and a gifted organizer who compiled in Punjabi the teaching of Nanak and his successors into the Sikh sacred book, the Adi Granth, was the first to cultivate the beginnings of political orientation. He built the Golden Temple, the Harimandir, with a sacred pool beside it, and around grew a city, Amritsar (the pool of nectar). Amritsar became the Sikhs' sacred place of pilgrimage. The Emperor Akbar helped the Sikhs, Arjun became a renowned leader, the religion and its followers of real importance. In a significant passage that shows the avowed religious feelings of the Sikhs, Arjun wrote:

> I do not keep the Hindu fast, nor the Muslim Ramadan.
> I serve Him alone who is my refuge.
> I serve the one Master, who is also Allah.
> I have broken with the Hindu and the Muslim, I will not worship with the Hindu, nor like the Muslim go to Mecca.

> I shall serve Him and no other.
> I will not pray to idols nor say the Muslims prayer.
> I shall put my heart at the feet of the one Supreme Being,
> For we are neither Hindus nor Mussulmans.

Akbar died and his successor, Jahangir, turned a jealous and angry eye on Arjun and the Sikhs. 'I fully know his heresies,' he wrote, 'and I ordered that he should be brought into my presence, that his houses and children be made over to Murtuza Khan, that his property be confiscated, and that he should be put to death with torture.'

Tortured Arjun was, but before he died he sent word to the Sikhs that his son Hargobind should be made his successor as the sixth guru, and this was done. Arjun's family were left at liberty in the belief that his death had subdued the Sikhs. But his martyrdom naturally had the opposite effect. It was the beginning of the Sikh transformation to militarism. Hargobind, aged eleven, by inclination or the advice of older and more experienced gurus, let it be known that henceforward they must be ready to defend their faith by force of arms. He trained a body of troops, and the Punjabis' martial spirit quickly responded to the new trend. Soldierly qualities were put before the old Sikh emphasis on virtuous living; meat eating was allowed, Hargobind became a military as well as a spiritual leader. Ten years later, in 1616, the agents of Jahangir were reporting that the Sikhs were changing in character from a peaceful rural people into a fighting one.

Sir James Roe, the English ambassador, spent this year persuading Jahangir to allow his own no less martial compatriots to establish their first trading stations in India. It would be nearly two hundred years before the British and Sikhs would see in each other the main obstacle to their mutual increase in power and territory. But from now on the character and beliefs of these two peoples set them on a collision course in India.

Hargobind instilled into his followers that they were well able to face the armed might of the Emperor. In clashes with the imperial troops victory went to the Sikhs. In 1645 he died, leaving them a rising military power with whom Shah Jehan, Jahangir's successor, might have to reckon. But Har Rai, Hargobind's successor as seventh guru, forsook the sword and emphasized anew the spiritual truths of the Sikh religion, while Hari Krishen, the boy who succeeded him was guru for a mere eight years before he died of smallpox at Delhi, whither he had been summoned by the Emperor Aurangzeb.

Tegh Bahadur succeeded him just as the Emperor began fierce persecution of the Sikhs, with the burning of temples, forcible conversion to Islam and the destruction of their political and military organization. Tegh Bahadur went into hiding. Captured, he was sentenced to death, but offered his life if he renounced the Sikh religion for that of Islam. He refused and was executed on 11 November 1675.

His son, Gobind Rai aged eleven, who succeeded him as guru, was brutally presented with his own father's head, for cremation. The shock left him with a fierce and abiding hatred for the great monarchy of Delhi. A poet, a leader of men, a priest and a scholar, he never forgot that he was also a son with a father to avenge. In his hiding-place, a small town among the foothills of the Himalayas, his own role as leader struck him with all the force of a spiritual vision. While still a youth, he stamped Sikhism forever with the mark of his personality. He proclaimed the faith anew, brought about a radical change in its character, laws and institutions by the abolition of caste and the introduction of social, religious and military reforms.

Gobind viewed the institution of the guru, meant to give unity to the Sikhs, as the cause of disunity, owing to quarrels over succession. With a stroke of genius he proclaimed himself the last guru. The sacred book, the *Adi Granth* was henceforward to be the source of all spiritual guidance. The traditional *panchayats*, or councils of five, would attend to secular matters.

Gobind set out to reinforce the sense of community among the Sikhs, to increase the power of the army and to lift his people from the status of a defensively orientated religious group to a dynamic socio-political movement, as it has been called, ready and willing to expand by force of arms. He instituted a new religious and military community, to be called the Khalsa, or the pure, united above all against the Muslim Mughal Empire of Delhi. In a baptismal ceremony of initiation, in which sugar was dissolved in water with a dagger, he abolished social distinctions among his followers, renamed all Sikhs *Singh*, meaning lion, and metaphorically warrior, by which all Sikhs have since been known. He gave them five symbols of their religion, the five *Ks*: hair and beard uncut, a comb in the hair, knee-length military shorts, a steel bangle on the right wrist, and a sword. Their energies were to be given to the profession of arms, and in war alone was merit to be gained. Rules of good conduct forbade them to smoke, to chew tobacco, to drink alcohol, to eat animal flesh unless it had been killed with one blow; or physically to molest Muslim women.

Gobind urged again that Hindus among them should forget and abandon all caste rules, mix freely, co-operate and not regard themselves as superior to any other. 'Do not follow the old scriptures,' he said. 'Let none pay heed to the Ganges and other places of pilgrimage which are considered holy in the

Hindu religion, or adore the Hindu deities, such as Rama, Krishna, Brahma, and Durga, but all should believe in Guru Nanak and his successors. Let men of the four castes receive baptism, eat out of the same vessel, and feel no disgust or contempt for one another.'[2]

This Sikh challenge to the established order in the Punjab led to a counter-challenge from the Emperor Aurangzeb's forces, who set out to destroy the Khalsa. Gobind fled with his family, but Mughal forces overtook him and in the fighting that followed killed his two eldest sons. Worse blows followed when his two younger sons were murdered by Wazir Khan, Mughal governor of the town of Sirhind. Gobind wrote to Aurangzeb protesting against the crime and set off to see him, but during his journey to Delhi the Emperor died. Later, while on a visit to Aurangzeb's successor, Bahadur Shah, Gobind himself was stabbed by two Pathans and died a few days later on 7 October 1708.

But the Sikhs were not subdued for Gobind had done his work well; the Khalsa, and the symbols of their faith remained to give them unity and raise their hopes.

By no means a state at this time, the Sikhs are best described as a commonwealth, military in character, based firmly on religion, with a hard core of almost a hundred thousand baptised members of the Khalsa, supported by more than a million sympathizers. And to assume temporal leadership and to revenge his murdered sons, Gobind had nominated a fanatic among his followers named Banda, also known as Lachman Das.

Banda launched a great uprising against the Mughal Government, which was fostered by the discontents and justified by the miseries of the peasantry of northern India. He

---

[2] *A Short History of the Sikhs*, Tej Singh and Ganda Singh.

promised protection to anyone oppressed by Muslim bigots, offered land to the landless and loot to all. Peasants armed with a few primitive firearms, spears, swords and hatchets flocked to his standards and Banda advanced northwards between the rivers Jumna and Sutlej on Wazir Khan's forces outside Sirhind, some seventy-five miles north-west. Despite their cannon and firelocks, the Mughal troops were shattered and overrun by the fanatic Sikhs; Wazir Khan was killed and the city of Sirhind razed. Banda had in fact unleashed a democratic agrarian uprising based on the religious and military beliefs of Sikhism. It spread across the Sutlej, where, reinforced by Punjabi nationalism, the whole region was taken except Lahore, the last remaining seat of Mughal authority. The social upheaval that followed is described vividly in *Later Mughuls* by W. Irvine:

> The reversal of previous customs was striking and complete. A low scavenger or leather-dresser, the lowest of the low in Indian estimation, had only to leave home and join the Guru, when in a short time he would return to his birthplace as its ruler, with his order of appointment in his hand. As soon as he set foot within the boundaries, the well-born and wealthy went out to greet him and escort him home. Arrived there, they stood before him with joined palms, awaiting his orders. A scavenger, from the nature of his duties, is intimately acquainted with the condition of every household. Thus the new ruler had no difficulty in exacting from every one their best and most valuable belongings, which were confiscated for the use of the Guru, or for his treasury. Not a soul dared to disobey an order, and men who had often risked themselves in battlefields, became so cowed that they were afraid even to remonstrate.

It was time for the Emperor to act again. Bahadur Shah stirred himself angrily and declared a jehad, or holy war, against the Sikhs. He sent his best troops under Firoz Khan against their peasant armies and scattered them, imposing his rule by the end of 1710 throughout the Malwa plains, between the Jumna and the Sutlej. Banda retreated into the southern foothills of the Himalayas. For the next five years he waged a hit-and-run war against the new Mughal Emperor Farrukh Siyar. But the Mughal forces advanced north and surrounded him. Finally after a long siege, Banda was starved into submission and surrendered on 17 December 1715.

He and his remaining troops were taken in cages to Delhi. During the march of retribution thousands of Sikhs were captured and executed, until their heads filled a procession of bullock carts. The bloody tumbrils entered Delhi with Banda in February 1716.

Tortured for three months, it is said, Banda was finally executed in June 1716, and still another wave of persecution was ordered by the Mughal Emperor.

Persecution certainly changed the character of Sikhism, but Banda, who saw himself as a scourge sent by God to punish the Muslim evildoers, bears most responsibility for its decline. It is a truism that all great movements become perverted when their leadership declines. The cry for religious freedom changes into the rasp of the inquisition, the martial spirit degenerates into mere savagery, praise of good grows into war upon imagined evil. The movement of peace and brotherhood that Nanak had founded some two hundred years earlier Banda changed into a rising of fanatical fury and barbaric butchery. Upon the Sikh peasantry it brought down the hatred even of Muslims and Hindus who hitherto were moved by the liberating appeal of the religion and its brotherhood. And from Delhi, the Mughal Emperor ordered the destruction of Sikhs everywhere. To save themselves, the weaker or less staunch cut hair and beards and for the time being swallowed their faith. The more resolute ones gave up their landholdings and fled to the mountains to live as outlaws.

In 1738 came the first sign of the break-up of the Mughal Empire. Nadir Shah of Persia swept down through Afghanistan and the Punjab, scattered the cumbersome elephant-born Mughal forces at Karnal, between the Sutlej and the Jumna, sacked and looted the magnificent palaces of the city of Delhi and massacred the inhabitants. Into his hands fell the wealth of centuries — the fabulous Koh-i-nor diamond and the jewelled peacock throne. But Sikh horsemen saw their chance when he returned home five months later and enriched themselves by a series of nightly hit-and-run raids on his baggage train. In a probably apocryphal story, Nadir Shah is said to have demanded of Zakarya Khan, Mughal Governor of Lahore, who were these raiders and where they lived. 'Their homes are their saddles,' Zakarya Khan answered. 'Take care,' came the warning. 'The day is not far distant when these rebels will take possession of your country.' For the next seventeen years the Sikhs faced ceaseless persecution from both Zakarya Khan and his successor. Thousands were executed, their sacred places defiled, but in face of it the Sikh faith was never broken.

In 1747 began the first of nine Afghan invasions of northern India under Ahmed Shah Abdali, lasting until 1769. The successive Mughal governors of Lahore, chief city of the Punjab, began to divide their allegiance according to what was expedient between the monarchs in Kabul and Delhi. Under this divided and uncertain authority the power of the Khalsa revived, though in the form of independent groups under chiefs. When the Afghans were defeated near Delhi and began their retreat across the Punjab, the Sikhs again worried them with hit-and-run tactics that brought much-needed horses and weapons. Now that no strong force existed to stop them, they began to spread throughout the Punjab and Malwa (the territory between the Sutlej and the Jumna) gradually, by permanent occupation of their territory, becoming a loosely knit federation.

The birth of a new power, the army of the Khalsa, next grew under the able leader Jassa Singh, and by 1754 it had become the strongest power in the Punjab and Malwa. But though the Khalsa was ready to challenge lesser leaders of the Afghan Dourani Empire, they feared the great Ahmed Shah Abdali himself and invariably dispersed before his army. In 1756 his Afghans again surged through the Punjab to sack Delhi and once more the Sikhs in turn pillaged the returning heavily laden columns.

In revenge, the Afghan Prince Taimur destroyed Sikh sacred buildings in Amritsar and forced Sikh prisoners to defile the foundations with the blood of cows. Then in 1760, the Marathas surged north, captured Delhi and swept on to drive the Sikhs from Lahore, only to be defeated at the Battle of Panipat by combined Afghan and Mughal forces. Ahmed Shah then returned to Afghanistan to deal with his own insurgent tribes. The Sikhs, now that there was no regular government in the Punjab, built forts and consolidated their power.

North and south of the Sutlej the *misls* joined forces in an army of 23,000 to defeat the regular forces of Zin Khan, Afghan governor of Sirhind, whom they killed, sacking the town in revenge for the murder there of Gobind's sons, seventy years earlier. The province was divided among the Sikh leaders. Ahmed Shah, acknowledging this new strength of the Sikhs, formally assigned the whole district to them on payment of agreed tribute. Thus, the Sikhs acquired a new status as rulers in the Punjab and the way to a great extension of their power lay open. But the democratic nature of their faith, their domination by predatory and mutually hostile chiefs made unity at this time impossible. The very lands they lived on constantly changed hands in this ceaseless clash of steel. 'Even within the borders of each confederacy,' writes Leppel Griffin, that nineteenth-century authority on Sikhism, 'the barons were always quarrelling, and first one chief and then another took the lead.'

Some *misls* — the *Bhangis* (they were addicted to *bhang*, an intoxicating drink made from Indian hemp); the Kanheyas, the Ramgarhias — grew strong enough to force their smaller neighbours to seek their protection, in return for which they were obliged to give military service when called upon, and, remarks Leppel Griffin, who lived among them:

> All that a Sikh chief asked in these days from a follower was a horse and a matchlock. All that a follower sought was protection and permission to plunder in the name of God and the Guru under the banner of the chief. There was little question of pay. All Sikhs were theoretically equal, and he who, like Amar Singh Majithia, could pierce a tree through with an arrow, or like Hari Singh Nalwa, could kill a tiger with a blow of his sword, might soon ride with followers behind him and call himself a sirdar... But all the great families, north and south of the Sutlej, have the same origin: the law of force, the keen sword and the strong hand were the foundations upon which Sikh society... was founded. To attract followers by his power and success was the main desire of every Sikh chief. Who they were, and what were their antecedents, were matters of no consequence if only they could fight and ride, which almost every Sikh could do... No man could consider his land, his horse, or his wife secure unless he was strong enough to defend them; for although the Sikh leaders were

best pleased with the spoil of Muhammadans or the capture of an imperial convoy, they were more robbers than patriots and plundered with frank impartiality…

Yet, while the Sikhs were undoubted robbers, and though cattle-lifting was the one honourable profession amongst them… their enthusiasm for their faith, their hatred to the Muhammadans who had so long trampled them under foot, who had killed their prophets and thrown down their altars, gave them a certain dignity, and to their objects and expeditions an almost national interest.

The Sikh chiefs, vigorously extending their territory in the Punjab, jealously challenging each other's conquests, were in 1767 frightened into a temporary unity by the sudden descent of Ahmad Shah from Kabul in a final effort to recover this most fertile of his provinces. But robbed by age of his old ferocious power to lead and to conquer, he instead sought to appease the Sikhs and awarded one of the chiefs, Amar Singh, the tide of Maharaja and the post of military commander of Sirhind in his name. Before he had completed this policy of trying to create a new reigning oligarchy of Sikhs loyal to him, his troops deserted and began a return march to Kabul in which the Shah had no choice but to join. Amar Singh founded the Patiala state in 1767, to become the strongest Sikh power east of the Sutlej. Thereafter, Ahmad Shah's successor, Timur Shah, made no serious attempt to destroy the de facto Sikh sovereignty in the Punjab. The Sikhs had come of age.

The British at this time, had disposed of the French, defeated Siraj-ud-daulah, Nawab of Bengal, at Plassey in 1757 and Mir Kasim at Buksar in 1764, to become the de facto rulers of Bengal and Bihar, the presidencies of Madras and Bombay and a long strip of coastal territory south of Calcutta. But they were not yet ready to expand towards the north-west or to challenge the military power of the Marathas. This martial race advanced north in 1768 and seized Delhi. The Sikhs, relieved of Mughal interference, were free to expand in the Punjab as they wished and by 1785 they were dominant from the upper reaches of the Ganges in the east to the Indus in the west.

The turbulent and chaotic post-Mughal period was bound sooner or later to produce a leader capable of uniting the divided Sikhs and preparing them militarily for their inevitable clash with the British, who were soon to embark on a new policy of expansion.

Ranjit Singh was this Sikh man of destiny.

3: Ranjit Singh

Ranjit Singh was born on 13 November 1780, son of the Sikh chief of the Sukerchakia *misl*, who let him run wild, spend his days riding, hunting, learning swordsmanship, the use of firearms and artillery. When he was five he was betrothed to the granddaughter of Jai Singh Kanhaya, chief of the strongest of all the Sikh *misls*. The betrothal, initial foundation of Ranjit Singh's later wealth and power, came about in an unusual way.

Maha Singh, Ranjit's father and Jai Singh, had fought each other to gain control of Kashmir. Jai Singh's eldest son was killed in the last of these skirmishes. Overcome by grief, Jai Singh tried to heal the enmity between the two tribes by an act of great magnanimity — the marriage between his dead son's daughter and the son of his greatest enemy. So, an act of which Nanuk, the founder of Sikhism, would surely have approved, made Ranjit heir to great territories and leader of thousands of horsemen, but an heir who could neither read nor write.

Ranjit's father died when he was twelve, leaving the *misl* to be ruled by his wife, the boy's mother, and one of her lovers. Ranjit, at this time, according to Baron Heugel, a German traveller, was short, with a thick muscular neck and broad chest, sinewy arms and legs, and one eye, the right one, having lost the sight of his left eye through smallpox, which had also pitted his brown skin. He was already a superb horseman, with an intense love for and understanding of horses, a passion which grew stronger as he grew older.

Jai Singh of the Kanhayas died in 1787, leaving the large territories he had acquired north of Amritsar — separated from those of the Sukerchakias only by the river Ravi — to his son's widow Sada Kaur, mother of Mehtab Kaur, to whom Ranjit Singh was betrothed. Described variously as a widow of great ability and unscrupulousness and as the most artful and ambitious woman in Sikh history, Sada Kaur clearly thought that by getting the young Ranjit Singh into her hands she could unite the lands of the two *misls* and gain control eventually of the entire Punjab for herself.

She is said to have initiated an unorthodox upbringing for the young chief, encouraging him to drink alcohol heavily and arranging for his seduction by Sikh women of beauty to try to divert him from his inheritance. But only partially were her ambitions realized, for though the youthful Ranjit showed an extraordinary thirst for women and wine, he turned out even as a boy to be one who commanded, one whom men obeyed. Thus the relationship was the reverse of the hopes and plans of Ranjit's mother-in-law. She became merely his adviser and counsellor, an *eminence grise* whose insight and vision showed him how to go about the dangerous task of subduing the other Sikh chiefs and gaining control of the entire Punjab.

When in 1796 the Afghans again invaded the Punjab, Ranjit emerged as a resistance leader and with his small force, scattered and defeated their much larger army. Furious at this defeat, the Afghan leader Shah Zeman sent a bigger force into the Punjab in 1798 with orders to spare no one. The Sikh chiefs still lacked the will to stand and fight, those beyond Ranjit's control fleeing to the hills and leaving the Afghans to occupy successively Gujerat, Gujranwala and Lahore. Ranjit again organized resistance and held the Afghans in the towns until Shah Zeman was forced to go back to Kabul to subdue a rising there. Ranjit and his forces then promptly attacked Lahore and after a short siege entered the city in July 1799. It was a turning point in his journey to power, for Zeman, tired of war, made him his deputy in Lahore. Henceforward, until his death and the subsequent war with the British, the story of Ranjit Singh is the story of the Sikhs.

In April 1801, proclaiming himself Maharajah of the Punjab, he won sovereignty over the entire geographical region and though he was not yet undisputed master of all the jealously independent Sikh chieftains, he now possessed the right to demand revenue from all who had in the past paid it to Lahore. In 1804 he extended his power in the west by seizing the Afghan province and city of Multan.

The British meanwhile, had in 1803 begun their inevitable trial of strength with the warlike Maratha people for the sovereignty of all India south of the river Jumna. Arthur Wellesley — later the Duke of Wellington — fought them in the Deccan, while General Lord Lake with an army of ten thousand met their challenge in northern India. Taking by storm the fortress of Aligah, between Agra and Delhi, he went on to defeat the French General Louis Borquin in command of their troops near Delhi.

Many steps nearer then were the British to a conflict with the Sikhs and to sovereignty in India.

But events now taught the aspiring Ranjit the truth about his military weakness compared with both the Marathas and the British. The remaining undefeated Maratha chief, Holkar, whose troops were trained by French officers, challenged the British. Defeated by Lord Lake at Deeg, Holkar retreated across the Sutlej into Sikh territory with fifteen thousand men and thirty guns during Ranjit's absence in Multan. Lord Lake, also without a by-your-leave, followed suit, both to discourage Ranjit from joining forces with Holkar and to encourage him to oppose the Maratha incursion, marching his army into the Punjab up to the river Beas, thirty-five miles from Amritsar.

Ranjit was now dangerously placed between the determined British and the desperate Holkar, who, he knew, was persuading the Afghans to ride down and join with him in a clash with the British on Punjab soil. Moreover, the Sikh chieftains were far from united in a wish to expel the intruders. Some favoured joining the British against Holkar as the price of their freedom from Ranjit's yoke. Others saw an alliance with Holkar a safer course than compliance with the British order to expel him, believing it an opportune time to challenge the power of the British, who were forever seizing more territory.

Before deciding what to do, the Maharajah made a personal inspection first of Holkar's troops, who were partially trained in European methods of warfare; and then, disguised as an ordinary soldier, but escorted by a squad of trusted swordsmen, made an inspection of Lord Lake's encampment on the Beas, carefully observing the drill and weapon training of the assembled redcoats, British and Sepoy.

He was recognized by his one eye and conducted to Lord Lake's tent, where the two are said to have had a private discussion. What passed on this occasion Ranjit Singh never revealed and Lord Lake at no time referred to it, but the outcome was a friendly agreement between Ranjit and the British, dated 1 January 1806. By it, Ranjit undertook to cause 'Jaswant Rao Holkar to remove with his army to the distance of thirty cos from Amritsar immediately, and will never hereafter... aid or assist him with troops or in any manner whatever'. The British agreed that as long as Ranjit Singh abstained from acts of hostility against them, their armies would never enter his territories or plain to seize his property.

The event coincided with a sudden reversal in official British policy in India from one of expansion to consolidation. The

British surprisingly allowed Jaswant Rao Holkar to return with his forces intact to his own domains. Lord Lake's army marched from the Punjab to stations further south, in a British India enlarged merely by the addition of Delhi and Agra, when the entire Punjab was open to them, Ranjit's forces then being little more than an undisciplined horde of cavalry.

Significant in this episode is British recognition for the first time of Ranjit Singh as ruler of the growing Sikh state in the Punjab.

During the next two years, 1805-7, the Maharajah made two expeditions across the Sutlej, ostensibly to mediate in the quarrels of the Malwa Sikh chieftains, but secretly with the aim of eventually bringing the entire region under his sway. From almost all the chiefs in the region he levied tributes by threatening force, moulding this loose and disorderly confederacy bit by bit into a well-ordered state. And at no time did the British feel that Ranjit had infringed the treaty.

But events elsewhere were indirectly now to change the British attitude. In May 1807, as part of a general diplomatic offensive in the Middle East, Napoleon signed a treaty with the Persians that paved the way for a possible French move towards India. It was followed by the visit of a French military mission to Teheran and by the middle of 1807 France had temporarily replaced England as the most favoured power in the Middle East.

Hardly fifty years ago had the British won the hand-to-hand struggle for European supremacy in India and it was only twenty-five years ago that the French Admiral Suffren had renewed the challenge. A mere nine years ago Bonaparte had moved as far east as Egypt and Syria, with the avowed aim of overthrowing British power in India — 'marching into Asia, riding an elephant, a turban on my head and in my hand the new Koran that I would have composed to suit my needs'. England had stopped him at the Battle of the Nile, but fears that the Corsican ogre's legions might follow the footsteps of earlier invaders down the dusty tracks of Persia, Afghanistan and the Punjab began to nag again.

When in July 1807, Napoleon and Tzar Alexander I, meeting on a raft on the river Nieman at Tilsit, signed that dramatic reversal of alliances, the Treaty of Tilsit, England was alarmed. This strange friendship seemed well and truly to open the road to Samarkand to Napoleon. But there were consequences of which the British took immediate advantage. Russia was an enemy of both Turks and Persians, so that Napoleon had lost all claims to friendship in their eyes. The pendulum swung back and a British understanding with these states became possible. In September 1807 the East India Company's Secret Committee in London instructed the Governor-General of India, Lord Minto, to seek alliances with Teheran, Kabul and Lahore against a Napoleonic invasion, one-sided arrangements for the defence of British India whereby the states involved would, if the worst came to the worst, take most of the kicks and get few of the ha'pence.

These instructions were anticipated by the Governor-General. In a letter written in March 1808, Minto reported to the Secret Committee his intention of dispatching envoys to Lahore, Kabul and Sind, in order to persuade their rulers to oppose a feared French attack on India in conjunction with Persia. Intelligence of the French anti-British intrigues at Teheran had reached Bengal before the instructions from London, which did not arrive before May 1808.

Ranjit's kingdom at this time stretched from Ludhiana in the east (just south of the Sutlej, in Malwa), to Multan in the west and beyond Gujerat in the north; and his immediate ambition was still to subdue the Sikh chiefs between the Sutlej and the Jumna — then the frontier of British India.

The Malwa chiefs went in daily fear that at any time they might awake to the crash of shot from Ranjit's twelve pounders through their rafters and the thunder of his cavalry. Singly too weak to oppose him, they were too suspicious of each other to fight side by side. Agreeing on one point, that 'between the lion and the wolf they had better come to terms with the lordlier beast', they sent representatives to Archibald Seton, Resident at Delhi, in March 1808, seeking British protection.

But they were two months too early. Lord Minto had not yet received the instructions embodying a change in policy that would enable him to intervene. And having just decided to invite Ranjit Singh to join in an anti-French alliance, he did not want to pave the way for it by squaring up to him in an area the Sikh leader regarded as properly part of his kingdom. The time for that might come later. So the Sikh chiefs went away with nothing more than polite wishes for their safety.

Hearing of their visit, Ranjit invited them to Amritsar, calmed their fears and persuaded them to join him rather than seek British protection; but this was less than the complete subjection he wanted. At the same time, he wrote to Lord Minto, suggesting an alliance, boldly naming the Jumna, rather than the Sutlej as the limit of his power, to which in view of the forthcoming diplomatic mission he received a suitably vague reply.

Ranjit neared now his first serious clash with the British; and since his unique leadership made the Anglo-Sikh wars possible, it is worth taking a close-up view of him. About twenty-eight, he had become a powerful, despotic ruler, seasoned in oriental diplomacy and surrounded by gifted Muslim and Hindu as well as Sikh advisers. Yet his looks were against him. Captain W. G. Osborne, who visited him, wrote that at first sight he looked strongly unattractive.

> A second look shows so much intelligence, and the restless wandering of his single fiery eye excites so much interest, that you get accustomed to his plainness, and are forced to confess that there is no common degree of intellect and acuteness developed in his countenance, however odd and repulsive its appearance may be. His height is rather beneath the usual stature of Sikhs, and an habitual stoop causes him to look shorter than he really is...
>
> Cunning and distrustful himself, he has succeeded in inspiring his followers with a strong and devoted attachment to his person; with a quick talent at reading men's minds, he is an equal adept at concealing his own; and it is curious to see the sort of quiet indifference with which he listens to the absurd reports of his own motives and actions which are daily poured into his ears... without giving any opinion of his own, and without rendering it possible to guess what his final decision on any subject will be till the moment for action has arrived.

This was the youthful chief who, though he could neither read nor write, had made himself the monarch of a turbulent nation by sheer force of intellect, personal magnetism and courage. He ruled with a rod of iron, and while it was said that he never took life, as was the custom then, he sentenced thieves and murderers to have hands, ears or nose cut off, leaving it to chance whether shock, or infection afterwards killed them. 'One blow of an axe, and then some boiling oil to immerse the stump in, and stop all effusion of blood,' writes Osborne, 'is all the machinery he requires for his courts of justice. He is himself accuser, judge, and jury; and five minutes is about the duration of the longest trial at Lahore.'

Contradictions — an abnormally large share of virtues and vices — dominated Ranjit's behaviour. He was openly and shamelessly drunken, a vice which he encouraged in his associates. Unlettered, he was yet intellectually alive and avid for knowledge. Mean to the point of avarice towards his subordinate chiefs, he was generous to a fault with foreigners. To Victor Jacquemont, a young French naturalist he gave five thousand rupees (£500) for his personal expenses, a fine horse, silk clothes and a miniature palace with fountains, orange trees and flowering gardens, as well as several beautiful girls to keep him company, and, wrote Jacquemont:

> A battalion of infantry was put on duty near me; the drums saluted whenever I put my head out of doors; and when I walked in the cool of the evening, in the alleys of my garden fountains played round me by the thousand. A most splendid fete was given to me; with an accompaniment of Kashmirian dancing girls as a matter of course; and although their eyes were daubed round with black and white, my taste is depraved enough to have thought them only the more beautiful.

Ranjit's love for his women, his horses and his army found humorous expression in his troop of about a hundred and fifty of the prettiest girls he could find from Kashmir, Persia and the Punjab, whom he called his Amazons. Magnificently dressed, armed with miniature bows and arrows, they were mounted on white horses, paraded for his amusement whenever he felt so inclined, and were not merely accomplished horsewomen, but singers, dancers and bed companions as well.

But Ranjit was no sloth. Whether in camp or palace he set out at sunrise in all weathers for an early morning gallop with a hundred and fifty of his personal guard, a horse artillery gun, several of his favourite horses saddled and bridled, his litter and his riding elephant. Two spare elephants followed, one laden with a tent made from silk shawls, together with awning, and the other with his chefs and a portable kitchen. He rode hard for about two hours in any direction he felt inclined and then stopped for breakfast.

Supported by silver poles, the tent was pitched in the shade of a grove of trees and Ranjit ate breakfast reclining in his litter, held on the bearers' shoulders, his table being the back of one of his kneeling servants. A tray with various curries, rice, boned fat quails, sweets and milk was placed on the man's back and the Maharajah set to with a good appetite, the meal being served in dishes made of fresh green leaves sewn together, beautifully cool and clean. After breakfast he rode another two hours, returned to his palace and sat in court until noon, hearing petitions, meting out justice, conferring with his councillors. Unless there was some other pressing business to attend to, he then gave the numerous women of his zenana the pleasure of his company until evening.

A heavy meal with visitors, friends and courtiers followed at about eight o'clock, after which there was usually a drinking bout. 'You have never been at one of my drinking parties,' he remarked to Captain Osborne. 'It is bad work drinking now the weather is so hot; but as soon as we have a good rainy day we will have one.' Osborne prayed for continued hot weather. Ranjit's wine, which he insisted on serving to the company himself, was vitriolic — 'as strong as aquafortis' — made from raisins and pearls ground to powder, a costly method of reducing acidity.

Lamenting that it was hard to avoid excess, Osborne observed that the Kashmirian girls never failed to attend Ranjit and his guests, when he would give way 'to every species of licentious debauchery… making the girls drink his wine and when he thinks them sufficiently excited, uses all his powers to set them by the ears, the result of which is a general action, in the course of which they tear one another almost to pieces…'

But it would be absurd to think of this great leader as only a debauchee. William McGregor, a British physician and surgeon who attended him later during the visit of Lord Auckland, depicts him also as listening to daily readings of the Sikh sacred *Granth*, and 'should the affairs of state require his attention, Ranjit is ready at all times during the day and night; and it is not unusual for him to order his secretary and prime minister to carry the designs on which he has been meditating during the night, into execution before daybreak.'

Referring to his lack of formal education, Jacquemont noted that he gained his knowledge by careful and persistent questioning of the many foreign visitors to his court:

> His conversation is like a nightmare… He is almost the first inquisitive Indian I have seen; and his curiosity balances the apathy of the whole of his nation. He has asked me a hundred thousand questions about India, the British, Europe, Bonaparte, this world in general and the next, hell, paradise, the soul, God, the devil and a myriad of others of the same kind.

Simply clothed in white muslin in summer and a long robe of saffron coloured cashmere in winter, Ranjit allowed no one to enter his court unless perfectly dressed, wearing their regalia and finest jewellery. Though he was creating a Sikh state, he gave equal opportunity to Muslim, Hindu and European and employed scholars of all races and religion. His foreign minister, Aziz-ud-din, was a Muslim Sufi mystic. His later prime minister, Dhyan Singh, was a Hindu Dogra; Raja Dina Nath, who later became finance minister, was a Brahmin.

But of all his interests, his soldiers were the greatest. Ever since seeing Lord Lake's troops manoeuvre, Ranjit had tried to train an army on western lines. Formerly, he had neglected infantry, cavalry being the main arm, plus a few guns, but after 1805 he began to build up a small infantry corps composed mainly of deserters from the Anglo-Indian army and from the Maratha forces. Even by 1809 however, these units were no match for properly trained and equipped troops. Guns had become one of his passions and in 1807 he established foundries for them in Lahore, but at first the bores of these weapons were faulty, nor was the shot standardized, so that too often they fired wide or short, while the carriages were made of wood and drawn by cumbersome oxen, rarely by horses. Of his method of acquiring guns, a British officer reported:

> The Rajah's attachment to guns and his opinion of their weight, are both so great, that he will never miss an opportunity of obtaining a gun. If he learns that there is a gun in any fort, he cannot rest until he has taken the fort to get at the gun, or until the gun has been given up to him to save the fort. He immediately dismounts the gun from the wall, and drags it after to him, as an addition to his field train.

By 1809, with a forward Indian policy again dominating the councils of the Government in Calcutta, the British were reconsidering their views about the Malwa Sikh territory, which lay north of Delhi and immediately south of the winding brown ribbon of the Sutlej. Bringing life to the thirsty land, this river was to be the decisive element, the boundary between peace and war. In a final effort to bring the cis-Sutlej Sikhs under his control, whatever the feelings of the British about it, Ranjit was now about to cross it at the head of his army.

Charles Metcalfe, aged twenty-three, a brilliant and earnest young political officer whose lush good looks were marred only by protruding dark eyes, had been appointed the British special envoy to Lahore, to negotiate an anti-Buonaparte alliance. Son of a director of the East India Company, he was fired with enthusiasm at being assigned the task of thwarting the ambitions of 'that infernal villain Buonaparte', and saw himself spreading a network of diplomacy that would baffle his intrigues throughout central Asia.

His discussions with Ranjit, in a small town in the southern Punjab specially chosen by the Maharajah to confine the British envoy as much as possible, began in September 1808. From the start he found it hard to convince Ranjit that he was really menaced by the French and besides, more urgent business beckoned the Maharajah. Early one morning, without telling Metcalfe he suddenly marched off with his army across the Sutlej and in succession occupied Faridkot, Maier Kotler, Patiala, Ambala, Shahabad — ever nearer to the British base only sixty miles away at Karnal. Having demonstrated that he ruled the entire area, he left garrisons in these towns, re-crossed the Sutlej with his army and arrived in Amritsar in December 1808.

It was a challenge that the British were not disposed to overlook, even although they had never before disputed Ranjit's legitimate interests in this Sikh region. When at the same time Napoleon met with setbacks in Europe that made an invasion of India remote and unlikely, Lord Minto,

Governor-General, decided to disregard Ranjit's usefulness as an ally — he was altogether too expansionist. 'The credit of the British Government,' Minto declared, 'is in a considerable degree concerned in affording protection to the chiefs south of the Sutlej,' thus replacing Ranjit's military power there 'by a confederacy of friendly chiefs, whose territories we could at all times command for defensive purposes'.

A remarkably swift and cynical bit of re-thinking, it was followed by the decision to extend protection to the cis-Sutlej chiefs, to require Ranjit to withdraw his troops — except a few needed for police purposes — and to establish a British military post near the frontier at Ludhiana. At the same time an army under Sir David Ochterlony was ordered to march from Delhi ready to go to war with Ranjit to enforce these demands.

Lord Minto sent Metcalfe a letter for the Maharajah warning him sternly to surrender all his conquests; and the joyful envoy called at the Amritsar palace to deliver it. He found the Maharajah celebrating with song and dance the fulfilment of his dearest ambition, the extension of his rule over the Malwa Sikhs, south of the Sutlej. He graciously accepted the letter Metcalfe gave him, but flatly refused to read it during his celebrations, and invited the envoy to join in. Metcalfe no doubt appreciated the bitter irony of the Maharajah's celebrating with Minto's ultimatum in his pocket and the steady tramp of Ochterlony's battalions bringing war ever nearer. Giving rein to his youthful thirst for physical pleasure he entered into the spirit of this oriental bacchanalia without saying a word of the truth. There were cups of Ranjit's devastating drinks to drive away mundane cares. The 'Amazons' were there and the dancing girls, tinkling gold bangles in time to grotesque movements. 'The evening was devoted to mirth and pleasure,' Metcalfe reported with modest understatement. 'I entered into the spirit of the scene as much as I thought proper. I took an early opportunity of retiring, but the Rajah and his friends were then evidently incapacitated for business.'

During the following days Ranjit firmly refused to comply with the British demands, and mobilized his troops. Metcalfe then played his trump card: a British force, he said, was marching up ready to expel the Maharajah's troops. At this, Ranjit angrily agreed to withdraw, but infuriated Metcalfe by changing his mind next day. The envoy then wrote directly to the British commander-in-chief, recommending invasion of the Punjab itself and the destruction of Ranjit's power.

But General Hewett saw no grounds for this sudden bellicose demand. It made him feel 'considerable embarrassment and uneasiness'. And these were also the feelings of the Government, for Napoleon's setback in Europe had changed the situation and British forces were to be used only to expel Ranjit's troops from Malwa and to prevent them from crossing the Sutlej.

Another event now helped Ranjit to decide what to do. Towards the end of February at Amritsar, the sepoys of Metcalfe's escort paraded their *tazias* — objects of tinsel and colour like carnival floats — round their tented camp in celebration of the Muslim festival of Mohorrum. A force of some thousand Akalis — fanatic Sikh shock troops — surged from the Golden Temple with drums beating and colours flying to attack them for this imagined affront.

Word reached Metcalfe, and his two hundred escort troops in their ragged red coats and tall blue caps were drawn up to repel them. The Akalis surged on and their fire began to drop the men in the ranks. Metcalfe then sanctioned Captain Popham's request to advance. Though heavily outnumbered, the sepoys launched a disciplined attack. Ranjit Singh, who arrived then to try to quell the Akalis, saw their disorderly retreat into the city with the sepoys' bayonets flashing behind them. Deeply impressed at the sepoys' bearing and combat in the English way, he is supposed to have asked himself how he would fare in a battle with thousands of the British themselves, and decided it should at all costs be avoided. He began then to act on Metcalfe's requests to withdraw his troops from newly conquered territory and at last the crisis began to cool. Metcalfe now called on Ranjit and coolly told him that 'authentic intelligence had been received of the French having suffered repeated defeats in Europe from his Majesty's armies and those of his allies; and of their being in embarrassments which would render impracticable the prosecution of those hostile projects against this country, against which it was the object of my mission to provide — that, consequently, there was no necessity for the conclusion of the treaty which I had formerly proposed, or for any specific engagements between the two states, who were already bound by the relations of amity and friendship.'

The speed and readiness with which Metcalfe, only twenty-three, had learned the use of diplomacy's weapons of hypocrisy, pretence, and threats of force must have shaken even Ranjit Singh, but he didn't show it. And so far as the treaty went, 'the Rajah did not express the disappointment which I had expected,' Metcalfe reported.

By the end of March, under the ever-present threat of military action, Ranjit had restored all but Faridkot and then, owing to regret at this setback to his prestige and his ambitions, he sought to escape with his women among the flowers and fountains of the gardens of Shalimar. To him, there, Metcalfe wrote reminding him of what he called 'friendship'. 'The Maharajah is revelling in delight in the Shalimar gardens, unmindful of the duties of friendship... I have nothing now remaining in my power but to require leave to depart. I, therefore... require my dismissal, and trust the Maharajah will furnish me with a proper escort to conduct me to the British armies...'

Ranjit replied in response to this new threat of military action, that the delights of the garden of friendship far exceeded those of a garden of roses and that Faridkot would be evacuated — he knew that Metcalfe had requested General St Leger to attack his troops there. He finally had them march out on 2 April, observing in a sarcastic response to Metcalfe, which echoed the envoy's tone: 'When matters are settled in an amicable and friendly way, to talk of armies and such things is neither necessary nor pleasing to my friendly disposition.'

Metcalfe's task was well and truly done. The British had ended one step nearer dominion over the whole of India, but Ranjit Singh now asked very firmly for a treaty with the British Government 'to obtain a security in its good faith against the consequences which might ensue from the establishment of the British power on the Sutlej.' Metcalfe reported that Ranjit believed that if the British would not give him this it must have hostile plans against him and that he would be always suspicious of their motives. 'This jealousy will always rankle in his heart, and will make him a most vigilant enemy.'

With these arguments the Governor-General on the whole agreed. The main British army was withdrawn, Ludhiana would be occupied permanently as a military outpost, and on 25 April 1809 a treaty was concluded leaving Ranjit with his older territories south of the Sutlej, where he would be allowed to maintain troops for police purposes. He was not to interfere with the cis-Sutlej Sikhs and the British agreed not to concern themselves with the territories north of the Sutlej. These two clauses are of importance, having regard to the war between British and Sikh later.

The agreement obviously fell far short of the original British wish for a treaty that would enable them at will to cross Ranjit's territory in defence of India, and in effect rob him of all freedom. This Ranjit escaped, but at the price of a British protectorate over the cis-Sutlej territories. With this, the British could claim to be well compensated for what they didn't get. They had, as well, an invaluable secret dossier on the Punjab that could not fail to be of use in the future.

In London, the Secret Committee, while accepting bravely this new burden of additional territory, wagged an admonitory finger, pointing out that it was hardly in accord with 'the principles laid down in Orders of the 19 October 1805, and 27 February 1806,' forbidding further territorial acquisitions; and that the Government at home should have been notified of the intention 'in terms more distinct and unreserved than those in which it was formerly conveyed Metcalfe, whose star was now one of the brightest in the Indian heavens, had done his work well. Edward Thompson in *The Life of Charles, Lord Metcalfe*, puts forward an additional non-political reason for his success which is worth mentioning. Many Englishmen then had Indian wives and mistresses and lived in regal style with them. (General Ochterlony had thirteen 'wives' when he was Resident at Delhi, who would take the air of an evening on thirteen separate elephants.) Metcalfe had one Indian wife, a Sikh lady, whom he met at Ranjit's court, and had three sons by her. Henry Studholme, his eldest son, Thompson discovered from old baptismal records in India, was born in 1809, baptised in 1813. 'I believe,' he says of this mysterious episode, 'that if we knew more we should understand better why Ranjit made his treaty and always cherished an affectionate memory of Metcalfe, almost as one who was a member of his own family.' The Sikh wife was possibly one of Ranjit's near relations.

But Ranjit seems never to have forgotten the humiliation he suffered, for the strengthening and modernizing of his armed forces along European lines henceforward became his ruling passion.

4: Militarization

The British had blocked him south of the Sutlej, so Ranjit had to look elsewhere for his conquests. Having an entirely military government and policy, he couldn't stop his campaigns even had he wished to do so. The Khalsa would have exploded. Moreover, he depended upon a constant supply of newly won territories to produce revenue to pay military commanders. His prestige had taken a hard knock among the jealous Sikh sirdars because of his surrender of Malwa to the British without fighting, but in 1810 he restored it by defeating the Gurkhas at Kangra, in the west, and driving them permanently from the Punjab. One by one the Sikh chiefs still free fell before his superior military talents, his strength and his ambitions. He turned again to Multan which he had already failed to subdue completely, having twice occupied the town but having failed to take the fort. In 1818, after a siege of several weeks, with the huge gun Zam-zan blasting 80-pound shot at the walls and his Akali shock troops storming the breaches, he finally took entirely this rich trading city. The beautiful Kashmir he next invaded, defeating the Afghan garrisons, making the region part of his kingdom in 1821 and destroying the last traces of Afghan rule in the Punjab.

The only power that he had cause to fear now was the British and — even though his army was now much improved — he set about creating a large first-class army on the European model. The strength of his regular infantry had risen from 1,500 in 1809 to about ten thousand in fourteen battalions of eight to eleven companies in 1821. Irregular infantry, used mainly for garrison and guard duties, had grown to some nine thousand, but there was much hostility to these changes. The feudal chiefs especially, whose power Ranjit was out to destroy, held that cavalry was the only possible arm for well-born men, infantry being for the lower orders, and artillery for artisans. The total strength of the regular army, as distinct from the irregular levies provided by the chiefs in payment for their estates, was not more than fifteen thousand, but henceforward it was to grow and keep on growing, until by 1845 it would be seventy-five thousand strong.

Indirectly, Napoleon at his zenith had earlier caused a reversal in Ranjit Singh's fortunes. In 1822, the Emperor was a broken idol with a disbanded army, but Ranjit's fortunes were aided by the aftermath of his downfall with the arrival in Lahore, in search of employment, of Chevaliers Jean Francois Allard and Jean Baptiste Ventura. Officers of the Grand Army, the fatal day of Waterloo sent them wandering through central Asia in search of work as soldiers of fortune.

Allard had been a captain in Napoleon's 7th Hussars, and aide-de-camp to Maréchal Brune; Ventura a colonel of infantry. Ranjit Singh employed them only after a careful examination of their abilities. Ventura, appointed to command the *Fouj-i-Khas* or model brigade — first in rank, discipline and equipment — became his right-hand man in converting the main strength of the army from irregular cavalry with little discipline to good disciplined infantry, the four infantry battalions of his brigade becoming models for the whole army.

Allard was commissioned by Ranjit Singh to raise and train a corps of cavalry dragoons on the French model. 'The men and horses were all picked,' wrote Lieutenant William Barr, who saw them on parade at Lahore, 'and amongst the former are to be seen many stalwart fellows, who appear to advantage under their cuirasses and steel casques. Particular attention seems to have been paid to setting them well up, and their accoutrements are kept in the highest order. Many of the officers wear brass cuirasses, and their commandant is perhaps the finest man of the whole body...'

Barr noted, as they manoeuvred, their uniform of dull red jackets with broad facings of buff crossed in front by a pair of black belts, one supporting a pouch and the other a bayonet. A cummerbund was partially concealed by a sword-belt, from which hung a heavy sabre with a brass hilt and leather scabbard, while their carbines rested in a bucket attached to the saddle. Trousers were of dark-blue cloth with a red stripe, turbans of crimson silk, slightly peaked in front, glittering with a small brass half-moon from which sprang a sprig about two inches in height. Smart as they were, the dragoons were put in the shade by their officers, dressed from top to toe in bright crimson silk and armed only with a heavy sabre.

Allard and Ventura took part in Ranjit Singh's campaigns almost from the time of their arrival. In 1823, when Allard had spent barely a year training his cavalry, the Maharajah one day ordered the Ghorcharas, his own irregular cavalry, to cross the Indus into Afghanistan. Plunging boldly into the torrent, without discipline or forethought, five hundred of them were swept away and drowned before Ranjit's shocked and angry gaze. Allard's turn came; mounted on an elephant, directing his carefully drilled cavalry by trumpet sounds, he moved them to a suitable crossing and to the other side without loss. Ranjit was so impressed by this simple act that he promoted Allard to the rank of general with a salary equivalent to £3,000 a year in money of the day, as well as the fine house he already had.

But the Ghorcharas, his own irregular cavalry, drawn mostly from among the sons of the Sikh nobility, remained Ranjit's favourites and he stinted money and equipment for Allard's dragoons, which, though they rose in strength to 4,345 by 1828, fell back to less than 4,000 five years later, owing to arrears of pay. Captain Osborne, Lord Auckland's Military Secretary, who visited the Punjab with the Governor-General, was in contrast to Barr, scornful of them.

> They are men of all ages, ill-looking, ill-dressed, and worse mounted, and neither in appearance or reality are they to be compared to the infantry soldier of the Punjab. One reason for this is that Ranjit personally inspects every recruit for his infantry, whilst the cavalry generally is recruited from the followers of the different Sirdars, and most of them owe their appointments to favour and interest, more than to their fitness or capability.

Allard settled down in Lahore and built himself a miniature palace in the Versailles style. His attractive personality, reliability and polished manners made him one of the Maharajah's close friends. He was given many costly presents, including a superb Persian sword with a hilt of solid gold studded with rubies and emeralds, and a blade for which Ranjit paid Rs 5000 (£500). Emily Eden, sister of Lord Auckland, Governor-General, who met Allard later at Ranjit's court, said of him: 'Allard wears an immensely long beard that he is always stroking and making much of; and I was dead absent all the time he was there because his *wings* are beautiful white hair, and his moustachios and the middle of his beard quite black. He looks like a piebald horse.' He was in fact a handsome man, with a warm intelligent expression and a flowing white beard parted in the centre into two horns twelve inches down his chest.

General Ventura — both he and Allard were later awarded this rank by the French King Louis Phillipe — had greater success with the Sikh infantry. In nine years it grew from seventeen battalions of about one thousand men each, to twenty-one battalions in 1831, giving a total strength then of more than twenty thousand. Training, discipline, weapons and welfare were improved. Thousands of flintlocks of the old Brown Bess pattern, 11 lb 2 oz in weight, barrel 46 inches long, bore 0.753 inches, were bought from the British to serve as design models and manufactured at Lahore. Ranjit invariably watched the parades and exercises, distributing gold necklaces to soldiers who excelled, fining or imprisoning idle ones. Osborne remarked of the Sikh infantry, who in a few years were to challenge the British:

> Went to the parade ground soon after sunrise. Ranjit came to meet us on his elephant about a mile from it, and we accompanied him to the right of his line of infantry. It consisted of about twelve thousand men and reached to the city gates, above two miles. I never saw so straight or beautiful a line with any troops. They were all dressed in white with black cross belts and either a red or yellow silk turban; armed with muskets and bayonets of excellent manufacture from Ranjit's foundry at Lahore. Their movements are very steady, but much too slow, and a European light infantry regiment would find little difficulty in working round them. This might easily be remedied by having a higher proportion of active European officers, but nothing can be worse than the system now in vogue. The commanding officer beats and abuses the major, the major the captains, the captains the subalterns, and so on till there is nothing left for the privates to beat but the drummer boys, who catch it accordingly.

There was at first another defect. Sikh discipline on the parade ground went to the winds on the battlefield, however hard Ranjit tried to enforce it. Though continually drilled, the Sikhs could not entirely subdue a fiery individualism that found outlet in the tumultuous uncontrolled charge, any more than they could forget their age-old urge for battlefield looting. 'The system of the British is so good that even if the enemy threw gold coins in the course of their fight, the soldiers would not even look at them,' Ranjit's official biographer Sohan Lal quotes him as saying. 'On the other hand, if the Khalsa soldiers saw mere corn, they would break their ranks, dash towards that and spoil the whole plan of operations.'

During one of Ranjit's campaigns against the Afghans, when the troops of both sides were locked in a fierce hand-to-hand struggle, Ranjit saw suddenly an opening for his reserve, which included his best regiments. He ordered a brigade to come up, but the only answer he received was 'an universal shout from the men that drill and manoeuvres did very well in peace time and on parade, but that they could not stand it now when they were really in action, and that they must fight their own way, or they would not fight at all. They accordingly all broke from their ranks, every man fighting for himself, and of course,' concludes Osborne, 'in a few minutes were completely beaten.'

An important cause of the uncontrollable urge to loot was arrears of pay. Ranjit, whose treasury was said to be worth over several million sterling in gold, used this indebtedness as a means of overcoming desertions to the forces of rulers in India who offered more. He once remarked to Osborne that he had disbanded some hundreds of men from the regiments at Peshawar for mutiny.

'When were they last paid?' Osborne asked.

'Eighteen months ago, and yet they are discontented.'

'Very odd,' Osborne rejoined ironically.

'What would you do in such a case?'

Osborne said that it could not have happened in the British army, where the men were regularly paid. Ranjit replied: 'So are mine — and more than that, the rascals have been living on plunder for the last six months.'

Despite their arrears, Osborne found, Ranjit's infantry kept their sense of humour. It was unbearably hot and oppressive during his stay at Lahore, with the temperature frequently over 110 degrees Fahrenheit. At daybreak he used to leave his bedroom in the Palace at the Shalimar Gardens and sit for an hour under the cool water of the great fountain. The Sikh guard at once turned out and presented arms in the most soldierlike way the moment he was seated. 'And there they persist in remaining under arms during the whole time I am bathing. And considering my dress, or rather the absence of it... it is a matter of considerable difficulty to return the salute with the proper degree of dignity.'

Conscientiously, Osborne never lost a chance of studying Ranjit's infantry. 'Proceeded as usual to the parade ground,' says one entry in his diary, 'and, as usual, found the Maharajah inspecting a brigade of infantry, cavalry, and horse artillery.' Ranjit insisted, as the force deployed to battle commands, that Osborne, beside him on another elephant, should point out differences from British methods. Osborne mentioned a mistake — making skirmishers fire together in volleys by command. Ranjit, apparently not having grasped the object of skirmishing, replied that it enabled them to fire more regularly.

> I explained to him that we considered the object of all skirmishing defeated by it, and that each man should fire individually, as soon as he had taken his aim, and felt certain of his mark, without waiting for his comrades. He considered for a few minutes, and then said, 'I think it would be better and I will try it;' and the next morning I saw his light infantry

practising individual firing, and skirmishing as well as any company's regiment could have done. There was only one other mistake which I pointed out to him, and suggested that the cavalry protecting his guns should be on the flanks and not in the rear. He saw the propriety of this at once, and the order for the change was given on the spot.

So certain were British officers of the superiority of their forces and so anxious were these perfectionists that the military art should be done properly, that they unhesitatingly passed on knowledge even to the ambitious ruler of a growing military nation.

Together with his treasury of gold and precious stones, Ranjit relished his artillery as the main source of his power. Only these — money and guns — came before women and horses. Three more foreigners, a Frenchman, an Italian and an American helped him to raise his gunnery to the European level. These were, General Claude Auguste Court, a Napoleonic army officer educated at the Ecole Polytechnique of Paris; General Paolo Bartolomeo Avitabile, a Neapolitan and an artillery officer under Murat in Italy; and Colonel Alexander Gardner, an American soldier of fortune who became an intimate of the Sikh court at Lahore and in this respect is the most interesting of the three. The first two arrived at Lahore in 1827.

Court, a short, thick-set man pitted with smallpox, with grizzled iron-grey hair and the looks of a rough-and-ready sailor, dressed casually in an open blue horse-artillery jacket with a red waistcoat heavily ornamented with gold lace, and an embroidered belt from which hung a heavy sabre. Apart from his two Sikh wives, he was a man of simple habits who lived alone in a small house in the garden of the mansion occupied by his family. Ranjit made him superintendent of his Lahore arsenal.

Before his time, most of Ranjit Singh's guns were sometimes liable after hard firing to burst and kill the gunners rather than the enemy, for neither the powder charges, the size and weight of shot, nor the bore of the barrels were standardized. At work in the foundry Ranjit had caused to be set up conveniently next to his Hall of Audience, Court, in the space of a few years, brought the Sikhs' guns to the level of the French or British, with howitzers, mortars and shells fused to burst accurately at eight or nine hundred yards over the target, or on impact. Ranjit awarded him thirty thousand rupees (£3,000) for manufacturing these shells, known then as spherical case shot, as invented in England in 1794 by Lieutenant Henry Shrapnel. (A hollow shell packed with shot and fused to burst where needed and pepper the enemy, it was not adopted by the British army until some years after its invention.) Lieutenant Barr, of the Bengal Horse Artillery, noted that the Sikh guns, as distinct from their carriages, were much heavier than those of the British, a Sikh four-pounder being often as heavy as a British six-pounder. Court, apparently, knew that additional weight and thickness of metal in the breech enabled heavier shot and shell to be fired and in Ranjit's military dictatorship, where forty-two per cent of annual revenue was spent on the army, the money for such refinements was always forthcoming.

Two British 24-pounder howitzers presented to Ranjit by Lord Willian Bentinck while Governor-General were at once copied. Barr noted in the foundry 'two very respectable-looking brass 24-pounder howitzers lately cast from the models of those presented to Ranjit Singh by Lord William Bentinck; the superintendent told us there were ready for service, in and around the immediate neighbourhood of

Lahore, seven hundred guns of various calibres.' When Osborne went one day at sunrise with Ranjit Singh to watch his artillery practice

> there were thirteen brass nine-pounders on the ground, protected by two squadrons of his regular cavalry, under the command of Raja Dyan Singh (his prime minister). After manoeuvring for about an hour... at a tolerable pace, they commenced practising with grape at a curtain, at two hundred yards' distance; the practice would have been creditable to any artillery in the world. At the first round of grape, the curtain was cut clean away, and their shells at eight and twelve hundred yards were thrown with a precision that is extraordinary, when the short period of time since they have known of even the existence of such a thing is taken into consideration.

This progress stemmed from Ranjit's unceasing determination to create an army that would one day, he hoped, match that of the British, and to this he brought a priest's zeal and a poet's passion. Lieutenant Henry Fane, visiting Lahore in 1837 with his father Sir Harry Fane (then commander-in-chief, India), to attend the marriage of Ranjit's grandson Prince Nihil Singh, tells of the Maharajah's review of the escorting British troops and — 'the extreme delight of the old man at the discipline of the men, and the explanation the General gave him of the movements... surpasses belief. He rode through and looked at every gun, examined the appointments of the men, counted the numbers in each square, and quite gained all our hearts by the interest he took, and the acuteness which he showed by his questions.'

He was only too aware of the shortcomings of his own gun crews, despite the great efforts of their instructors, for he was quite astonished, says Fane, at the speed with which a British troop of horse artillery carried out the routine drill of breaking down and re-assembling a gun.

> It was ordered to be done by a six-pounder... thrown on the ground, dismounted from its carriage, taken all to pieces, remounted, men on their horses, and again in full gallop, in the space of five minutes. He could not, for some time, believe that it had really been taken to pieces, and would have it that they only stopped because some of the harness had been broken; and it had to be again performed before he could quite believe what he saw.

Avitabile too, helped to raise the quality of Sikh gunnery, but realizing his talent for administration, Ranjit made him governor first at Wazirabad, then at Peshawar in the north, where the Afghan danger lay. Barr described him as 'a fine tall stout man, upwards of six feet high, with a pleasing yet determined cast of countenance, from which you can see at once he never issues an order without its being promptly obeyed, or woe be to the man who neglects it.' With a grey beard halfway down his chest and moustaches like twisted bayonets, he dressed with flair and imagination. Barr says 'his costume consisted of a long green coat... ornamented with a profusion of lace and three rows of oblong buttons of solid gold; trowsers of scarlet cloth, with a broad gold stripe down the seams, and a green velvet cap, with a band also of gold lace and a tassel of the same material, but no peak. This he invariably retains on his head, whether indoors or not.'

Avitabile showed Barr several long matchlocks or camel guns known as *zambureks* about seven feet long, which he had just had made. Used also as wall-guns, they fired a heavy one-inch calibre ball over a mile with much accuracy. He later transformed the fort at Peshawar into an impregnable citadel with comfortable barracks and stores 'a vast number of ten-inch shells at one end of a gallery and a complete hill of bullets at the other...'

Colonel Alexander Haughton Gardner, commander of Ranjit's artillery at Lahore, who arrived there in 1831, was born in Wisconsin near the source of the Mississippi in 1785, the son of a surgeon of Scottish descent and an American lady, daughter of a Major Haughton. Dr Gardner, the father, who was a friend of George Washington and the Marquis de Lafayette, fought on the American side against the English in the War of Independence. His son, Alexander, a tall lean man with a determined, fiery look on his bony features, left America on the death of his parents and began his life-long travels in central Asia as a soldier of fortune. He wore invariably a simple uniform of his own design, later made from plaid bought from Scottish regiments in India.

Gardner sold his military services to one central Asian chief after another, notably in Persia and Afghanistan. Fighting there for a chief who opposed the ruler, Dost Mahommed Khan, Gardner was presented with a fort, which he called his *castello*, and given charge of a mountainous region in the west. He married a beautiful Afghan girl, by whom he had a son, but his happiness was short-lived, for during his absence fighting elsewhere, his fort was taken and his wife and son slaughtered. Heart-broken, he left Afghanistan for a time, but later made his peace with Dost Mahommed and then journeyed to the Punjab with the hope of military service with Ranjit. General Avitabile, at Wazirabad, gave him a note of introduction to General Ventura and to Ranjit's prime minister, Raja Dhyan Singh. Gardner describes two incidents which show something of his determined character. The first took place when he was waiting outside the Shalimar Gardens to be presented to the Maharajah.

> A certain Nand Singh, an officer of the Maharajah's cavalry, rode his horse intentionally against mine and endeavoured to jostle me into the ditch, which was deep and filled with running water. I touched the rein of my good steed, gave him half a turn, pressed him with my sword hand the veriest trifle on the loins, and in an instant Nand Singh and his horse were rolling on the ground. I calmly expressed a hope that the fallen man was not hurt, and was treated with much civility during the remaining time that I was kept waiting. Shortly after, I was summoned to the Maharajah's presence, and was graciously received by that great man. Much as I had heard of the insignificance of his appearance, it at first startled me; but the profound respect with which he was treated, and the extraordinary range of subjects on which he closely examined me, speedily dispelled the first impression.

Gardner believed that the Maharajah was 'one of those masterminds which only require opportunity to change the face of the globe'. He made 'a great and powerful nation from the disunited confederacies of the Sikhs, and would have carried his conquests to Delhi or even farther had it not been for the simultaneous rise and consolidation of the British empire in India'.

At the time of his arrival in Lahore, the Maharajah urgently needed a good artillery instructor, Colonel Court being employed principally as superintendent of the gun-factory. A few days after Gardner's audience, Raja Dhyan Singh, the Prime Minister, showed him the two guns that Lord William Bentinck, Governor-General at the time, had presented to Ranjit Singh, pointing out the shells and fuses, and asking Gardner if he could explain the use of this kind of projectile, or fire them. Accustomed to the more primitive round-shot, Gardner was at first a little puzzled, but luck was with him.

> I found in one of the tumbrils, enclosed in a bundle of fuses, a small printed slip of paper giving instructions as to the time of burning, time of flight, etc. Having read this I told Dhyan Singh that I hoped to be able to fire them and to satisfy him as to my knowledge of their proper use. I, however, asked to be allowed to cut and burn one fuse first, which at his desire I did in his presence. The result agreeing with that shown on the printed slip, there seemed to be no further difficulty... I was ordered to get ready to fire three or four of the shells at different distances in the presence of the Maharajah Ranjit Singh. I took a few soldiers in hand, and in a few days' time all this was done with a degree of success unexpected even by myself, the shells bursting exactly as required at 600, 800, 1,000 and 1,200 yards... I received a considerable present and was enrolled in the Maharajah's service with the rank of colonel of artillery, and was placed in full command of a camp of eight horse-artillery guns, two mortars and two howitzers. I was likewise deputed to teach most of the principal officers attached to artillery, at the head of whom were General Sultan Muhammed and several colonels... For two or three months Ranjit Singh witnessed with much interest their firing of shell, shot, cannister, red-hot shot, etc., all receiving presents from his Highness according to their proficiency or merits.

Gardner thereafter took part in all Ranjit Singh's campaigns, including the capture of Peshawar from Dost Mahommed Khan in 1835 by a Sikh army eighty thousand strong led by Ranjit himself. It included the self-contained model brigade known as the *Francese Campo*, consisting of Ventura's four battalions of infantry, Allard's two regiments of cavalry and a troop of artillery of twenty-four guns, which Gardner commanded. It became the pattern for the Khalsa of the future.

Ranjit Singh's military achievement, in short, was to seize upon the masses of brave but militarily ignorant horsemen of the Punjab and with the help of foreigners organize their transformation into a disciplined regular army of forty thousand with an artillery of nearly four hundred guns, plus an irregular army of some thirty-eight thousand. It had weaknesses which he could not overcome — doubtful loyalty and poor quality of officers, serious discontent owing to irregularity and arrears of pay among men, but it was a formidable army.

The Frenchmen Allard and Court, the Italians Ventura and Avitabile, and the American Gardner had done their work well. How well, the bloody struggle in which the Sikhs were soon to be locked with the British will show.

The ambitions of the British and of Ranjit Singh's Sikhs were in the 1830's conflicting more and more. Twice in the few years before his death at the age of fifty-nine, the Maharajah yielded to the British. In 1836, he wished to extend his territory down the Indus to the coast by occupying Sind (now part of Pakistan). Though he guessed that the British secretly would like to move in and probably would object, his son Prince Kharrack Singh and his grandson Prince Nao Nihil Singh were both, towards the end of the year, ready on the Indus to invade with large armies. Then Captain Wade, British Resident at Ludhiana, confided that the invasion might well end in war with the British and advised him to call it off.

Ranjit's chiefs protested, urged him not to yield as he did over the Malwa states, insisting that nobody could see where the English demands and advances would end. Had they not occupied Ferozepore the year before? Ranjit is said to have reminded them that the Marathas fought the English once —

'and where are their 200,000 spearmen now?' He yielded, and to show that his friendship with the British was still as good as ever, invited the Governor-General, Lord Auckland, to the marriage in 1837 of his grandson Prince Nihil Singh, whose wedding gift from the Maharajah was to have been the territory of Sind.

The celebrations were a great success, especially the Hindu festival of the goddess Holi, when it was usual for celebrants to douse each other with vermilion coloured liquid. Ranjit started the fun by emptying a large dish of cold saffron soup over Sir Henry Fane's bald head, after which he was smothered head to toe in vermilion.

Fearing a Russian, instead of a French invasion of India now, the British resolved at this time, 1838, to depose Dost Mohammed Khan, the ruler of Afghanistan and to replace him by Shah Shuja, a former monarch, who they wrongly believed, would be a more reliable ally. The assistance, or at least, the neutrality of the Sikhs was vital to the enterprise — even though it involved a British puppet state of Afghanistan on Ranjit Singh's western frontier, so that he would be surrounded.

The mission to urge Ranjit that this improbable undertaking would be to his advantage included William Macnaghten, the scholarly and ambitious political secretary to the government, later to be assassinated in Kabul by the subjugated Afghans, and Captain Osborne, Military Secretary to the Governor-General. They met the Maharajah at Adeenanagar — little more than a large garden, irrigated by a canal which kept the shrubs and flowers fresh and green, with a moderate sized palace where he usually spent the hot weather.

The Maharajah greeted them with a friendly embrace in the main hall of the palace, beneath a silk canopy embroidered with gold and precious stones supported by gold pillars. He seated them, inevitably, on gold chairs and sat on another gold chair opposite. Dressed simply in white, he wore no ornaments, Osborne says simply, except 'a single string of enormous pearls round the waist and the celebrated Koh-i-noor, or mountain of light, on his arm (the jewel rivalled, if not surpassed, in brilliancy by the glance of fire which every now and then shot from his single eye as it wandered restlessly round the circle)...'

Intricately, the negotiations dragged on for three weeks. Ranjit Singh demanded a high price for his collaboration — Shikapore in Scinde, or Jellalabad eighty miles west of Peshawar, in Afghanistan. But this the British refused and finally Macnaghten told Ranjit that with or without his co-operation they intended to place Shuja on the throne at Kabul. This plain statement, bluntly said, took Ranjit aback. He is said to have paused, and then in his usual quick emphatic manner asked for the treaty to be drawn up for him to sign. It was agreed that Shuja, when on the throne, should pay him £20,000 a year tribute to compensate him for the lack of Jellalabad, as well as 'fifty-five highbred horses of approved colour and pleasant paces'; scimitars and poniards, and a delicious list of fruit — 'grapes and pomegranites, apples, quinces, almonds, raisins, pistoles or chronuts, an abundant supply of each'.

The Tripartite Treaty, as it was called, had for its object a joint expedition by Shah Shuja's British-trained irregulars and the Sikh armies to subdue Afghanistan and replace Dost Mohammed by Shah Shuja. It did not pledge the aid of British arms, but the sheer logic of events soon forced the Governor-General to commit British troops substantially. An army of twelve thousand assembled at Ferozepore and on 12

December began its twelve hundred mile march by way of Shikapore to Kabul.

Four drawbacks to the enterprise were overlooked. First, that Dost Mahommed was king and accepted as king, whereas Shah Shuja, a former king, was hated by the Afghans. Secondly, under these circumstances he would have to be kept on the throne and the Afghans held in subjection by an occupying force. Thirdly, Ranjit Singh feared on the Kabul throne a king who would be a British puppet, but he had no other course but to yield, and he might not therefore fulfil his obligations. Fourth, the British forces in Kabul would be separated by some fifteen hundred miles of mountainous country from their supply bases.

All these were to lead to the biggest military disaster the British had known in India and to doubts in the Sikh mind about British military pre-eminence, which encouraged the Sikhs to go to war later.

The campaign was launched by a ceremonial meeting between the Governor-General, Lord Auckland, and Ranjit Singh, at Ferozepore, one hundred miles south-east of Lahore, across the Sutlej. A veritable field of the cloth of gold, Ranjit's bodyguards were drawn up there in a lane through which Lord Auckland had to pass, one troop dressed in yellow satin with gold scarfs and shawls, the other in cloth of gold, scarlet, purple or yellow, their heads enveloped in gold muslin brought over their beards to protect them from the dust. Ranjit and Auckland met in this riot of colour amid scenes of 'indescribable uproar and confusion'. Henry Fane, son of the commander-in-chief, wrote that 'the crowd was what one might expect from the meeting of upwards of one hundred elephants within the space of as many yards wide, and the crush awful; elephants trumpeting, gentlemen swearing, and each one trying how he could best poke out his neighbour's eye with the corner of his howdah: while the confusion was not a little heightened by the cannon firing within three yards of one…'

Among the presents of swords, guns and pistols Auckland presented to the Maharajah were two fine nine-pounder guns beautifully inlaid and carved with a medallion of Ranjit's own head in the centre of the barrel. In his eagerness to inspect them, the frail Ranjit in his long robes of crimson cashmere stumbled and fell. There was a murmur of horror from his assembled chiefs at the ominous sight of their ruler flat on his face before the British guns. Auckland's entourage of diplomats helped him to his feet and one of them instinctively relieved the tension by observing that, 'If his Highness did fall before the British guns, the highest representatives of the British Government helped him to his feet'.

Ranjit then set an example in the festivities that followed, drinking huge quantities of his favourite new drink made from orange spirit, crushed emeralds and brandy — 'a horrible spirit, one drop of which actually burnt my lips,' confessed Emily Eden, Lord Auckland's sister. Ranjit stood a day or two of this in the great heat and then suffered a stroke that left him partially paralysed and hardly able to speak. 'We took leave of Ranjit Singh yesterday,' Osborne wrote on 3 January 1839. 'He has been very ill, but is better. It was thought at one time that he would have died; and although better he cannot last much longer…'

Ranjit lasted another six months and died on 27 June 1839.

He was placed on a pyre of sandalwood. His chief wife sat down beside him and put his head on her lap, three of his other eighteen wives and seven of his slave girls, bravely or dutifully, arranged themselves around him. Prince Kharrack Singh, his eldest son and his proclaimed heir, set fire to it, the flames crackled, the smoke arose, music was played and all were cremated.

The British went on to occupy Kabul. Shah Shuja was installed as king of Afghanistan, Dost Mahommed fled to the mountains, led a vigorous resistance for two years, then surrendered. It soon became clear that only British bayonets would keep Shuja on the throne. Every month the hatred of the Afghans for the regime grew stronger. Military and political mismanagement as well caused the eventual disaster the British suffered in this country where every man and every boy was a marksman and a swordsman.

Also at this time the British were at the mercy of the Sikhs, for their supply convoys were passing through the Punjab, but the confusion and conflict that followed Ranjit Singh's death probably saved them from attack then.

Ranjit's throne, his victories, the tradition of his power and greatness, all these ended with him. He left no one able to control the Khalsa and the turbulent chiefs upon whom he had imposed his imperious will. Anarchy and murder flourished in the Court on a scale beside which the bloodiest Elizabethan drama pales into a faded frieze, and enabled the Khalsa eventually to seize power.

5: Murder

The causes of the First Anglo-Sikh War were far more complex than the effect of British imperialist expansion, though later this was to become a potent factor. Weary of war, for the time being, after the Afghan disaster, the British in India were also short of money, fairly content with the Sutlej as the northern frontier, and restrained by a new climate of educated opinion in England that opposed the seizure of more territory in India. This policy of restraint was, of course, modified by the ambitions of Governors-General who, looking for glory, chanced their arm, provoked war and told London afterwards. But in the 1840's expansionism was a stronger urge among the Sikhs than among the British. Controlled southwards in Ranjit's time, after his death this urge became in that direction stronger and more imperative as murder in Lahore ended the lives of politicians and heirs to the throne alike. Eventually, the Khalsa became supreme in the land, an uncontrolled power eager for war, like a hungry wolf pack sniffing winds bringing the taste of blood from the southern horizon. How this happened, while dramatic in itself, reveals as well much of the course of the first Sikh War. (The Sikh names of the several assassins and their victims need not be confusing if first read carefully.)[3]

---

[3] Prince Kharrack Singh: Ranjit Singh's only legitimate son. Prince Shere Singh: one of the Maharajah's illegitimate sons. Prince Nao Nihil Singh; son of Kharrack Singh. Chet Singh: Kharrack Singh's confidential adviser. Raja Dhyan Singh: prime minister or vizier. Hira Singh: Dhyan Singh's son, vizier after his father's death. Gulab Singh, Suchet Singh, Dhyan Singh's brothers. Udam Singh: son of Gulab Singh. Chand Kaur: wife of Kharrack Singh, later Maharani. Ajit

The trouble first arose owing to Ranjit's successor's unfitness to be King. The Maharajah had proclaimed his only legitimate son, Prince Kharrack Singh, heir to the throne, and Raja Dhyan Singh prime minister. Kharrack Singh, says Colonel Gardner, who was present throughout these bloody scenes, was 'a blockhead, and a slave to opium: at the time of his succession to the throne he passed the whole time in a state of stupefaction.' Inevitably, there were other contenders for power, plotting in secret. Chief of these were Raja Dhyan Singh, Ranjit's trusted prime minister, and his brother Gulab Singh, who had together determined to murder, one by one, as the time was ripe, all Ranjit's successors, place on the throne Hira Singh, Dhyan Singh's son — a handsome youth who had been Ranjit's intimate and favourite — and rule through him.

Another contender for power was an ambitious chief named Chet Singh, Prince Kharrack Singh's adviser. He also sought to rule behind the scenes and three months after Ranjit's death tension between him and Dhyan Singh had reached the point of no return. 'See what will become of you in twenty-four hours,' Chet Singh rashly threatened Dhyan Singh in a whisper, during an audience at Court, according to Gardner. 'Your humble servant, sir; we *shall* see,' answered Dhyan Singh, who had already sought the overthrow of Chet Singh by drawing round him a net of conspirators, including Kharrack Singh's wife, who spread rumours that he was a traitor in British pay. Dhyan Singh now plotted to kill Chet Singh, force Maharajah Kharrack Singh to withdraw from public life, and place his son,

---

Singh, Uttur Singh, leaders of the powerful Sindhanwalia family and contenders for ruling power. Tej Singh: later appointed Sikh commander-in-chief. Lal Singh: later prime minister. Maharani Jindan: a wife Ranjit married a year before dying. Maharajah Duleep Singh: her son, born 1836. Jowahir Singh: her brother, vizier in 1844.

the next victim, Prince Nao Nihil Singh, aged eighteen, on the throne, as second in line of succession.

On the night chosen for the murder, Gardner — 'Gordano Sahib' as the Sikhs named him — was ordered by Dhyan Singh after dark to place artillery with trusted gun crews ready for battle at all the palace gates. This done, he was ordered to accompany Dhyan Singh, his two brothers Suchet Singh and Gulab Singh, Prince Nao Nihil Singh, Ajit Singh and Uttur Singh, the heads of the Sindhanwalai family, with two or three trusted chiefs, into the palace through a secret door opened to them by dissatisfied ladies of the harem. 'We stealthily crept our way in the dark up a flight of stairs, over a place called the Badshah-i-Takht, and thence to the immediate vicinity of the royal apartment,' noted Gardner.

> At this moment a man started up, and seeing us, called out and tried to run off. Suchet Singh shot him dead, and was himself instantly almost knocked down by a tremendous cuff on the ear dealt him by his brother, Gulab Singh, who cursed him under his breath for his imprudence. On looking over the parapet we saw two companies of the Maharajah's guard. Dhyan Singh quickly went down the staircase to the place where they were stationed, and was accosted by the subadar in command, who said, 'Why did you fire?' I had followed Dhyan Singh, and stood immediately behind him. He simply showed his right hand (on which he had two thumbs) and put his finger to his lips. On seeing the well-known peculiarity the subadar whispered, 'Lie down,' and the whole of the two companies noiselessly lay down at full length and pretended sleep. The subadar then pointed with a mute gesture to the room of the doomed man, the door of which had been left ajar. There was a light in the room. Dhyan Singh approached and entered it, followed by the whole party. Lo! There sat Maharajah Kharrack Singh on his bed washing his teeth. The

adjoining bed, which belonged to Chet Singh, was empty. When asked where his Minister was, Kharrack Singh simply replied that he had gone out on hearing a shot fired... His own son and some four or five Sikhs held him down while we proceeded in search of the fugitive... Lal Singh called out that he saw the glitter of a sword in one corner, and there cowered the wretched man, his hand upon his sword... Dhyan Singh, dagger in hand, slowly advancing towards his enemy, said, 'The twenty-four hours you were courteous enough to mention to me have not yet elapsed.' Then with the spring of a tiger the successful counter-plotter dashed at his enemy and plunged his dagger into his heart, crying out, 'Take this in memory of Ranjit Singh!' Dhyan Singh, his face radiant with gratified purpose, then turned round to his party and courteously thanked us for our aid.

Kharrack Singh was then deposed and, says Gardner, 'gradually poisoned with the connivance of his son Nao Nihil Singh. Kharrack Singh cherished the greatest affection for this unnatural son, and in the agony of death called for Nao Nihil Singh so as to pardon him: the young prince, however... treated him with the greatest brutality and insolence.' Kharrack Singh died, aged thirty-eight, in November 1840, and Nao Nihil Singh was proclaimed Maharajah.

The rule of the new Maharajah, who even before his father's death had ordered moves to counter British encroachments in the cis-Sutlej states, was short indeed. The next day he attended his father's cremation, a barbarous ritual in which two of the dead man's wives and eleven of his slave girls were burnt with him, one of them, who fought for life, being literally flung on to the flames. Nao Nihil Singh stood briefly before the blazing pyre in the open space opposite Ranjit Singh's mausoleum and then, defying deeply venerated religious etiquette, left the scene of smoke and flames before cremation was completed and strode off to a bathing place a hundred yards away to perform the ceremony of ablution. 'I was present, standing close by in attendance on Raja Dhyan Singh,' Gardner says.

> Before the new Maharajah left the spot I was directed by Dhyan Singh to go and bring forty of my artillerymen in their fatigue dress: I was not told, nor have I ever ascertained, what they were wanted for. When I returned the catastrophe had just occurred. Maharajah Nao Nihil Singh had passed through an archway on his return from bathing, and just before entering it he took the hand of his constant companion, the eldest son of Raja Gulab Singh: the two young men entered the archway together. As they emerged from it a crash was heard; beams, stones, and tiles fell from above, and the Maharajah and Udam Singh were struck to the ground. The latter was killed on the spot, and Nao Nihil Singh… was injured in the head, but presently attempted to rise and cried out for water… Nao Nihil Singh was carried into the palace, the doors were closed, and admission denied to all… Admittance even to the fort there was none, still less into the Maharajah's apartment. None of the female inmates, not even his wives, were suffered to see him.

Gardner, who seems to imply that the artillerymen were ordered by Dhyan Singh to bring down the archway on top of the Maharajah, saw a small wound above his right ear, bleeding slightly, as he was carried in to the palace, but later, when his death was announced, he saw a deep head wound. Dhyan Singh lay on the floor prostrate with grief and Nur-ud-din, the royal physician, was wringing his hands and lamenting the fact that all remedies had been useless.

Ranjit Singh's legitimate line ended with Prince Nao Nihil Singh. Only Prince Shere Singh and one or two other princes born out of wedlock, though acknowledged by the Maharajah, now stood in the way of Raja Dhyan Singh's ambitions. Described by the British as 'an amiable voluptuary', Shere Singh was now proclaimed Maharajah, with Dhyan Singh's backing, and Nao Nihil Singh was cremated with two of his wives on his father's still smouldering pyre.

A woman now stepped boldly into the arena. Chand Kaur, Raja Kharrack Singh's widow, and mother of Raja Nao Nihil Singh, on the grounds that a widow of her dead son would in due time give birth to an heir, now claimed the regency of the Punjab pending the child's birth. At this, Gardner asserts, the brothers Dhyan Singh and Gulab Singh pretended to quarrel and to take opposite sides. Gulab Singh and his nephew Hira Singh supported the widow, while Dhyan Singh seemingly stood behind Shere Singh, who had assumed the title of Maharajah. The issue was complicated by the chiefs of the powerful Sindhanwalia family declaring for the widow, in the hope that they would in time be able to seize control of the country from her. Civil war now loomed.

The Khalsa meanwhile were growing unruly and mutinous. The men overruled the officers, threatened them and sometimes forced them to resign. They set up small committees called *panchayats* on the pattern of village councils in every unit from troops battery and company to brigade level, to run the Khalsa in opposition to the officers — a revolutionary form of democratic control that stirs echoes of Cromwell's army. The men of the Khalsa were beginning to see that they held the keys to power.

The British were now watching the struggle for power and the state of public feeling in the Punjab with the utmost care. The north-west frontier agent, George Clerk, stationed at Ludhiana, wrote at this time that reports in Anglo-Indian newspapers had convinced the Sikhs that the British army was to assemble at Ferozepore, south of the Sutlej for the conquest of the Punjab. 'Since the receipt of this intelligence,' he told the Government, 'little else has been thought of for the last few days, and a great sensation has been produced in the Durbar Court; Raja Dhyan Singh remarked on the Khalsa having stood by the British Government on the advance through the Khyber and (which God forbid) should the Russians create any disturbance then the friendship of the British and Khalsa governments would become manifest.'

Thus the Sikhs still felt a strong sense of common interest with the British.

Clerk, whose intelligence reports were a model of restraint, added:

> I cannot divest my mind of the feeling that the dissolution of all government in the Punjab, which formerly need not have affected the British Government, would now affect it…; and that in consequence… it may be expedient that, if the British Government be not early called upon to restore tranquillity it should not delay to call upon the Sikhs authoritatively to do so… Various are the elements of discord now raging at Lahore; and various are the parties, powerful among themselves, whose distractions may involve consequences that would compel the British Government to interfere for the restoration of order… General and violent disorder in the Punjab may ensue… This turbulence might in several ways materially affect the interests of the British Government… and would therefore require to be promptly met and suppressed.

This suggestion, that British forces might soon be needed to 'enforce law and order', was to be put forward frequently by Clerk during this period of anarchy and bloodshed. For the time being, Lord Auckland, the Governor-General, merely agreed that the situation might compel such interference, which the British Government 'has sought and still seeks, wholly to avoid'.

Early in December, the widow Chand Kaur brought matters to a head in Lahore by having herself proclaimed Maharani. Shere Singh fled the capital, followed a month later by Raja Dhyan Singh, but by mid-January Shere Singh had gathered enough followers to re-assert his claim to the throne once more. He marched on the capital at the head of a small, well-armed force. Chand Kaur, Gulab Singh, his nephew Hira Singh, and the American Colonel Gardner, determined to resist, barricaded themselves in the fortified palace of Lahore with about three thousand men and forty guns. Far north in his ancestral home in Jammu, Dhyan Singh stayed carefully out of the way until the time would be ripe for his return.

Shere Singh now sent messengers throughout the country calling on the whole Khalsa to join him, offering as an inducement an increase in pay and the traditional right of every Sikh soldier to bring four relations to join in pillaging the enemies of the State. Additionally, he gave them leave to execute what Gardner calls lynch-law upon their private enemies, a dangerous and retrograde step that aggravated the spirit of mutiny and brought a wave of cruelty and violence.

The Italian General Ventura also now played an influential role in the struggle for power. Before Dhyan Singh had left for Jammu, he had, says Clerk, urged the General to 'attend to the public duties in concert with Raja Gulab Singh...' The Maharani tried to bring him over to her side with costly presents from the Palace treasury — a sword set with jewels, an elephant, a horse with a silver saddle, a valuable pearl necklace, a gold armlet and ten thousand rupees (£1,000).

According to Clerk, whose secret agents were close to the highest personages in the Court, Ventura told the Maharani that the Khalsa power would dissolve into nothing if Dhyan Singh did not return, and the whole country would rise up for plunder and that the British were close at hand at Ferozepore watching. At this she presented him, in addition, with a pair of gold armlets set with jewels which had belonged to her dead son Nao Nihil Singh.

But Ventura nevertheless declared for Shere Singh and was soon followed by Court. Lacking any money to pay his troops, Shere Singh was reported by Clerk to have borrowed two lakhs of rupees (£20,000) from a wealthy courtesan. 'The citizens... desire Shere Singh to be ruler,' Clerk wrote, 'but as yet they all wear a double face. The wealthy in the town are hiding their cash and jewels.'

The Khalsa flocked to Shere Singh's standard, eager for loot — for the gold said to be worth more than two millions sterling, for the fabulous jewels, including the Koh-i-noor diamond held in the treasury in the fort. The dusty plains and the hills outside Lahore were a blaze of camp fires. Spies brought Clerk intelligence that twenty-six thousand infantry, eight thousand horse and forty-five guns with their crews, were with Shere Singh. Chand Kaur, fearful of what might now happen, handed out £20,000 to the defenders to try to buy their loyalty.

This state of imminent civil war the British watched anxiously. Safe passage for their supplies through the Punjab to Afghanistan was essential and they were aware that a total breakdown in government would endanger it. They advanced troops to the Sutlej in readiness. From Kabul, William Macnaghten, now envoy to the new monarch Shah Shujah, proposed that the Tripartite Treaty, which he had taken such pains both to father and deliver, should be abrogated, and the Punjab be split into two parts to be ruled by the predominant chiefs in each. Lord Auckland, however, did not approve; Britain wanted a strong, united and friendly Punjab as her western neighbour.

On 16 January 1841, Shere Singh advanced in great state with General Ventura and Court, all on elephants, to the city walls and planted his standard upon an overlooking hill. Inside, Alexander Gardner, in charge of artillery for the Maharani, heard the thunderous salutes of the troops — 'Shere Singh Badshah (leader)! Dhyan Singh Wazir! Death to Chand Kaur!' At dawn next day the besieging army surrounded the city walls. The troops of the city guard, having accepted fifty thousand rupees (£5,000) from the Maharani, now took a bribe from Shere Singh as well and opened the gates.

Shere Singh's troops surged with a frenzied roar through Lahore's narrow streets up to the barred gates of the royal palace and fort. Within, Gardner had ordered heavy wagons to block the passages leading to them through the walls; and to make quite sure, had sighted at point-blank range on the gates two 12-pounders loaded to the muzzles with grapeshot. Gulab Singh's infantrymen lined the parapets. Outside on the broad road facing the fort, Shere Singh's gunners deployed forty horse-artillery guns and sighted heavy siege guns at the walls. Marksmen swarmed to the minarets of the nearby Badshahi mosque.

Treachery now threatened Gulab Singh and the Maharani. First, the Sindhanwalias deserted with several hundred men, then the city guard went over to Shere Singh. 'The treachery of Tej Singh was so conspicuously and pointedly base,' wrote Gardner, '... that we all swore to a man to kill him if fate put him in our way.' Tej Singh, a chief and military commander of whom more will be heard later, arranged for the gates of the outer fort to be opened. Shere Singh entered with Ventura and Court and took shelter in an underground room. So far, except for the occasional sniping, both sides had held their fire. 'Every moment,' relates Gardner, 'we expected to see the spark of a port-fire and to hear the crash of the cannonade. Gulab Singh's keen eyes peered anxiously through the opening: still there was no noise and not a musket fired.'

Gardner sidled along the dark passages blocked with wagons to look through a chink of one of the gates and saw fourteen guns within twenty yards aimed straight at the gates, with the gunners at the ready. 'The little fort was surrounded by a sea of human heads,' he noted.

> Gulab Singh on the parapets… roared out to Shere Singh, demanding that he should surrender. There was a brief, but breathless pause, and I had not time to warn my artillerymen to clear out of the way when down came the gates over our party, torn to shreds by the simultaneous discharge of all the fourteen guns. Seventeen of my party were blown to pieces, parts of the bodies flying over me. When I had wiped the blood and brains from my face, and could recover a moment, I saw only one little trembling *Klasi*. I hurriedly asked him for a port-fire, having lost mine in the fall of the ruins. He had just had time to hand it to me, and I had crept under my two guns, when with a wild yell some three hundred Akalis[4] swept up the Hazuri Garden and crowded into the gate. They were packed as close as fish, and could hardly move over the heaps of wood and stone, the rubbish and the carts, with which the gateway was blocked. Just at that moment, when the crowd were rushing on us, their swords high, I managed to fire the two guns, and literally blew them into the air.

---

[4] Religious shock troops and fanatics.

In the pause which followed I loaded the guns with the aid of the three of my artillerymen who survived, and our next discharge swept away the hostile artillerymen who were at the fourteen guns outside, who had remained standing perfectly paralysed by the destruction of the Akalis. Then... grievous carnage commenced. The Dogras, always excellent marksmen, seemed that day not to miss a man from the walls... In the Hazuri Bagh we counted the bodies of no less than 2,800 soldiers, 200 artillerymen and 180 horses. And now the whole park of artillery opened upon us that day, and for the three days following, tearing the walls of the fort to rags. They mounted their heavy guns on high houses, the walls of which they pierced to command the fort. Many a time did Shere Singh attempt a parley; but Gulab Singh knew his countrymen too well to believe any protestations. He said, 'Wait until Dhyan Singh comes!' At last that noble Minister did arrive, furious, as it seemed, with Shere Singh for his rashness...

The brothers Gulab Singh and Dhyan Singh, with Prince Shere Singh, now arranged terms. Shere Singh was to be Maharajah and Dhyan Singh was to keep his posts as prime minister and war minister. The Maharani was to be given a pension of seven lakhs of rupees (£70,000) a year and a house. But meanwhile, unknown to Shere Singh, she had sent Ajit Singh Sindhanwalia across the Sutlej to George Clerk seeking British intervention on her behalf in exchange for the transfer of Kashmir to them. But the Governor-General still drew back from war against the Sikhs.

In Lahore, events followed a characteristic course. It was agreed that Gulab Singh and his troops should quit the fort with honour at midnight on 19 January 1841, but when Shere Singh discovered that the treasury was almost empty, he ordered that the defenders should be searched, all but ten rupees each to be wrested from them. Angrily Gulab protested that being a Rajput who wielded the sword, it would not become his character to allow his followers to be searched and he therefore demanded to be allowed to depart unmolested with them. This was agreed and during the night his men marched out with more than twenty thousand rupees, while Gulab Singh himself removed from the treasury a fortune in gold and silver and jewels. The next day Shere Singh entered the fort and palace on an elephant with a silver howdah, Court and Ventura followed on another elephant and sixteen more elephants all gorgeously caparisoned carried his chiefs and generals. Gardner, oddly enough, continued in command of the Lahore artillery.

Shere Singh was enthroned on 27 January 1841, after the Maharani had been requested to leave the palace and to hand over the keys of the treasury, which very naturally she did with tears in her eyes. The dead were removed, the palace gardens washed, Ranjit Singh's terrified concubines, living there on pension, were consoled, and Shere Singh begged the Maharani's pardon, promising her he would treat her like his own mother.

Had the army been disciplined and under control, all would now have returned to normal, but the Khalsa was like a mob of bandits, plundering merchants, attacking citizens, murdering officers who interfered. Shere Singh gently requested them to cease, says Clerk. 'The troops replied that it was owing to their help and good offices that he had got the throne and that he must now indulge them.'

George Clerk, whose special duty it was to watch British interests in the region, became more and more concerned about the clear inability of Shere Singh's government to stop the Khalsa behaving as if it was a rival power in the land. Camel convoys of food, ammunition and treasure for the

British Army in Afghanistan were endangered. Major George Broadfoot, a paranoiac Scot with pebble spectacles and red hair, leading a convoy of Shah Shuja's two hundred women through the Punjab to Kabul with an escort of Muslim sepoys, dealt with the danger aggressively by ordering immediate attacks on any armed Sikhs who came within gunshot range and delivered the Shah's women safely to their new harem.

Clerk had already been authorized to agree to any request for a British force to march to the aid of Shere Singh to suppress disturbances and twelve thousand British and Indian troops were now held ready at Ludhiana for the purpose. On 14 February, when the Sikh soldiers in Lahore were still looting and stabbing, Clerk wrote the Governor-General saying that these outrages had destroyed the peace and security that ought to exist on the borders of a friendly state. 'The time seems therefore to have arrived, when it is incumbent on the British Government to require the restoration of order by the head of the State, to threaten, if he fails, to interfere to restore it, and to be prepared to undertake to do so.' Shere Singh duly received a warning that the British Government had no wish to interfere in the internal affairs of his country, but unless outrages ceased and order was restored it would have no alternative. Dhyan Singh partially solved the problem by sending large numbers of the troops on their annual leave.

Meanwhile, naturally grieved at finding the treasury in the Lahore palace more or less empty — even the fabulous Koh-i-noor diamond, now part of the British Crown jewels had disappeared — Shere Singh personally led searches first to the Maharani's home in her native village and later to an estate nearby belonging to Gulab Singh. The Maharani freely confessed to having the Koh-i-noor and tearfully handed it over. She was warned that if she continued to intrigue against the Maharajah with the Sindhanwalias her annual pension of £70,000 would be cancelled.

Shere Singh's heart must have leapt for joy at the fabulous hoard discovered at Gulab Singh's home during his absence in Kashmir. The list included: nine large gold bricks, each weighing three pounds; two hundred gold saddles set with jewels; ninety-two pairs of solid gold bangles; the Maharani's jewels, valued at ninety thousand rupees (£9,000); a ruby valued at sixty-five thousand rupees; nine bags filled with diamonds and emeralds; a pearl necklace valued at seventy-five thousand rupees, five hundred silver saddles; sixty-one gold plates; two hundred and seventy-five gold and silver plates; five gold chairs, eleven silver chairs; five hundred thousand rupees belonging to the Maharani and forty-five thousand gold ducats. For good measure six nine-pounder guns, two hundred matchlocks, two mortars, forty horses, seventy bullocks and one hundred and eighty buffaloes were taken off as well. But this was a mere fraction of the treasure the prudent Ranjit Singh had seized in his lifetime from rival chieftains, and reputedly worth more than twelve million pounds sterling at the time.

Events had destroyed the legend of British military invincibility in Sikh eyes, and brought war nearer. By the end of 1841 the British army occupying Kabul faced disaster. Led by Akbar Khan, son of Dost Mohammed Khan, the king whom the British had deposed, the Afghan tribesmen throughout the country surged into Kabul and in face of the gross incompetence of the sick and ageing British commander, General Elphinstone, seized stores and provisions in a fort outside their cantonments and starved them into surrender. Instead of agreeing to his officers' pleas to fight, General Elphinstone signed a treaty of surrender with the Afghans that committed the British army, women and children, with camp followers, to a march through the icy, snow-blocked mountain passes in mid-winter. The long procession, twelve thousand strong, set out from Kabul on 6 January 1842. By 13 January, a week later, all apart from two hundred prisoners, were dead but one man, Dr Brydon, who rode wounded and barely conscious into Jellalabad, in western Afghanistan, held by a British force.

The legend of British invincibility was dealt by this stupid and unnecessary defeat a damaging blow. In the popular judgement, the British presence in Kabul at all was encirclement of the Punjab, as a step towards extending the Empire. Among the Sikhs, there were many who saw this as a favourable moment to cross the Sutlej, and attack the British, at the same time waging war on the new British army of retribution under General Pollock which was crossing the Punjab on its way to the Khyber Pass. But Marahajah Shere Singh remained steadfastly loyal, guaranteed as well as he was able the undisputed passage of Pollock's army and placed fifteen thousand of his own troops at British disposal against the Afghans. This total force reinforced the British at Jellalabad, defeated Akbar Khan and withdrew from Afghanistan after the honour of British arms was felt to have been vindicated.

But it by no means removed the new doubts in British invincibility in the minds of the Sikh soldiery.

Maharajah Shere Singh, however, still maintained a sincere friendship for the British, which Lord Ellenborough, the new Governor-General, publicly praised, declaring that 'the loss sustained by the Sikhs in the assault of the Pass which was forced by them is understood to have been equal to that sustained by the troops of Her Majesty...'

Raja Dhyan Singh had now become the most powerful figure in the Punjab. 'It is commonly supposed,' wrote Clerk, 'that his scheme is by some means or other to possess himself of the throne... Certainly his rivals were eliminated. The Maharani Chand Kaur had been intriguing against both him and Shere Singh. Dhyan Singh had in revenge caused her pension to be cancelled. On the night of 11 June 1842, she was murdered. Her slave-girls beat her head with stones while she was lying in her bath. They were caught, but before they could talk their tongues were cut out on the order of Dhyan Singh and they were executed. He and his brother Gulab Singh shared in the dead Maharani's property.

Meanwhile, Lord Ellenborough was bringing to his duties as Governor-General, a thirst for glory and a keen appreciation of military needs.

6: War

Even before he set foot in the white neo-classical building in Calcutta called Government House, Ellenborough had recognized what he believed was the danger to British India of an independent Punjab. Perhaps as much as anything, the brilliant military campaign of the Sikh General Zowahir Singh, who in June 1841 had crossed the high Himalayas and invaded Chinese Tibet, cutting British links with Lhasa, had alerted him to the danger. George Clerk, the British agent in the northwest provinces, had demanded an immediate withdrawal. The Sikhs denied that the move was a breach of their treaty obligations, stayed put and only the need to reconquer Afghanistan at the time stopped British counter-action. Then the snows came; ill-equipped for winter warfare the Sikhs fell victims in the high altitude to cold, hunger and Chinese attacks. Zowahir Singh was killed as they fought their way out. In the spring of 1842 a fresh Sikh force invaded, but in face of renewed British protests they signed a treaty with the Chinese and withdrew.

Ellenborough, meanwhile, had gone as far as studying the most promising way to attack the country, appointing Lieutenant Henry Durand, an engineer officer who was later to become Governor of the Punjab to examine the terrain and make a report for submission to the Duke of Wellington. 'I am most anxious to have your opinion as to the general principles upon which a campaign against the country should be conducted,' he wrote to the Duke in October 1841. And later: 'At present some 12,000 men are collected at Ferozepore to watch the Sikhs and act if necessary.'

At the same time, Ellenborough decided to pull the British armies of retribution out of Afghanistan as soon as they had done their work, justifying it, in a letter to Sir Jasper Nichols, then commander-in-chief, with the remark that it was erroneous 'to suppose that a forward position in Upper Afghanistan would have the effect of controlling the Sikhs...' The Punjab, he declared, was liable any day to be actively hostile and the sole alternative to withdrawal from Afghanistan was the conquest of the Sikhs and annexation of their country, a move then militarily impossible.

Ellenborough's next move, after the death of Shah Shuja, the British puppet king in Afghanistan, was without telling the Sikhs, to revoke the Tripartite Treaty, which Ranjit Singh had been persuaded to sign, and to allow the Sikh's inveterate enemy Dost Mahommed — whom the British had driven out — to return to Kabul. At this, even Maharajah Shere Singh's pro-British feelings cooled, and Anglo-Sikh relations worsened. Perhaps suspecting that the British had made a secret anti-Sikh agreement with the Afghan ruler, he gave Dost Mahommed an impressive reception and signed a separate treaty recognizing him as king of Afghanistan when the exile returned to his homeland through Lahore.

The humiliating disaster the British had suffered at Afghan hands had meantime convinced Sikh soldiers that the British, who had earlier checked them in Malwa, Sind and Tibet, no longer led invincible troops. For the Khalsa, the issue was therefore brutally simple: they must wrest power from the Court, cross the Sutlej, subdue the British, seize Delhi and conquer India, for they believed no other troops except the Redcoats could think of challenging them.

Such were the dreams of these soldiers who gathered in homage around Ranjit Singh's tomb in Lahore, excited by hopes of loot, inflamed by a growing hatred of the ever-watchful British. In March 1843 they had still more reason for hatred, and fear, too. The British seized Sind, the province on the Indus whose outlet to the sea Ranjit Singh had wanted so much. Wishing to control the Indus for the vessels British merchants hoped would carry wool, skins and furs down to the sea from the north, Ellenborough used the ruthless General Sir Charles Napier to provoke a war with the family oligarchy known as the Amirs of Sind so that he could annex the province — even though a British treaty was supposed to guarantee its independence. Vainly, the Amirs pleaded and protested. 'God knows we have never thought of opposing the British nor thought of war or fighting. We have not the power,' one of them lamented to Napier. 'I am now and shall continue to be a suitor for justice at your hands.'

Napier, a soldier first and foremost, swiftly found a reason for war. He accused the Amirs of suborning his sepoys; their tribesmen of attacking British-protected territory. Invading with a small force of two thousand infantry and twelve guns, he routed the Sindian army of twenty-two thousand, killed five thousand, exiled the Amirs, annexed the province and personally took £70,000 in prize money from the property seizures that followed. Cynically, he called the affair a bit of 'humane rascality'.

For the Sikhs, it was an alarm signal. Their turn, it seemed, could not but be next.

But fresh bloodshed now came with dramatic suddenness at Lahore. Ajit Singh Sindhanwalia, who earlier had tried to seize control of the country by backing the Maharani Chand Kaur, had been forgiven by Maharajah Shere Singh and allowed to return from British India. On 14 September 1843 he arrived in Lahore with fifty newly trained cavalry troopers for Shere

Singh to review next day. The Maharajah rode out on horseback with a few attendants through the Roshnaee gate of Lahore and passed along the line of cavalrymen in their brilliant array. Ajit Singh thereupon offered him a present of a fine new English rifle, which Shere Singh took eagerly, squinted along the sights, and passed it to one of Ajit Singh's retainers to load and fire. Ajit Singh nodded, and the man shot the Maharajah in the heart. He fell and Ajit Singh struck off his head with one blow of his sword and stuck it on his spear. Lehna Singh, Ajit's brother, killed young Prince Pertaub Singh in a garden nearby and decapitated him. Both then rode into Lahore with their followers, carrying their grisly trophies.

Raja Dhyan Singh, believed to be involved in the plot to eliminate the Maharajah, pretended to be shocked when he saw the heads of both Shere Singh, and his son, and straightway reproved them for killing the young prince. Shrugging his shoulders, Ajit Singh said that 'what is done cannot be undone', and more to the point, asked — 'Who is to be king now?' Dhyan Singh answered cryptically, 'There is no one but Duleep Singh.' (The infant son allegedly of Ranjit Singh and Rani Jindan, one of his wives.) Ajit Singh said: 'And so he is to be made king and you become prime minister, while we get nothing for our pains?'

A revered holy man, Guru Goormukh Singh, now lent his spiritual authority to still another murder. 'What is the use of words?' he whispered to Ajit Singh. 'Remove the Raja as you have done Shere Singh and his son, then your path will be clear.'

Ajit Singh then shot Dhyan Singh in the back and killed him, rushed into the royal palace at the head of his followers, burst into Shere Singh's harem and in the bloodiest of scenes murdered all his women. The Sindhanwalias' three thousand troops now surged into the fort, the gates were closed and Ajit Singh proclaimed seven-years-old Duleep Singh Maharajah and himself vizier.

Thus was Dhyan Singh overwhelmed in the wave of murder he had originally launched.

Hira Singh, his son, promising the Khalsa extra pay, attacked the fort and for two days artillery hammered the ancient walls, until the troops surged in, Ajit Singh was killed by a Muslim soldier and all the defenders were slaughtered. 'The whole of the inside of the fort is red with blood,' the British *Punjab Intelligence Report* said precisely. Hira Singh now kissed seven-years-old Duleep Singh's feet, proclaimed him Maharajah and himself as prime minister. The body of Rajah Dhyan Singh was burnt with the Rani and seven other women of his household on the funeral pyre. A British force of fourteen thousand was brought forward to protect the frontier, and distributed between Ferozepore, Ludhiana, Roopur and Bussean and Ambala.

The treble killing of Maharajah Shere Singh, his son and Dhyan Singh, the prime minister, was to lead soon to the last spate of murder in the Punjab and to the unleasing of the Khalsa.

Ellenborough, a zealous advocate of what was called the 'forward' or expansionist policy in India, watched this collapse of government in the Punjab like a hungry lion, and in regular letters told Her Majesty Queen Victoria about it. A letter from General Ventura forecasting renewed anarchy and bloodshed — a copy of which was sent to the Queen — caused Ellenborough to advise her in a letter on 20 October 1843 that it was 'impossible not to perceive that the ultimate tendency of the late events at Lahore is, without any effort on our part, to bring the plains first, and at a somewhat later period the hills, under our protection or control.'

Writing to the Duke of Wellington on the same day Ellenborough stressed the dangers of the lack of effective political control over the Khalsa, and set out his ideas as to the probable government of the Punjab under the British, and the treasure it would bring in:

> The army is paramount. Everything is managed by the regimental committees, which correspond and act in concert. The donations and pay can only be paid for a short time out of the accumulated treasures. When these fail all will be confusion. Heera Singh has no real authority… We adhere to the policy pursued for so many years; and for my own part I desire the continuance of a government in the Punjab like that of Ranjit Singh. The thing, however, will not be; and the time cannot be very distant when the Punjab will fall into our management… The Khalsa lands are worth half a million, and the payments from the Jagheers may be as much. There would also be lapses of estates.

The British were far from ready for war and Ellenborough made clear his dissatisfaction with the army at this time. To the Secret Committee he said in an anxious letter on 11 February 1844:

> Our position with respect to the Punjab can now be viewed only in the light of an armed truce — the contest, whenever it may take place, must be on both sides, not for Empire only, but for life, and I must frankly confess, that when I look at the whole condition of our Army I had rather, if the contest cannot be further postponed, that it were at least postponed to November 1845. Let our policy be what it may the contest must come at last, and the intervening time which may be

given to us should be employed in unostentatious but vigilant preparation.

In particular, he wanted first-class artillery — he told the Duke of Wellington that the British would encounter a very powerful artillery if it were obliged to meet the Sikhs 'and it is very necessary that every possible measure should be previously taken to make our artillery most efficient.' He emphasized in another letter: 'I earnestly hope that we may not be obliged to cross the Sutlej in December next. We shall not be ready so soon. The army requires a great deal of setting up after five years of war. I am quietly doing what I can to strengthen and equip it.'

Overshadowing this Anglo-Sikh drift towards war was the army of mercenaries dominating the Mahratta state of Gwalior, lying south of Agra, between the rivers Chambal and Jumna. Fearing a dangerous combination of Sikh and Mahratta against the British, Ellenborough now ordered the assembly of the 'Army of Exercise' under the new commander-in-chief, Sir Hugh Gough, strong enough to defeat them so quickly that the Sikhs would have no time to intervene. 'It is a matter of great moment,' he wrote to Queen Victoria on 19 December 1843, defending this policy, 'to reduce the strength of the army maintained by the Gwalior State... The existence of an army of such strength in that position must very seriously embarrass the disposition of troops we might be desirous of making to meet a coming danger from the Sutlej.'

Upon the Treaty of Burhampur (1804), which gave the British power to aid in maintaining order, Lord Ellenborough based his right to interfere and on 26 December General Gough advanced with a force of four thousand eight hundred infantry, thirteen hundred cavalry and three hundred and eighty guns. The senior officers' ladies were mounted on elephants to witness the battle, but the gunfire, and the explosion of a powder dump nearby stampeded the beasts, trumpeting wildly, across country. They were found towards evening and none the worse the ladies were taken to a tent for tea on ground held earlier by the Mahrattas. Suddenly, a squad of British soldiers rushed in and carried them out. They were hardly clear when an enemy mine exploded and the tent was blown to pieces. The campaign ended in forty-eight hours with the total defeat of the Mahratta army of fifteen thousand, and Ellenborough celebrated by presenting each of the ladies with a commemorative medal like that given to the troops.

Ellenborough was still anxious about the army, but the East India Company directors in London had become far more anxious about him — about the aggressive trend of his policy, in face of the need for peace which they had urged upon him; about the arrogant tone of his letters, and about his open favouritism of the army at the expense of the civilians. They decided to act. In June 1844, despite Queen Victoria's opposition, Ellenborough was recalled, and replaced by General Sir Henry Hardinge, aged fifty-nine, a former war minister and veteran soldier who, at Vimiera, Albuera, Ligny and other battles of the Napoleonic Wars had proved his worth, though mainly as a staff officer.

If the directors hoped for a less war-minded man Hardinge was a strange choice. 'Without doubt,' wrote his son, also his private secretary in India, 'the selection of a distinguished soldier, who also possessed the experience of a cabinet minister, rather painted to the anticipation of war.' Nor did Ellenborough, a kinsman by marriage and a close friend, anticipate any significant changes. 'You will have heard that the Court of Directors have thought fit to recall me,' he wrote to the warlike Major George Broadfoot, whom he had recommended to succeed Colonel Richmond as north-west frontier political agent. 'My successor will carry out all my views. He is my most confidential friend, with whom I have communicated upon all subjects for thirty years.'

In fact, as we shall see, Hardinge obeyed his orders to avoid war to the extent that Gough's hands were tied when the crunch came.

At Lahore meanwhile, the rule of Hira Singh and his Hindu mentor Pandit Julia was threatened by the mutinous Khalsa and more seriously by Maharani Jindan. Queen Mother, she was determined to seize power and rule through her lover Lal Singh and her brother Jowahir Singh, if necessary murdering Hira Singh to reach this objective for her son's sake. The Maharani, of whom Lord Ellenborough said, 'she seems to be a woman of determined courage, the only person at Lahore apparently who has courage,' had no alternative but to rule through men. Outside private apartments, in Court especially, a screen, as well as a veil, separated her from courtiers, a handicap that made trusted intermediaries, or lovers, essential. The daughter of one of his officers, Ranjit had gone through a form of marriage with her during his last year of life. Gardner constantly refers to her as a woman of extraordinary beauty and talent.

When Hira Singh, on economy grounds, dismissed two or three hundred Khalsa officers in December 1844, Maharani told the military *panchayats* that he and Pandit Julia were guilty of treason, adding that her own life would be in danger if these two knew of her loyalty to the troops. It was a clever move and it succeeded, for the *panchayats* began to clamour for the lives first of Pandit Julia and then of Hira Singh, too. The Khalsa was now a formidable force, Captain J. D. Cunningham of the north-west frontier agency having recently estimated its strength at eighty thousand infantry, thirty-one thousand cavalry, more than five thousand gunners, five hundred field guns and nine hundred swivel guns. Colonel Richmond's *Punjab Intelligence* reported at this time that one of the Khalsa's generals had informed Hira Singh a few months earlier that they were ready to cross the Sutlej and take the British bases of Ferozepore and Ludhiana as soon as orders were received, but that Hira Singh was unwilling.

During December, the Khalsa learned that Pandit Julia, finance minister, had declared that the state could no longer support them, and on 21 December thousands of troops gathered outside the palace clamouring for Hira Singh's and his blood. For these two it was the end. They escaped, fled the city on horseback with a bodyguard but were detected, chased and after a running fight over nine miles, caught and cut down. The troops paraded their heads on spears through the streets of Lahore.

So, in this traditionally violent way, died Hira Singh, of whom Sir Henry Hardinge had written only a few weeks earlier: 'He is the handsomest man in the East, twenty-four years of age, and has shown considerable ability. He is brave and reckless, and it is probable that among people so ferocious he will not long escape a violent death…'

There was no one now even to try to control the Khalsa but Maharani Jindan and her drunken brother Jawahir Singh. He bribed the Khalsa in what had become the traditional way, increasing its manpower still more and encouraging it to look to the day when it would fight the British. Major George Broadfoot had begun his stormy period as political agent at Ferozepore. He was dependent for information upon a *vakeel* (agent) and an official newswriter at the Lahore Court, just as was this Court upon similar British sources at Ferozepore, Delhi and Calcutta. A system of indirect representation it put the two nations at the mercy of agents — foreign ones, for the British — for whom it was worthwhile to keep excitement and suspicion at fever pitch; and of course, there were spies. It would seem to have been one of the causes of the misunderstandings and suspicion between British and Sikh at this time.

Broadfoot, an intensely ambitious and hot-headed Scot, was a dangerous man indeed in this very sensitive situation. Paranoiacally liable to see grave insults to the British Government where none were intended he was also arrogant, pompous and bellicose. In private letters to Lord Ellenborough in England, he adversely criticized Sir Hugh Gough, commander-in-chief, for ordering movements of reserves forward to join the brigades at Ferozepore. When a young officer, Lieutenant Ellice, disappeared for a few days in a region of the cis-Sutlej states controlled by Lahore, Broadfoot indulged in a foolish display of sabre-rattling because the Lahore authorities said that this was the officer's own fault — he was drunk. At the same time Broadfoot was carrying on with Lahore a correspondence on issues affecting the foundation of the relations between British and Sikh.

Hardinge reproved him, sought to bring him under control, telling him: 'It is the desire of the Governor-General to shew all forbearance and consideration to the young Maharajah in the present unhappy state of parties at the capital and on no account to make the misconduct and notorious immorality of his advisers... an occasion for the breaking of these treaties which have hitherto existed between the two governments.'

But on Broadfoot, a strong believer in 'sword government', this good advice went unheard, for he was soon stirring up trouble with reports on, of all things, Maharani Jindan's sex life — or as he called it, 'misconduct and notorious immorality' — which more than anything, he knew, would help to strengthen the wish to impose 'Christian government' in the Punjab.

The Rani's lover, Raja Lal Singh who controlled the Khalsa, and Jawahir Singh, her brother, and prime minister, had quarrelled, he reported in July, owing to Jawahir Singh's jealousy over the resumption of Lal Singh's visits to the Maharani after his recovery from cholera, of which there was then a serious epidemic in Lahore. Lal Singh, aware that the Maharani had a passionate desire for him, tried to undermine Jawahir Singh's standing with his sister by letting her know that he was afraid to visit her because he might be attacked. Cleverly, she brought them together and reconciled them. Then, Broadfoot reported, to celebrate the reconciliation, she presented each of them with a beautiful slave girl, both of whom she had just received from a Sikh chief who knew of her fondness for attractive girls, and with the girls she sent word that she expected they 'would do proper honour to her gift'. Lamented Broadfoot: 'Such is Sikh morality, for Lal Singh is one of the Rani's lovers.'

Nero fiddled while Rome burned; the Maharani and her ministers plunged into orgies while war loomed and the Khalsa smouldered ominously like a furnace about to burst into flames. Of this, Broadfoot reported:

> Jawahir Singh is always drunk… I believe he has for some time formed a drunken design or vision of war with us after the Duserah… to avert from himself the wrath of the army as a means of finding money to pay them… It is quite impossible to see what may be the issue of dealings with such a drunk acting on such troops.

> I sometimes feel as if I were a sort of parish constable at the door of a brothel rather than the representative of one government to another. The state of parties is seriously changed. The cause is the Rani's mind having become seriously affected by her excesses. Messalina picked big men and Catherine liked variety, but what do you think… of four young fellows changed as they cease to give satisfaction passing every night with the Rani. She has become stupid instead of clever and lively — is sometimes for days in a state bordering on fatuity and though at times she revives, chiefly when stimulated by drinking, she has but little concern in the public business compared with what she used to do.

Early in August 1845, towards the end of the monsoon, when the frogs croaked in the torrential rain and the peacocks shrieked as thunder rent the damp air, Broadfoot complained that he was unable to get a reply to his letters because the Rani, Jawahir Singh and Rajah Lal Singh were all drunk, together with the Khalsa generals. 'They listened to no business, but sending for dancing girls, Jawahir Singh dresses himself as one and dances with the rest.'

Nevertheless, one or all of these three had given the orders and supplied the money, for the Khalsa was preparing. Broadfoot reported at this time unusual vigour in military preparations:

> Artillery is the object of special attention — new guns have been cast, carriages are in course of construction, the old carriages are under repair and the artillery draft cattle are sent out to graze. Ammunition and stores of every kind are also under preparation. Muskets, swords and gunpowder are ordered to be bought and manufactured in large quantities and unless something occurs to divert the attention of the Durbar, the army will as to material be more efficient next cold weather than it has been for some years.

> These preparations are undoubtedly made with reference to possible collision with us and yet I think... that the suspicions of the Durbar are greatly less than they were and are still decreasing... The utmost total dispersion of the army for the first time for many years shows... that though preparation is thought prudent there is no belief in immediate hostility being intended by us.

But this dispersion of the Khalsa was caused not by trust of the British, but by a march north to Jammu to put down a rebellion by Gulab Singh, who had declared himself independent. Gulab Singh was certainly not so foolish as to weaken himself now in a useless struggle with the Khalsa if he could fight later with advantage, when it was caught up in its inevitable struggle with the British — to whom, indeed, he had already offered his services in the event of war.

So he submitted to the Khalsa, flatteringly declared that he was its servant and not that of the Court, and returned to Lahore with it, promising himself threefold revenge for the abduction of hundreds of women and boys by the Sikh troops, the rape, the theft and the destruction. Fined sixty-eight lakhs of rupees (£68,000), he managed to settle for twenty-seven lakhs, then regained his freedom, went back to Jammu and sent an agent to Broadfoot assuring him that when war came he would attack the Sikhs from behind with forty thousand men.

Hardinge now decided that in October he should start on the long journey from Calcutta to the British base of Ambala so as to be able to be on the spot to control things. 'When the finances of the [Sikh] state shall be found insufficient to pay the troops, a state of things may arise at any moment requiring the instant decision of the highest authority...' He also quite clearly had decided that Broadfoot — whom he greatly admired — did need direct control of the kind only he could give, for during the few months since his appointment, Broadfoot had decisively worsened Anglo-Sikh relations — had he wished for war he could not have done more. He had unilaterally declared the Maharajah's extensive lands south of the Sutlej — apart from Sikh territories mentioned in the treaty of 1809 — to be under British protection, and to be liable to escheat or confiscation should the young Maharajah die or be deposed. He had ordered troops to oppose a small party of Sikh mounted police after it had legally crossed the Sutlej to relieve those legally stationed there, ordered them to return and when they did not comply quickly enough with this illegal order, charged them and killed one. When Sikh peasants in the sparse land south of Ferozepore had refused to supply large quantities of forage because they had not even enough for their own needs, he made ready to send troops to enforce his demands. Only Hardinge's warning that the matter must be settled peaceably stopped military action.

Each of these belligerent acts angered the Sikhs and made it harder for the Maharani's frail government to control the Khalsa.

Hardinge reproved Broadfoot, but this the Sikh Government at Lahore was not to know; Broadfoot was the accredited British agent; his attitudes and bearing were assumed to be those of his masters. Broadfoot was hostile where in the interests of both governments he should have been friendly and constructive. That he was hard-working and energetic only increased his harmfulness. This, Hardinge seems to have realized, for in August he ordered Broadfoot to avoid all decisions as far as possible until he himself arrived to take over in October, and truthfully to give this as the reason. But instead, Broadfoot added to Sikh suspicion and hostility by refusing discussions on various issues 'so long as the Durbar maintained its present posture', thus increasing tensions.

Gulab Singh's offer to join in an attack on the Punjab, and the requests of Sikh chiefs of the anti-war group that the British should intervene to restore ordered government, or to establish a protectorate like that over the Sikh states south of the Sutlej, Broadfoot properly reported. The reply he received from the Government dated 10 September 1845 is the best evidence of the British feelings about the warlike situation which the combined efforts of their hostile envoy and an unemployed Sikh army had created.

> The Governor-General in Council is convinced that a strong Sikh Government as in Ranjit Singh's time, united to us by a common interest in resisting Mahommedan aggression, is the most prudent mode of occupying the Punjab, instead of advancing the British outposts three hundred miles beyond our present frontier... If any sudden outbreak on the part of the Sikh troops should cause proposals to be made to you, and on the terms stated in your Dispatch, you will express your conviction that the Governor-General will not assent to that arrangement...

This, together with a reminder that the best British policy was not to interfere by force of arms, and that he was not to conceal British military preparedness, was precise and unmistakable; had Broadfoot sought to advance the Government's policy, he would at this juncture have got authority to meet the Sikh government to try to heal the breach. But Broadfoot was moved by a spirit of enmity; and the Governor-General, still new and uncertain of himself in the field of Indian politics, let himself be too much led.

Early in September Broadfoot wrote to Sir Hugh Gough about numerous sepoy deserters from British forces crossing the Sutlej and enlisting with the Sikhs at Lahore. Broadfoot added that 'men are now actually employed in trying to seduce the sepoys to desert; at any rate the Durbar is paying men for this purpose.' He asked that no fakirs from the Punjab should be allowed to stay in the frontier cantonments.

Broadfoot had in fact discovered the formidable Sikh attempt to sow the seeds of mutiny throughout the Indian army — persuasion that, under Sikh leadership India could be retaken from the *feringees*, and that to achieve this they had merely to desert and enlist at Lahore, when they would at once receive double pay. The message must have been attractive to the Hindu sepoys — the democratic faith of Sikhism and an army ruled not by high caste foreigners but by regimental committees elected by the soldiers themselves. Sir Henry Hardinge had noted this danger and had observed in a letter to Lord Ellenborough that 'self-preservation may require the dispersion of this Sikh army, the baneful influence of such an example is the evil most to be dreaded...'

Baneful it was and Broadfoot now warned his assistant Captain Peter Nicholson to watch certain Punjabis in his employ who had secretly undertaken to corrupt the sepoys. 'One month's espionage for the Durbar, if much approved, will gain one of these men more than he will make honestly by us in all his life.' Artillerymen, all Hindus, he said, had been sent from Lahore disguised as fakirs to enter the British cantonments to persuade the sepoys to go over to Lahore. 'Diligently watch all fakirs... Watch also all brothels and other places of resort by sepoys, and all strangers frequenting them...' Jawahir Singh, terrified that he might, as he put it 'die a dog's death, like Hira Singh' because the army hated him for allegedly having murdered Prince Peshaura Singh, among other crimes, was offering big gold payments to successful emissaries. He had other reasons to want war — lack of money to pay the army, now increased to some seventy thousand men.

In mid-September, he ordered three brigades of troops to the Sutlej with specific instructions to seek a conflict with the English, but, Broadfoot's spies reported, the Guru Bhae Ram Singh urged the troops not to leave Lahore and to avoid at all costs a breach with the English. He predicted too, that Jawahir Singh would be murdered on or around 23 September 1845.

Bhae Ram Singh personally tried to dissuade Jawahir Singh from seeking war, but found that he was in every way determined, believing that whether he himself lived or died there would shortly be a rising against the English at Delhi and other cantonments owing to his subversive preparations. 'The English power,' he was reported to have told a conference of Khalsa generals, 'is small and scattered, and by rapid movements it might be overwhelmed.' The generals said that even if he took Delhi he would not have defeated the English. How would he fare if he led them into such an enterprise without success? Jawahir Singh said that they would murder him, but before that he would shoot himself rather than die like a dog. He continued to urge the immediate march of troops to fight the British.

His ablest counsellors pointed out the folly of throwing away friendship of forty years' standing and the calamity it would bring upon the country. Ponderously Bhae Ram Singh, the guru, asked: 'How can a powerless ant contend with an elephant in rut?' The *panchayats* said the Khalsa might march against the English, but not at the bidding of a fool. Jawahir Singh reproached them and then, terrified, began to prepare the fort of Lahore for defence. The *panchayats* accused him of transgressing the rule made after the death of Raja Dhyan Singh that all important affairs should be settled by discussion between the Durbar, the chiefs and the Khalsa. They claimed that he had overruled them and met to deliberate on his fate.

Matters had now reached flashpoint. The military *panchayats* decided to kill Jawahir Singh and take over government of the state themselves. On 20 September 1845 the Khalsa formally took over all powers. As its first act it ordered the Maharani, with her son and all government officials to attend at the Khalsa camp outside Lahore to hand Jawahir Singh over to them for justice.

Colonel Gardner, commanding Lahore artillery, the troops and their officers were ready to obey the summons. Jawahir Singh wanted to resist. 'I had one interview with him,' Gardner says, 'and could hold out no hope, but told him to behave like a man and face the peril.'

The next morning, Gardner, the artillery and the infantry, left the fort and marched to the Khalsa camp. The Maharani, her son Maharajah Duleep Singh, Jawahir Singh and three or four hundred of his own cavalry bodyguard remained there. When this was known, four battalions of Khalsa troops left the camp with orders to destroy everyone still in the fort.

Finally persuaded it was useless to resist, Jawahir Singh took the young Maharajah on one state elephant, the Maharani followed on another and the members of the Durbar came on a third, with the escorting cavalry behind. On the way, in the late afternoon, with the sun low in the western sky, they encountered the four advancing infantry battalions, who turned about and in silence escorted them to the long lines of tents and the assembled troops. Gardner was ordered to greet Maharajah Duleep Singh and the Rani with his artillery.

> An ominous salute ran along the immense line of the army — one hundred and eighty guns were fired... After the salute had died away, not a sound was heard but trampling of the

feet of the royal cavalcade. Duleep Singh was received with royal honours: his mother, the Maharani Jindan, in miserable terror for her brother, was seated on her golden *hauda*, dressed in white clothes and closely veiled. As soon as the procession reached the middle of the line one man came forward and cried out, 'Stop,' and at his single voice the whole procession paused. A tremor ran through the host: many expected a rescue on the part of the French brigade; but not a man stirred. The great *Panch* (Military Council) was still sitting on the right of the line. Four battalions... now removed Jawahir Singh's escort to a distance... Ten of the Council then came forward; the Maharani's elephant was ordered to kneel down, and she herself was escorted to a small but beautiful tent prepared for her close by.

Then a terrible scene took place. The Maharani was dragged away, shrieking to the army to spare her brother. Jawahir Singh was next ordered to descend from his elephant... Duleep Singh was placed in his mother's arms, and she, hiding herself behind the walls of her tent, held the child up above... crying for mercy for her brother in the name of her son. Suddenly, hearing a yell of agony from a well-known voice, she flung the child away in an agony of grief and rage. Fortunately he was caught by a soldier... Meanwhile the bloody work had been done on the hated minister. A soldier ... had gone up the ladder placed by Jawahir Singh's elephant, stabbed him with his bayonet and flung him upon the ground, where he was despatched in a moment with fifty wounds.

In the dusk, the whole of the government were slain or imprisoned. Next day, the Maharani came out of her tent with her son to where lay Jawahir Singh's body, almost cut to pieces, and broke out into violent lamentations, which moved the soldiers so much that they allowed her to take it to the fort. It was carried to the burning-place, where amid a great crowd, four of his wives were to be burned with it. As they approached the funeral pyre, the Sikh soldiers on duty brutally ripped off their jewels and ornaments, thereby both dishonouring them and depriving them of their last holy offerings to the priests. 'Suttees are sacred and receive worship,' Broadfoot wrote.

> Their last words are considered prophetic, their blessings eagerly sought for, their curses dreaded. The Rani and others prostrated themselves before the suttees and asked their blessing. The suttees blessed them, but cursed the Sikh *Panth* (Military Council). At the pyre they were asked the fate of the Punjab. They declared that during the present year its independence would cease, that the Sikh sect would be conquered, the wives of the Sikh soldiery be widows, and the country desolate, but that the Rani and her son would live long and happily, and that the Maharajah would continue to reign. These prophecies made a great impression on the superstitious multitude.

Two days later the Maharani took over the government and made friendly overtures to the British, but next day a brigade demanded as the price of recognizing her as Regent to be led to war against the British. There were two factions in the army and either one might win.

For the time being the Maharani seduced them into restraint by appearing before them unveiled, dressed as a dancing girl. The men, says Gardner, were so charmed that they agreed to confirm her in government if she would move into their camp and let them see her unveiled whenever they thought proper.

Since his arrival, Sir Henry Hardinge had greatly strengthened the British frontier defence forces, acting on Sir Hugh Gough's insistent advice, and despite warnings from London against any move which might add to the risk of war. The force now numbered twenty-two thousand fighting men, of whom most were now British. Five thousand men alternately sweltered and froze in airless brick barracks at Ludhiana (Brigadier Wheeler), seven thousand at Ferozepore (General Littler) and ten thousand at Ambala, Kassauli and Subathu (Major-General Sir Walter Raleigh Gilbert), with sixty-eight guns, mostly modest little six-pounders. At Meerut, one hundred and thirty miles south-east of Ludhiana, where there were another twenty-six bigger guns, still another nine thousand men drilled on the dusty parade ground and waited.

Ambala, where Sir Hugh Gough and most of the force were stationed, was eighty miles from the frontier at Ludhiana and a hundred and sixty miles from Ferozepore. A flat, sandy and appallingly dusty plain was the country between, with only a few wells to moisten the parched lips and throats of men and animals. The tracks — there were no roads — made hard labour of marching; only camels moved easily. Villages, mainly mud huts surrounded by a defensive mud wall, were few, while camel-thorn and low jungle trees flourished, with here and there a giant banyan.

In the sense that it could fight where it stood, the British army was always ready, but getting to the chosen field of battle was another story. Dependent upon animal transport, it could not start until this was at hand, but beyond a small number at each station, the animals — camels, elephants and bullocks — were hired or requisitioned, often a lengthy matter.

Thus while the Khalsa was shouting for war, British forces were dangerously dispersed, relatively weak, and their military preparedness hampered by a Governor-General who at first put approval by the Court of Directors in London before all else.

Desertions of sepoys to the Sikhs in twos and threes continued. A party of fakirs visited the Ferozepore lines in daylight and, after blowing on a conch shell to call out the Hindu troops, urged them in the name of God to desert the British, and a few did. It was rumoured that as soon as the Sikh army crossed the Sutlej all the sepoys would join them. One qualified observer remarked that Hindu India at this time looked to the Sikh army for the expulsion of Christianity from the East. Captain Peter Nicholson, one of Broadfoot's assistants, was saying: 'The sooner we put down the rabble army the better. We are too near it for the example not to be detrimental.' This was the real trend of British fears.

Now, while the Sikh treasury was almost empty, the army raving for still higher pay and clamouring for war, the Sikh government, on behalf of the young Maharajah Duleep Singh, wrote hopefully to the Governor-General: 'By the Grace of God the hands of friendship and unity of the two exalted Durbars are constantly multiplied... and this Garden of Unity and Friendship by the watering of the Divine Bounty is and will remain fresh and ever flourishing...'

Not quite yet had the Maharani reached the point where she would shrug her fine shoulders at the uncontrollable soldiers and tell them to attack the British if they wished, in the hope that their power would be destroyed. Still she hoped that the peace party led by herself, the Guru Bhae Ram Singh and some of the chiefs would prevail.

Sir Henry Hardinge, now at Agra, and still believing there would be no invasion, on 24 October 1845 ordered the hire of animal transport for seven regiments of cavalry, eighteen battalions of infantry and eleven batteries of artillery. He said however, that he had not considered it necessary to engage transport for 'a field hospital or an artillery battering train or any establishment which offensive operations would imperatively require. The pacific policy of the Government remains unaltered... If as I expect, the tone of the Durbar should continue to be more friendly... I shall be anxious... gradually to diminish the scale of the present preparations...'

Sir Henry's pacific policy or his lack of logic was hampering the proper equipment of the army. Even allowing for the wide differences between nineteenth and twentieth-century outlook on these matters, how can failure to provide transport for a field hospital be justified?

To complicate the situation, Broadfoot's intelligence was conflicting. On 20 November he reported to Sir Hugh Gough that the Sikh generals had formed their plan of campaign, dividing their army into seven divisions of eight to twelve thousand men each, one to stay at Lahore and the rest to march at once to cross the Sutlej under the overall command of Tej Singh.

Sir Hugh, without referring to the Governor-General, at once ordered HM's 9th Lancers to march from Meerut and the 16th Lancers, two troops of Horse Artillery, the 3rd Regiment of Light Cavalry and HM's 10th Foot to be ready to march and cross the Sutlej, without delay. The next day, reflecting probably the oriental impasse at Lahore between Court and Khalsa, Broadfoot reported that the astrologers had chosen 11 am on 19 November as most auspicious for the Khalsa to march, but not a chief had stirred from his house.

Officers and men of the *panchayats* crowded to the Durbar to know why. The Rani tried to soothe them, saying that the fortunate hour was long passed and the march could not be undertaken till the astrologers found another. The soldiers demanded that this should be done instantly and the Court astrologer was ordered into their presence to find the proper time. An odd scene took place. He pored through his tables, while the Rani sought to divert the attention of the military mob. At length he announced that the next favourable day was the 28 November. The military were furious and declared that he was an impostor. Terrified, the astrologer said that the 20th was also a favourable day. Under pressure he next named the 23rd as favourable and the army prepared to march then, but halted twelve miles south of Lahore because having got their pay many soldiers went home.

So three days after his warning of invasion, Broadfoot reported that it had been postponed. 'Things are in extreme confusion and there is no saying what they may attempt,' he wrote on 23 November to Brigadier Wheeler, at Ludhiana. 'With their strength in irregular cavalry they can of course isolate both Ludhiana and Ferozepore when they choose… but I feel no sort of uneasiness about either station' — hardly reassuring intelligence for this isolated commander.

On the same day Broadfoot strangely told Sir Hugh Gough at Ambala that 'the project of marching against us seemed more than ever likely to be set aside' and he therefore suggested that the commander-in-chief should forward his important orders for reinforcements to the Governor-General. 'You will give him the option of forwarding them or withholding them according as the advance of the troops may fall in or not with any plans he may have decided on with reference to the Lahore movement.'

Sir Hugh agreed, but told Broadfoot he hoped that Sir Henry would not halt the troops — 'the arrangement is good, whatever may be the finale.'

The wishes of the commander-in-chief, which would have brought reinforcements to the Sutlej before the first guns began firing were not to be. The Governor-General, almost it would seem neurotically anxious to obey the Court of Directors and avoid causes for war, on 24 November countermanded all the orders and the 9th Lancers rode back to Meerut. Two days later Sir Henry, a suave Englishman, and Sir Hugh, a mercurial Irishman, met at Kurnal and the commander-in-chief was persuaded to give formal agreement, no doubt in the belief that to do otherwise could do nothing but harm. 'I like him much, and he appeared ready to place every confidence in me,' Sir Hugh wrote to his son a few days later. 'But he is very anxious not to fall into the error of Lord Ellenborough, of making war without ample cause for doing so.'

On 28 November, Broadfoot reported significantly that Rani was against the war, but the Guru Bhae Ram Singh had told her: 'In future be silent. If the soldiery demand to march let them do as they like.'

Bhae Ram Singh was then said to oppose the war too, but three days later, Broadfoot was saying that Sikh confidence that Indian soldiers would desert to their side had made everyone, including the guru, support going to war.

On 2 December he reported that the policy of the Maharani, Lal Singh and the chiefs was now to establish the army on the Sutlej and bring on a war so that they could get freedom from the rebellious Sikh army. Two days later, when the army had still not marched, the Maharani told the chiefs that the Treasury was empty, revenue fallen, expenditure doubled and twenty thousand men added to the army. There was now nothing for it but to move forward, when a battle with the English would take place and the army perish of itself. 'But in spite of orders continued for twenty days the army does not march,' she was said to have complained.

Sir Henry Hardinge arrived with his modest entourage of sixty elephants and two hundred camels at Ambala on 3 December and the next day among other developments he reported to the Secret Committee that Broadfoot, having received no reply to his protest about the 'recent unusual proceedings' in Lahore, had been instructed to see the Sikh envoy in the camp and ask for an explanation. The envoy assured Broadfoot that he had not had a reply. Broadfoot, pointing out the discourtesy and the construction which must be placed upon it, said that until a reply was received the envoy must go, and would not be given any further interview. The Sikh envoy then left the British camp; the diplomatic link was broken now.

Sir Henry, fully supporting Broadfoot's brash move in breaking off relations at this critical moment — in cutting the only lifeline — told the Secret Committee that this procedure was the mildest he could adopt 'consistent with the dignity, position, and interests of the British Government.' He went on:

> The Rani and the Sirdars (Tej Singh and Lal Singh) are becoming more and more urgent that the Army should advance to the frontier, believing that... the only hope of saving their lives and prolonging their power is to be found in bringing about a collision with the British forces. The Sikh Army moves with evident reluctance. My own impression remains unaltered. I do not expect that the troops will come as far as the banks of the Sutlej, or that any positive acts of aggression will be committed; but it is evident that the Rani and the Chiefs, are for their own preservation, endeavouring to raise a storm which, when raised, they will be powerless either to direct or allay...

Extraordinary, in so experienced a person as Sir Henry

Hardinge, was his letting the bellicose Broadfoot become in effect the arbiter of peace or war. The only explanation is his belief that to meet and talk to the Sikhs himself in an effort to avert war would be beneath his dignity and that of the British Government.

Also hard to understand is his under-estimation of the Khalsa in refusing to believe that it would cross the Sutlej, when even on 4 December, four days before the event, Broadfoot's assistants, Captains Mills and Nicholson, were reporting that it was already moving advance cavalry units across to attack and cut off Littler's small force. Gulab Singh too had warned the British that the Sikhs intended war — and that he himself would support them.

Could war have been averted then, granted that neither the Court of Directors in London nor the Governor-General wanted it — and that at the last moment, the Sikhs themselves shrunk back from it? Not as things were, for there had been a calamitous failure in communication, leading to a crisis notable for a complete lack of reason. No single rational move towards avoiding fighting had come from the British; for example no conference, to examine the issues, if any, that divided the two governments, not even the suggestion of one, or the most tentative peaceful gesture, despite a professed wish for peace.

Sir Henry Hardinge, it would appear, believed a constructive diplomatic effort to avert war beneath the 'dignity, position and interests' of the British Government. He had no conception of the statesmanship that the great post of Governor-General called for. He was afflicted by a kind of mental paralysis — he had been too long a soldier in uniform. In face of instructions not to go to war his sole act was the blind military one of refusing to reinforce troops on the frontier, to avoid alarming the Sikhs, when they had already been frightened out of their wits.

So Sikh suspicions worsened, their mistrust deepened, their fears grew and their Government, undermined by the lack of support given to it by the British, fell more and more into the hands of the restless Khalsa.

In these conditions of ineptitude war was inevitable.

On 2 December, General Sir John Littler, commanding seven thousand men at the exposed and unfortified cantonment of Ferozepore, became so concerned about reports of Sikh troop movements that he asked Sir Hugh Gough for another British regiment. The commander-in-chief supported his request, but tied hand and foot, sent it on to the Governor-General, whom it reached at Ambala on 3 December. Sir Henry agreed, but unaccountably failed to sign the vital command for another three days and HM's 80th Foot did not march for still another three days.

By then, 10 December, it was too late. At Ambala the British were dancing while Sikh cavalry and skirmishers were crossing the Sutlej at Hariki, opposite Ferozepore. They were followed by the main armies under Tej Singh on a flotilla of small boats. Somehow, General Littler's spies and cavalry reconnaissance failed utterly to detect this vast movement of men, animals, stores and guns. His seven thousand troops were cut off by a Sikh army of fifty thousand. 'I got the consent of the Governor-General too late,' Sir Hugh Gough complained, 'as the Sikh army were between me and it (Ferozepore) before they (the 80th Foot) had even moved.'

In this state of confusion and muddle among the British, conflict and treason among the Sikhs, the war began.

7: Mudki

When, too late, General Littler heard early on 12 December 1845 that advance cavalry of the Sikh army were drawn up in battle array some three miles away, he hurriedly deployed his forces behind a line of hastily dug trenches and awaited the expected attack with some alarm. Of his force of eight infantry battalions and two cavalry regiments, only one infantry regiment was British, the 62nd Queen's, together with two troops of horse artillery (twelve guns), and two light field batteries (also twelve guns). The Sikhs had tried hard during the past year to subvert the Indian troops. Littler therefore feared that he might during an attack by this much bigger force have to deal with treachery by disloyal sepoys as well. It was a chilling prospect.

No useful account has been left of those suspenseful days, with the British artillerymen sleeping by their guns and the few hundred British infantrymen expecting the disaffected sepoys to turn on them directly the Sikh war drums and the sweep of scarlet-clad cavalry heralded their attack. Littler waited one, two, three... six days; and still no action. On the evening of the sixth day, 18 December, he heard the distant rumble of a cannonade north of Mudki, and knew that the British and Sikh forces there had joined battle, but even then no attack came.

A surgeon with the British forces, Dr W. L. McGregor, who subsequently talked with many Sikhs, recorded that they 'pressed Lal Singh to lead them against Ferozepore repeatedly, but he refused... His excuse... was that he wanted to fight the commander-in-chief and considered anyone else below his notice.'

It was an excuse for treason. Lal Singh, prime minister, and Tej Singh, commander-in-chief, were both in the field hoping to see the British destroy their own troops, the uncontrollable Khalsa. The victors would then, they expected, maintain them in power as reliable ministers in a dependent state. According to Captain Peter Nicholson, one of Broadfoot's political assistants, Lal Singh had already in a letter requested the British 'to consider him and the *bibi sahiba* (Rani Jindan) as their friends and cut up the *burchas* (ruffians of the Khalsa) for them.' So there was no point in Lal Singh and Tej Singh compromising themselves by destroying Littler's small British force.

Nicholson, according to contemporary authorities, had also received a letter from Lal Singh after the crossing, affirming his friendship with the British and asking what he should best do. Nicholson is said to have answered: 'Do not attack Ferozepore. Halt as many days as you can, and march towards the Governor-General.'

Lal Singh took Nicholson's advice and split his army, leaving Tej Singh with one part to threaten, but not attack Littler's force, while he led the other part south to face the British at Mudki. Thus, for the time being, the Sikh leaders' treason had saved Littler's battalion of British infantry and his artillerymen from a possible massacre.

Meanwhile, in Lahore, the Maharani went in fear of her life. Those of the Khalsa who remained there terrified the inhabitants with their own brand of martial law. All but one of the foreign officers had fled across the Sutlej to safety. Only Colonel Gardner was prepared to stay and fight on the Sikh side. 'The ignominious departure of Avitabile and Ventura at this critical juncture,' he wrote, 'much disgusted the army... There was no necessity to leave that I saw. I was always treated with honour and respect.' Gardner started for the Sutlej with the Khalsa, but the Maharani recalled him with his artillery to Lahore. She wanted an efficient protector.

> She specially insisted that I was wanted to hold Lahore against the Khalsa. I was privately told to bring back no Sikhs, but as many Mussulmans as I had with me… The Muhammadans, hating the Sikhs, were enchanted at the recall, and on our return I was, as it were governor of Lahore… The resolve of their ruler to destroy the army, anyhow and by whatever means, was known even by the Sikh army itself; but such had been the stern discipline of the *Panch*, such were the hopes of loot from Delhi, such the real belief that the intentions of the British were aggressive, such the domestic incitements of their families to plunder and such their devotion to their mystic faith, that one single dogged determination filled the bosom of each soldier. The word went round, 'We will go to the sacrifice'.

Meantime, on 11 December, after the ball, Gough's army had marched off from Ambala, along the sandy track that led to Ferozepore. During the day an officer caked in dust galloped up to him with a message that the Sikh army, estimated at fifty thousand with about a hundred guns, had crossed the Sutlej. No doubt, Sir Hugh had been expecting this. He quickened the pace. That day, through the clouds of penetrating dust raised by the rattling gunwheels and the tramp of boots, the force marched sixteen miles: eighteen miles the next day, twenty on the third, thirty on the fourth and incredibly thirty miles again on the fifth, making one hundred and fourteen miles in five days in the blinding dust and parched air. Food and water were scarce. The camp followers had fallen behind and the marching men did not reach the reserve grain dump until the fifth day.

In India then, a division of ten thousand took the field as fighting men only; there were no storemen, clerks, drivers, cooks, sick-bay attendants and mobile bath operators with them; mostly men who fought on foot, on horseback or with artillery. But they depended for all the necessaries of life upon a vast army of camp followers, a system the British inherited from the fallen Mughal regime. So the force General Gough was hurrying desperately forward from Ambala wagged a tail of nearly forty thousand followers and a vast horde of elephants, camels, bullocks, horses, ponies and carts.

According to his rank, every officer was allowed from ten to twenty-five personal servants to look after his clothes, his equipment and his laundry; to pitch his tent, prepare, cook and serve his food and his drinks as well as to oversee all those who performed these tasks. If he kept a palanquin — and senior officers often reclined in them rather than ride all day in the hot sun — he needed six bearers. For every horse he was allowed two servants, a groom and a grass cutter; and for every elephant another two. For each three camels he hired to carry his personal baggage he had one servant — camels and elephants were marks of status, and senior officers would have forty or fifty of each.

As if these were not enough, every regiment was accompanied by six hundred stretcher, or dooly bearers; camel-doctors, water-carriers, saddlers, blacksmiths, cobblers, tailors, milk-girls, and often, for entertaining the sepoys, nautch girls and fiddlers. Six thousand camels carried enough grain to feed eight thousand horses for a month, but thousands more camels and bullocks carried ammunition, gunpowder and rations, apart from special personal baggage. Sometimes this was considerable for unexpected reasons.

An English journalist, J. H. Stocqueler, editor of *The Bombay Times*, had six years earlier travelled with the army invading Afghanistan and had offered a few boxes of cigars as a present to the officers' mess who had entertained him. Politely, he was advised that they would scarcely be valued. 'Our mess has two camel-loads of the best Manilas,' he was told.

Lieutenant-Colonel Burlton, who, as the Indian Army's Commissary-General defended the camp-follower system, described it thus:

> First comes a bevy of elephants... laden with the tents of European soldiers; then follow long strings of camels, carrying the spare ammunition... and the tents of the native troops. Then again, more camels, carrying hospital stores, wines, medicines, quilts, beds, pots and pans... Imagine a county infirmary, its contents, stock, furniture and stores, to be removed daily some ten or fifteen miles on the backs of camels, and you have some faint idea of this very small portion of our luggage.
>
> Then came doolies, or litters... Another long string of camels carrying the day's supply of grain for the cavalry and artillery horses comes next, as well as what are called troop stores — horse clothing, head and heel ropes, pickets, nose bags, spare shoes, etc. The supply of grain for the day for two hundred horses, would need two hundred camels, and for the troop stores as many again. And now comes the private baggage and the tents of the sybarite officers. Finally, the varied groups of women, children, ponies, mules, asses, bullocks and carts laden with all sorts of things...

No less surely was it an established rule that troops were not to be ordered into the field without the sanction of the Governor-General or the Government, though once war had begun, their handling was usually left to the commander-in-chief. But not on this occasion. Contrary to the Governor-General's expectations, the Sikhs had crossed the river. Desperate to retrieve the dangerously exposed position of the British forces that his 'no preparations' policy had caused, Sir Henry — who had ridden on a day's march ahead of Gough's forces — rashly went on with a small escort up to the unguarded Sutlej frontier and along to the outpost of Ludhiana. Here, without consulting Sir Hugh Gough, he ordered Brigadier Wheeler to march his troops to the grain depot of Bussean, to protect the supplies there, and within twenty-four hours the five thousand infantry, two regiments of cavalry and twelve field guns were on the move, leaving only a few hundred 'old and infirm men' to hold Ludhiana, an important frontier post.

Conflict and mistrust existed and would grow between the ambitious Sir Henry Hardinge and the mercurial commander-in-chief, Sir Hugh Gough. Already, for Sir Henry's sake, Sir Hugh had forced his men to trudge sixty miles in two days. 'I have possibly overworked the advance,' he wrote to Sir Henry, 'but I really do not like your position. It would be a fearful thing to have a Governor-General bagged.'

On 17 December the Ludhiana troops met the Ambala force at Charrak, making an army of between eleven and twelve thousand men — five regiments of cavalry, five troops of horse artillery, two field batteries with forty-two guns, and thirteen battalions of infantry, of which but four were British. It was now brigaded into one cavalry division under General Thackwell and three infantry divisions under Generals Harry Smith, Sir Walter Raleigh Gilbert and Sir John McCaskill, but only Smith's division was up to strength, the other two being little more than brigades.[5]

---

[5] Cavalry Division, Brigadier-General Thackwell. Brigadier Mactier's

For most of the way the unfortunate troops marched on half-filled stomachs; the over-cautious Hardinge had refused even to let Gough lay in reserve supplies and build up dumps along the line of march. When the Sikhs made their surprise move, Hardinge desperately ordered Broadfoot and his assistants — Robert Cust, Peter Nicholson, Edward Lake and Charles Abbott — to purchase, by force if necessary, every available sack of grain in the area. Cust, an Etonian of twenty-two who wrote an absorbing diary of the campaign, noted that guns had to be trained on the gates of the villages before they were opened and access given to the granaries. Riding into Bussean on an elephant on 14 December, he seized the fort and granary.

> We opened three vast pits containing the stores of the last harvest, and for the whole day these pits were giving up their treasure to the vast multitude who were to be fed. The impolicy and danger of bringing up the Army so imperfectly supplied with stores and so hurried along became daily more manifest, and anxiety began to show itself on the faces of some — the question was asked, how will men starving be able to fight?

Cust had soon to learn as a matter of fact that British troops then always fought well, whatever the conditions.

Brigade: 9th Irregular Horse, 14th Light Cavalry. Brigadier Gough's Brigade: 5th Light Cavalry; Governor-General's Bodyguard. Brigadier White's Brigade: 3rd Light Dragoons, ½ 4th Light Cavalry. 1st Infantry Division, General Smith. 1st Brigade (Brigadier Bolton) 31st Foot, 24th and 47th Native Infantry. 2nd Brigade (Brigadier Wheeler) 50th Foot, 42nd, 48th Native Infantry. 2nd Infantry Division. General Gilbert. 3rd Brigade: 45th Native Infantry, 2nd Grenadiers Native Infantry. 4th Brigade: 16th Grenadiers, Native Infantry. 3rd Division: General McCaskill. 5th Brigade: 9th Foot and 73rd Native Infantry. 6th Brigade: Nil.

At daybreak next day, 18 December, the 3rd Light Dragoons led the army on a march of twenty-one miles to Mudki, south of Ferozepore, towards the Sikh armies, for on the flat jungly plain somewhere between these places, cutting off Sir John Littler's troops, was their main force. In the early morning sunshine, just as Cust found the Governor-General enjoying some breakfast under a tree, there was a sudden alarm. 'Quartermaster Crabtree of the 3rd Light Dragoons,' says Cust, 'came back from the advance, which had gone ahead with Broadfoot, and gave notice that the enemy had appeared, upon which we formed line, and the commander-in-chief and staff proceeded onwards... We allowed the cavalry to advance, and sat down under a tree to await the advance of the infantry column.'

Half obscured in the dust, an indistinct mass of red and white through which bayonets glittered, the lines of infantry tramped past. Sir Henry Hardinge, Cust noted, was thoughtful and silent. Eventually, he remarked: 'Will the people of England consider this an actual invasion of our territory and a justification for war?' No one apparently answered. The Sikh army, after all, was camped just south of the Sutlej in territory that, according to the treaty of 1809, belonged to them. Second thoughts seemed to be troubling Hardinge, involved willy-nilly in war against the wishes of the East India Company.

An officer rode up and told Hardinge that the alarm was unfounded. He and his staff, with five hundred cavalry of the Bodyguard, then mounted and rode ahead through the low tamarisk bushes to the outskirts of Mudki, a large village of mud huts and a fort surrounded by a defensive wall, north-west of which, astride the road to Ferozepore, the British advance cavalry and horse artillery had halted. It was just after midday. Everyone was hungry and thirsty. Cust rode into the village and ordered the merchants to open their shops for the sale of grain. Gough, who had received a report that the enemy were near to Mudki, had again changed his infantry from column of route to order of battle. Exhausted, and suffering badly from thirst, they were trudging through the sand and dust two or three miles outside the village. Trooper N. W. Bancroft, of the Bengal Horse Artillery, helped to groom the horses and lead them to water 'but it was so foul that thirsty as they must have been... the poor animals refused to drink it.'

At about 3 pm some camels with rations arrived and then the tired and dusty infantry. Smoke from hundreds of cooking fires, the clatter of pots and pans signalled their first meal of the day. Bancroft and a corporal chose this moment to quarrel and stepped outside the camp to pummel each other. Sir Hugh had meantime sent his military secretary, Captain (later Field-Marshal Sir Frederick) Haines to find out from cavalry scouts where the enemy were. Haines rode to the right front where Captain Quin of the 3rd Dragoons excitedly pointed out clouds of dust rising behind a low jungle two or three miles away.

The Sikhs were advancing, ready to fight. Raja Lal Singh, commanding a modest force of two thousand infantry, twenty-two guns and eight to ten thousand horsemen, had seen the smoke from the British fires and sent his men forward at this useful moment to attack. Haines rode back fast, only to find that the commander-in-chief had already received the news and was taking measures. The first battle against the Sikhs had begun.

Still exchanging blows, Bancroft and the corporal suddenly heard the trumpet shrilly sounding the *alarm*. Stripped to the waist, they raced for the guns and standing at the ready with their comrades saw the Governor-General and the commander-in-chief gallop past the lines, preceded by the trumpet major of the 4th Native Lancers, blowing loudly. A party from each gun ran to bring up the horses, which were soon harnessed to the gun trailers.

Brigadier Brooke, commanding artillery, rode up to his twelve field-battery nine-pounders and his thirty horse-artillery six-pounders, and, says Bancroft, he shouted: 'Now my men, when at the gallop, if you see me drop the point of my sword, *so*' (suiting the action to the word) 'go as if the devil were after you: when I raise it *so* (indicating the motion) pull up; and when I give the flourish, *so* (and here he gave a tremendous one indeed) come about and unlimber!'

Riding to the front the Brigadier shouted: 'Advance in column of troops from the right!' The five troops of horse artillery galloped in line to the front, followed at a more leisurely pace by the twelve nine-pounders. They had not advanced far towards a jungle nearly a mile ahead, when they saw the smoke and heard the boom of the Sikh artillery, and, noted Bancroft, 'round-shot from the enemy's artillery began rolling and plunging among the horses' legs like so many cricket balls, but were not quite so harmless as they looked, for they broke several of our horses' legs.'

> A hair-brained lieutenant (Wheelwright) took a fancy that he might stop one of their balls and return it to them; he made the trial, and had the mortification of having his right arm disabled as the result of his experiment, and he returned to his guns, cursing his ill-luck at being thus disabled before having had an opportunity of using the splendid Damascus blade which he had just received as a present from his father at home. The major reprimanded him sharply for his language and ordered him to the rear.

Behind the cavalry and the artillery General Harry Smith's 1st

Infantry Division — only a few companies of the other divisions were ready — had formed up. Officers commanding batteries shouted — 'With round-shot load, and blaze away!' Beside the breeches of the guns, the blue-coated gunners stood with lighted port-fires — the quick burning match set to the vent to fire the charge. 'Fire!' The air was rent with a metallic crash, the shell began its parabola, the wheels rolled back with the recoil, and another gunner thrust a wet sponge on a long rod the length of the smoking barrel to damp out dangerous sparks. 'Load!' Powder and shot were thrust home. 'Fire!'

The cannonade crashed loudly on both sides and the Sikh shot, now in range, whistled among the British gunners. Ahead, through the dust and the blue haze of the short winter afternoon they saw the long line of the opposing infantry ready and deployed on the verges of a low sparse jungle in a flat plain dotted with sandy hillocks — 'in a beautiful and regular order of battle', according to Lieutenant John Cumming of the 80th Foot — 'about 20,000 cavalry in well-formed columns covered the plain, their sabres glittering in the setting sun like a sea of silver. But their artillery and most of their infantry were concealed from our view, masked by brushwood and little sand hills.'

BATTLE OF MOODKEE, December 18, 1845.

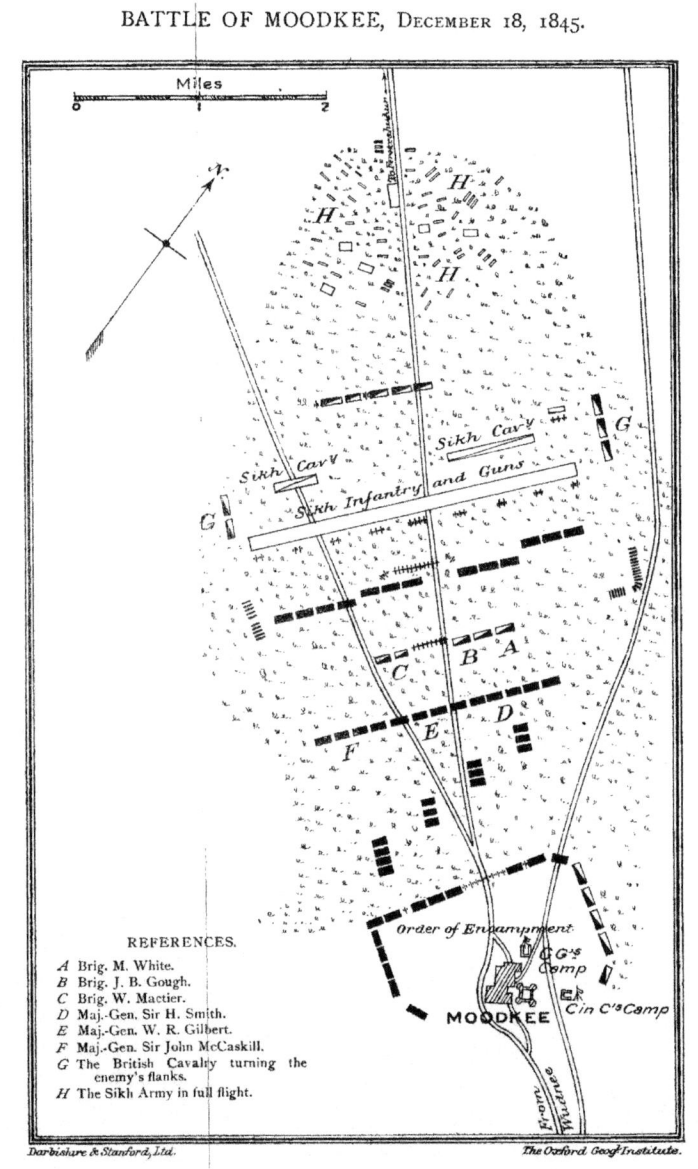

REFERENCES.
A Brig. M. White.
B Brig. J. B. Gough.
C Brig. W. Mactier.
D Maj.-Gen. Sir H. Smith.
E Maj.-Gen. W. R. Gilbert.
F Maj.-Gen. Sir John McCaskill.
G The British Cavalry turning the enemy's flanks.
H The Sikh Army in full flight.

Battle of Mudki, 18 December 1845

General Gough, in his dispatch, stated that on 18 December 1845, receiving the news that the Sikhs had taken up their positions he immediately pushed forward the horse artillery and cavalry, directing the infantry, accompanied by the slower and heavier field batteries, to move forward in support. To resist their attack and to cover the formation of his infantry into line, he advanced the cavalry under Brigadiers White, Gough and Mactier rapidly to the front in columns of squadrons. The thirty horse-artillery six-pounders, each with forty-six rounds and weighing with limber and carriage more than twenty-seven hundredweight, were galloped up to within two or three hundred yards of the Sikh positions in the jungle. 'The enemy,' says Gough, 'opened a very severe cannonade upon our advancing troops, which was vigorously replied to by the battery of horse artillery under Brigadier Brooke, soon joined by the two light field batteries.'

One can imagine the scene — clear bugle notes sounding the 'advance', sullen drumbeats reinforcing iron discipline that drove officers and men forward into a hail of shot, hoarse shouts of seasoned NCO's to terrified young soldiers to 'close up' as whistling grapeshot cut their comrades down; knowledge, for the first time comprehended by untried lads from the green fields of the British Isles that they must kill or be killed; the screams of men and animals, the swirling dust, the deafening crash of the guns, the confusion, the horrible wounds.

Bancroft, then a young gunner in action for the first time, saw the casualties mounting as he served the guns blazing away at the Sikh artillery hidden three hundred yards away in the jungle, in his first gunnery duel.

> A ventsman of one of our guns was actually running about disembowelled; the powder-pouch worn on his side had been

struck by a shell and exploded. Some of the escapes were miraculous. A corporal had the port-fire in his hand shattered with a round-shot while he was in the act of firing his gun, and he also had to be reprimanded for the language he used on that occasion... On looking back to our wagon-train, the writer saw that another of his comrades had fallen... shot through the right eye: looking to his left he saw a gunner, an old friend of his, sitting up in his saddle after a round-shot had passed through his breast; he had to be lifted out... put into a doolie and carried to the rear. These sights were not the most pleasant and were calculated to make a young soldier rather squeamish than otherwise...

What Sir Hugh Gough calls 'the rapid and well directed fire of our artillery' at their only target — the bursts of smoke in the jungle — slowed down the Sikh cannonade. Masses of their cavalry, extending well beyond the British front, began advancing on either flank in an enveloping movement. Through the dust clouds and the blue late afternoon haze, General Gough saw the danger as it began and sent two aides, one to Brigadiers Gough and White, on the right, and the other to Brigadier Mactier, on the left. Gough himself rode out with the aide on the right and galloped forward two hundred yards with Brigadier White, urging the 3rd Light Dragoons and the units of the 4th Light Cavalry to stop the Sikh threat at all costs.

Together with the Bodyguard and the 5th Light Cavalry commanded by Brigadier Gough, their long red and white plumes streaming from tall black shakos, the Dragoons swept out in a long deadly charge against the advancing Sikh horse. Brigadier Mactier's units of the 4th Light Cavalry and the 9th Irregular Cavalry, crouching low in light blue coatees and dark blue turbans, levelled their long bamboo lances and tore into the ranks of the lighter and less disciplined Sikhs.

Both charges succeeded brilliantly. The Sikh horse on both sides fell back, the British cavalry turned the enemy's left, and in a charge that earned the 3rd Light Dragoons the name of the *Mudkiwallahs*, galloped with swords flashing along the entire lines of enemy artillery and infantry, silencing the guns for a time and putting their cavalry to flight. 'Oh, how I wished for a thousand more good British horse to join that whirlwind charge,' wrote Lieutenant John Cumming, of the 80th Foot. For numbers of the cavalry were shot down by Sikh infantry hidden in the dwarf tamarisk trees, then slashed with the sword as they lay wounded or dying on the ground.

Now the British infantry line had been formed, with General Sir Harry Smith's division on the right and Sir Walter Gilbert's and Sir John McCaskill's incomplete divisions on the left. While they were marching up over the rough ploughed land Brigadier Brooke ordered up his horse artillery again. 'Soon after,' says Trooper Bancroft, 'we found ourselves pretty close to a rather dense jungle of low stunted bush. Here we unlimbered again and the cannonade was renewed on both sides with terrible effect. Limbs and heads were carried away in all directions, and in many instances men were literally cut in two.'

Less than an hour of daylight remained when the long line of twelve battalions of British and sepoy redcoats marched forward towards the enemy infantry and artillery sheltered in the jungle. The Sikh infantry responded with disciplined volleys, while sharpshooters in the trees picked off officers and enemy guns kept up an unceasing blast of grapeshot. Lieutenant Robertson of the 31st Foot (Brigadier Bolton's Brigade) ran forward into the jungle into a tremendous fire of musketry and guns.

We were much broken by the bushes, which would have done well for Light Infantry, but for nothing else, and the men were beginning to get hit. The first person I saw on the ground was Bulkeley, who looked quite dead... I saw a batch of them (sepoys) behind a big tree, firing straight up into the air... The last words I heard Bolton say were, 'Steady 31st, steady, and fire low for your lives!' Cockins, the bugler, was trying to hold the grey horse, when they were all three hit and went down together. This was from the first volley by the enemy. Shortly after Willes was hit, and I took command of No 1... He said he was hit from behind by the sepoys. Young was hit in the back of the neck, and the buckle of his stock saved him, as the ball came round and out in front. Hart and Brenchley were both hit in the body, and did not live long. We soon get into a regular mob, blazing away at everything in front of us, and nearly as many shots coming from behind us as in front.

Captain Arthur Hardinge, riding with his father, Sir Henry, and Robert Cust, towards the advancing infantry, saw a regiment of sepoys firing indiscriminately into the air. 'Their officers seemed to have no control over them. The men had lost their heads and I am afraid this was not the only instance...'

Frightened by warfare more furious than they had ever encountered in India, many of them, at once disloyal and terrified, wavered in the heavy fire, turned and began to run. Sir Hugh sent Captain Henry Havelock after them and Havelock rode round them shouting — 'the enemy are in front of you, not behind you!'

It was a confused encounter, fought now in twilight, darkened still more by the heavy clouds of dust and the low jungle, in which the enemy could only be discovered by his fire. In this gloom, Lieutenant-Colonel John Byrne, commanding the 31st Foot, fell with a severe wound and two officers carrying the colours were shot down. Seeing them unable to rise, Quarter-Master Sergeant Jones sprang for the colours, raised them high and kept them unscathed throughout the hottest fire — he was awarded an immediate commission as a reward.

All this time the Sikh gunners, recovered now from the British cavalry attack, their batteries carefully placed in the jungle, were blasting the British with round-shot and grape. The outcome of this strange encounter was still in doubt. The British had gained no permanent advantage and in face of heavy losses their infantry lacked the impetus of the first charge. When the Sikh cavalry threatened their flank, Brigadier Wheeler's brigade, on the left, had formed a square, stuck in a vulnerable defensive position. Sir Harry Smith, the divisional commander, rode up furiously and ordered them to advance. This the 50th Foot did, but the two regiments of sepoys for some minutes refused to break and reform, firing wildly, some bullets hitting in the back the men of the advancing 50th in front of them.

When things were at their worst, the brigade commander, Brigadier Wheeler, fell with a mortal wound, but Sir Harry Smith on his celebrated black Arab Jem Crow, seized one of the 50th's colours and planted it, as he said, 'in the very teeth of a Sikh column, and gloriously did the Regiment rush on with the bayonet...'

Sir John McCaskill, another veteran commander, now fell, shot in the heart. The British line, especially the 31st and 50th on the right, upon whom the brunt of the fighting had fallen in this battle against hidden foes, lost their forward movement again in the blast of the Sikh fire. Sir Hugh Gough rode up, his white fighting coat flying behind him, aware that upon the capture of the Sikh batteries hung victory, urging officers and men as only he could, with the shout, 'We must take those guns!' But in this nightmarish melee no one knew where they were. 'Law was standing near us with his legs wide, shouting out, "Charge! Charge!" and hitting the ground with his sword, and sometimes the men's toes (just as he used to set Growler on Shaw's dog),' Lieutenant Robertson noted.

> I called out to Sir Hugh Gough: 'Where are the guns, and we will soon take them?' and Somerset[6] put his hat on his sword and called out, 'Thirty-first, follow me!' We rushed after him through the smoke, and had the guns in a moment. On we went and came upon two light guns which the enemy were trying to take off the field; but some of our shots hit the horses and brought them to a stand. They then took a shot at us, not twenty yards off; down we went on our noses at the flash, and the grape went over our heads in a shower. I felt it warm; then a rush, and the guns were ours, the gunners not attempting to run away, but cutting at us with their tulwars. I think those two guns were taken away by the Sikhs that night, as I never saw them afterwards.

Robert Cust meantime, rode through the smoke and dust with Sir Henry Hardinge and Major Broadfoot after the advancing British infantry, hearing their continuous volleys, their cheers as they took the first battery. 'We then… passed through the battery just taken, over the bodies of the dead and dying. We found Hillier, one of our ADCs, lying on the ground wounded… We left two *sowars* to look after him and passed on in the direction of the second battery, which was now vomiting forth at a fine rate showers of grape.'

Cust, a civilian, found it 'unpleasantly hot' with Sikh fire whistling past his ears, men falling all around and the cheers

---

[6] Captain A. F. W. Somerset, Grenadier Guards, Lord Raglan's eldest son and Military Secretary to Lord Hardinge.

and screams as the 31st surged onto the second Sikh battery. He rode back with Mr Coley, a clergyman 'amid a shower of round-shot, which before had passed over our heads and now fell all about us.' They reached the Horse Artillery and found Sir Robert Sale lying wounded upon one gun wagon and upon another Captain Dashwood, one of Cust's friends. 'I went up and found he was shot through both the arm and the leg. I lent the doctor a penknife to rip open the sleeve of his coat and assisted in roughly bandaging up the wound.'

Meantime, the five-to-one British infantry superiority had told. The Sikhs were driven back. 'Their whole force,' remarked Sir Hugh Gough, 'was driven from position after position with great slaughter and the loss of seventeen pieces of artillery, some of them of heavy calibre; our infantry using the never-failing weapon, the bayonet, whenever the enemy stood…'

Lieutenant (later Field-Marshal) Herbert Edwardes, found it harder going: 'The last two hours of the battle were a series of dogged stands, and skirmishing retreats on the part of the Sikh troops, of sharp struggles, gun captures and recaptures, and a British pursuit over five miles of the worst ground that armies ever fought for.' Lieutenant Robertson noted that long after the bugles were sounding the 'cease fire' in all directions, the firing continued, the men blazing away at nothing, or at each other. At last it stopped, 'and we got something like a regiment formed but no colours, or bugler to sound the regimental call.' A sepoy bugler was ordered to try, but just as he got out a squeak someone nearly knocked the bugle down his throat. It was Sir Harry Smith, demanding why they were making such a row. 'We were a long time collecting the men, and then marched back towards the camp, but were halted some way in front of it, and had to sleep on the sand till morning.'

The British had driven the Sikhs back to their camp at Ferozeshur. It was a victory, of sorts, bought at great cost from a weaker force, British losses in five or six hours being 215 killed and 657 wounded, those killed including thirteen British and two Indian officers. Cavalry losses were worst, with eighty-one killed and eighty-seven wounded, the 3rd Light Dragoons, charging with 497 men, having no less than two officers, fifty-six men and one hundred horses killed as well as thirty-five men wounded. The artillery losses were relatively almost as high, twenty-seven men being killed and forty-seven wounded, testifying to the accuracy of the Sikh counter-battery gunnery. Also a high proportion of senior officers were killed, including Generals McCaskill, and Sale ('Fighting Bob', who had survived the Afghan and so many other campaigns) and Brigadier Bolton; while severely wounded were Brigadiers Wheeler and Mactier and the Deputy-Adjutant General, Major Pat Grant.

Part of these losses, of all ranks, as Sir Hugh Gough remarked in a letter to his son, was caused by corps firing into one another.

Sir Henry Hardinge, in a critical letter about the action, said that having been collected from various points, and constantly engaged in marching, the troops had only been brigaded on paper. 'The troops therefore were not in that state of organization and formation so essential to discipline and field movements. The Brigadiers and their staff were unknown to the men, and the men to the Brigadiers, while at Mudki the confusion of the attack, combined with the facts above noticed, had created a feeling that the army was not well in hand.'

Written by the Governor-General to the President of the Board of Control, this letter appears to be the start of those stealthy attacks that Sir Henry was throughout the Sikh war to wage against the commander-in-chief, for, it will be remembered, he had expressly forbidden Sir Hugh to assemble his troops near the frontier in formations. The responsibility for the fault about which he complained was therefore the Governor-General's. 'You are aware,' Sir Hugh wrote to his son on 19 December 1845, 'that however expedient in a political point of view, I had it not in my power to arrest this evil.'

Until 2 am, Sir Hugh and one or two of his staff studied the battlefield, picking their way by torchlight among the broken guns, the dead and wounded men and animals, tracing the course of the fighting by the rows of the fallen of the various regiments, noting faces of young and old they had known and faces unrecognizable from the savage mutilation, hearing the groans of the wounded still unattended; for the Governor-General had early in December mistakenly countermanded transport for a field hospital and this essential service had still to arrive.

That remarkable soldier and man, General Sir Harry Smith, also surveyed the field when the smoke had drifted away and the moon had risen. He observed that so hidden was everything in the battle that it afterwards appeared that the bulk of the Sikh forces passed in column along the front of the 1st Brigade of the 1st Division. When repulsed by its 2nd Brigade and a brigade of the 2nd Division they were driven again across the front of the 50th, the advance of which was pushed by Smith himself. When the troops were halted and the atmosphere cleared, the 1st Brigade 1st Division formed an obtuse angle with the rest of the army. 'This brigade,' Smith noted proudly, 'had gone right through the Sikh repulsed columns.'

The exhausted and battle-weary troops reached their camp at 12.30 am. The gunners unlimbered the guns and left the horses in harness with blankets over them. The entire army threw themselves, wrapped in their cloaks, on the ground, ready for any sudden attack. That day, they had marched more than twenty miles, fought a battle, and now without having eaten or drunk since the evening of the day before, they slept thankfully, content, no doubt, to be alive.

Soon after daybreak, bugles piercingly sounded reveille in the cold dry air and parties were sent to bring in the wounded. Cavalry outposts were pushed forward to cover this and to enable the gunners to bring in the captured Sikh artillery. Young Robert Cust, who noted the war's tragedy equally with its heroism and glory, visited the small fort at Mudki into which the wounded were taken. The place was now overflowing with wounded and every corner was occupied.

Sikh sword blows were dreaded. Bearing *tulwars*, heavier and usually sharper than the British cavalry sword, and the regulation infantry sword, the Sikhs did not merely strike with the edge but simultaneously drew the weapon back with a cutting motion that trebled the wound's length and depth. Remarkable it is, not that so many wounded men died, but that any survived at all, for surgery was unbelievably primitive.[7]

During the morning of the 19th the troops had their first meal for thirty-six hours, then sat in the hot sun smoking their pipes and, noted Bancroft, 'chatting about our lost comrades who had been left on the field where they fell, and were lying stark and stiff under the rays of a scorching sun without a chance of being buried.'

---

[7] See Note on Wounds.

Suddenly the bugles sounded the alarm, there was a scramble for arms, the entire army except reserves formed up and marched in columns to a position in front of Mudki. Cavalry outposts had brought reports that a large body of Sikh cavalry was advancing to attack. The battalions deployed into line, artillery and cavalry on each flank. Cursing and sweating in the hot sun, they stood waiting.

8: Ferozeshur

The army stood to arms until midday, when scouts galloped in to report that the mass of Sikh cavalry had turned about on seeing it drawn up in line and had returned to the village of Ferozeshur (inaccurately so-called by the British in place of the Punjabi name Pheerooshuhur), where they had established a strongly fortified position and camp, with good water supplies for men and animals. There, about nine miles north-east of Mudki and halfway to Ferozepore, Sir Hugh Gough decided to attack on the 21st.

In the evening, reinforcements were joyfully played into camp. They had marched nearly two hundred miles in nine days over the arid, waterless country and Sir Henry Hardinge had thoughtfully sent out fifty of his personal elephants to help carry in the footsore early that morning, as well as a number of his camels with water. The British force was now strengthened by HM's 29th Foot, about nine hundred men; the 1st European Light Infantry, of the Company's army, about eight hundred men; a detachment of guns (two eight-inch howitzers and two elephant-drawn 18-pounders) and two sepoy regiments, about 1,500 men.

Plans for the next day's attack went on. The gunners prepared ammunition for the howitzers; but the 18-pounders — the only heavy guns the British had with them — it was decided for some reason to leave behind at Mudki. One of those quite bewildering decisions was this, for, against the British light artillery, six and nine-pounders, the Sikhs had guns of very heavy weight, up to 24, 32 and 48-pounders. This blunder compares with General Keane's allowing his artillery commander to leave behind at Kandahar the 24-pounders he would need to attack the fortress of Ghazni, strongest in central Asia, during the invasion of Afghanistan five years earlier. It would cost the British casualties, but in contemporary accounts it was glossed over.

There was some re-organization now. Colonels Ryan and Hicks replaced Wheeler and Bolton as brigadiers in General Smith's 1st Division, while the skeleton brigades of the 2nd and 3rd divisions commanded respectively by Generals Gilbert and Wallace (who had succeeded McCaskill) were able to be reinforced. Most interesting, Sir Henry Hardinge, who was junior to Sir Hugh Gough in the army, waived his civil rank as Governor-General for the occasion and offered himself as second-in-command. 'In addition to the valuable counsel with which you had in every emergency before favoured me,' the commander-in-chief said in euphemistic phrase, in his dispatch of 19 December, 'you were pleased yet further to strengthen my hands by kindly offering your services as second-in-command of my army. I need hardly say with how much pleasure the offer was accepted.'

Poor Gough — he had no alternative but to accept, short of insulting Hardinge by a refusal. He knew well enough that Hardinge was out for glory and, a brave man and a soldier at heart, would assume a general's authority in any case, so that less harm might be done were he to be given some specific role. Hardinge, of course, had no rightful place on the battlefield. Only a commander-in-chief as good natured as Sir Hugh Gough could have let himself be burdened in this way. Inevitably on the eve of battle, two days later, it led to a costly confrontation between the two.

Meanwhile, the Sikh forces were still split, one part, thirty thousand men under Tej Singh, still watching Ferozepore and

Sir John Littler's force of some seven thousand men; the other, under Lal Singh, about twenty thousand men and about a hundred guns, entrenched at Ferozeshur, waiting for the British to attack.

Sir Hugh Gough's objectives were threefold: to keep his lines of communication intact; to engage Lal Singh's and Tej Singh's forces separately; and, if possible, to have Sir John Littler's force at Ferozepore somehow elude Tej Singh and join him, so as to strengthen his own forces still more. But to do this he would have to attack Lal Singh's strong army at Ferozeshur — an attempt at a southerly march round it to join forces with Littler would probably have led to the British being surrounded.

The day before, General Littler had received news of the battle at Mudki from the Governor-General, who, pursuing the role of military supremo, suggested that Littler should march out to meet Gough's army at Sultan-Khanwalla, ten miles from Ferozepore, if he could do so without risk. Littler was about to march off secretly at dawn next day when Tej Singh's troops threatened an attack and obliged him to stand-to, after which it was both too late and inexpedient to march — he would most likely have been seen. This was in fact, very fortunate, because Gough had made no plans whatsoever to march towards Ferozeshur on 20 December; and without this strong support Littler's small force would have been open to attack by both the Sikh commanders.

Before midnight Littler received another message from the Governor-General, ordering him to march, if possible without being seen or heard, at 8 am next morning and meet Gough's army at a point south of Sultan-Khanwalla, which would take four or five hours. Both of these messages show clearly the dangers of divided command, because Gough's plans depended on being ready for battle much earlier than Littler could arrive. Hardinge had become a self-appointed overlord and short of a blunt assertion of his authority and an outright row on the eve of battle there was nothing Gough could do about it.

Well enough aware that Littler's manoeuvre could be detected, and lead to a clash with Tej Singh's stronger force which the Sikhs were likeliest to win, Gough decided he must attack and defeat Lal Singh at Ferozeshur as soon as possible next day, with or without Littler's aid. Only thus, could he be quite sure of preventing the two Sikh armies re-uniting to form an immeasurably stronger force.

That same evening, the commander-in-chief summoned his brigade and divisional commanders to a briefing on the next day's battle, notifying the Governor-General, as his second-in-command, of this important meeting. But Sir Henry, perhaps stopped by his pride from attending — he would be taking second place; or regretting his quixotic move, sent his military secretary, Colonel Blucher Wood. Sir Hugh told his commanders what he knew of the Sikh positions, based on intelligence received from his own men and the political department. It cannot have amounted to much; reports of British cavalry reconnaissance are conspicuously lacking.

That evening, at dinner, written orders were given to captains commanding companies to go silently to the men's tents with their junior officers to wake them at 1 am — the whole army was to be on parade an hour later. Excitement ran high among the officers, who are reported as talking freely among themselves of the decisive battle next day. To Captain Thomas Box, of the Bengal European Regiment (later the Royal Munster Fusiliers), who had shown himself a fearless soldier in many a fight, it brought silence and unusual low spirits. 'I feel I shall get a shot right slap in the face' he confessed, when asked the reason. It seemed so unlike him that all present laughed at what seemed a rough-edged joke, rather than a presentiment.

By 2 am the whole force except two Native Infantry regiments protecting the wounded and baggage, had stumbled out of their tents into the darkness, for a quite extraordinary breakfast — coffee, onions, and what the men called 'elephants' lugs' — huge cakes of rice, bran and chopped straw made for the elephants. Each man was then issued with a piece of stale bread, a hunk of cooked meat and enough water to fill his can. An hour later, carrying sixty rounds each, the redcoats marched off silently in their blue trousers and white-covered shakos with a white neck-curtain, across the Mudki battlefield towards the Sikh positions at Ferozeshur, eight or nine miles north-west.

Moving in line of columns ready to deploy at once, they made slow progress in the pitch black, frequently forced by jungle to make detours, held up by halts in front while the line of march was checked, stumbling now and then over the bodies of comrades who had fallen two days before. 'We set about digging graves for the poor fellows,' Trooper Bancroft noted, 'but were disturbed in our work by the arrival of the commander-in-chief, who quietly remarked that "this was no time for such business".'

Seven hours later, at 10 am, the army had marched to within about three miles of the eastern face of the Sikh entrenchments, the weakest side of a roughly shaped parallelogram, or oval, about a mile and a half long from north to south and about a mile wide, west to east, with the west side facing Ferozepore. About half past ten the troops ate their bread and meat, watching the Sikh entrenchments from a distance, while the commander-in-chief carried out a personal reconnaissance.

The hour of battle seemed near. Major Broadfoot's department had already reported the northern, southern and western sides to be strongly entrenched and defended by guns of very big calibre, with belts of jungle and low trees hampering the approaches to these three faces. The entrenchments followed the contours of clusters of low hillocks encircling the village some ten feet above the level of the plain. Ensign P. R. Innes, Bengal European Light Infantry, who was present, noted that the Sikhs had thrown stumps and branches of trees over a sort of ditch, to camouflage it.

The commander-in-chief was able at half-past ten that morning to base his plan of attack upon the knowledge that Sir John Littler had marched, though at the late hour of 8 am, the time stated by the Governor-General. Littler was therefore unlikely to join forces with him before midday. But the news convinced Gough again that Lal Singh's force must be fought and scattered at once, otherwise he would face what he most wished to avoid — a unified and much stronger Sikh army. Moreover, he had to attack early both because 21 December was the shortest day in the year — by late afternoon it would be dusk — and because, having been up since 1 am and having marched several miles since, his men's fighting capacity would soon fall off rapidly. But were he to wait until Littler's force had joined him and had been deployed in line with the main army, it would be late afternoon.

He decided to treat Littler's force of about six thousand men as a reserve, to attack the Sikhs immediately, and on the eastern face, where the terrain was certainly easier for the attack. This battle-tried old soldier, whose actions were based as much on intuition, imagination and experience as logic, and whose colours were tied to high morale and an indestructible will to victory, believed he could shatter Lal Singh's force with a bold attack from the eastern side and drive the remnants westward to further destruction by Littler's approaching force.

He rode back to inform Hardinge, his second-in-command, of this decision. Now took place an incident worthy of place in a Gilbert and Sullivan military musical comedy — while also supporting the view that to some extent history depends upon fortuitous events.

Sir Hugh found Sir Henry and his staff sitting down under a tree sharing a picnic of the ample provisions they had brought with them in holsters and saddlebags. Shattering the calm of this alfresco scene, Gough said confidently: 'Sir Henry, if we attack at once, I promise you a splendid victory.'

No one present recorded whether Hardinge choked over his food at the commander-in-chief's words. Probably he did, for there is the indignant remark of his son Arthur, that 'it was with no small surprise that the Governor-General found himself confronted with such extraordinary proposals.'

But Sir Hugh Gough could hardly have been less surprised himself when Sir Henry — presumably resigning his temporary rank of second-in-command — opposed this plan. He wanted to wait for Littler to come up even though it meant the loss of valuable hours of daylight and the army's freshness. An argument developed. Both generals stood their ground, until Sir Henry, brushing the crumbs aside, rose and motioned to the commander-in-chief, his own son and one or two of their respective staffs to talk under a small grove of trees about fifty paces away.

Here Sir Hugh stated his reasons vigorously: it was vital to attack now so as to avoid the dangerous night fighting that proved so costly at Mudki. Littler was on the way — his force should be given the role of a reserve. And now that Tej Singh's force had no reason to stay at Ferozepore, Lal Singh's army must be overcome at once before the two could unite.

Sir Henry Hardinge was, above all, noted for courage during his relatively short period of active service in the Napoleonic Wars, but he had seen no fighting since the Battle of Waterloo, twenty-five years earlier, and his entire experience was that of a staff officer, always bravely in the thick of the battle, honoured by the Duke of Wellington, invested with authority without the responsibility of command and promoted direct to Major-General from Lieutenant-Colonel when appointed a liaison officer between the allied armies in the field at Waterloo. There his hand was shattered by a round-shot, his arm was clumsily amputated. He turned to politics, sat in the Commons and in 1829 became Secretary of State for War.

Now in 1845 he found himself in this unknown continent, able once more to reach after the military glory he had yearned for in his youth, using his civil authority to supersede his commander-in-chief and place himself at the head of this army upon which the fate of India depended. And there is no doubt that he did so with the fullest conviction that destiny had earmarked him for the role of saviour of a British India lumbered with an unreliable commander-in-chief.

Hardinge, moreover, had seen the Sikhs in action at Mudki and had wondered at their discipline and courage, their morale, equalled only in the finest British regiments. Faced now with a much bigger and stronger Sikh force entrenched with guns far heavier than the British, in this war which he had already spoken of with feelings of guilt and doubt, his own morale temporarily failed him. He doubted the confidence and the will to victory of Gough, a fighting soldier, fresh from five years commanding British forces in the China campaign and inspired with the belief that even without Littler's reinforcements he could vanquish the Sikhs. It seemed to Hardinge desperate and foolhardy. He therefore opposed Gough's arguments — insisted that the army should meet and unite with Littler's force before attacking.

Gough was almost bowled over by this proposal. 'What!' he is said to have protested. 'Abandon my communications with India and my wounded at Mudki?' For this indeed is what a march in the direction of Littler's force would have risked. Under the shade of the trees, with the army massed around them, Gough went over again the overwhelming case for an immediate attack. The Governor-General 'in the most positive manner declined to entertain it', his son noted. Gough reminded him who was commander-in-chief. Hardinge exploded: 'Then, Sir Hugh, I must exercise my civil powers as Governor-General and forbid the attack until Littler's force has come up.'

Sir Henry had placed himself in an unenviable position. First, having been ordered by the Secret Committee to avoid war, he had let himself be led into it by total diplomatic failure. Secondly, he had weakened his commander-in-chief's army by countermanding orders absolutely necessary for the safety of the British position — including those early in December for the 9th Lancers to move up to Ludhiana from Meerut. (Sir Henry had sent them back and they were still moving up for the second time, their absence a general subject of regret, for, as Captain Humbly observed then, 'It is not possible to calculate the value of the services which this strong corps might have rendered in the hour of need.') Having thus weakened the army, Sir Henry, using his powers as Governor-General, for the first and only time in British-Indian history overruled the plans of his commander-in-chief in face of the enemy.

It must have been the last straw for Gough, after struggling for months against the futile acts of his over-anxious superior. But he knew well enough that this so-called second-in-command could not, in fact, shed his supreme civil powers, or his ultimate responsibility. He therefore accepted the situation as well as he could, mounted his horse and ordered the army to march in the direction of Ferozepore until it sighted Littler's force. With mounting weariness the men tramped off anew in a dangerous move, 'almost crossing the front of the enemy's position,' Sir Harry Smith noted. They escaped disaster by a hair's breadth, saved only by divisions in the enemy camp. The embattled Sikhs clamoured at this moment for an immediate flank attack upon the vulnerable British, but the treacherous Lal Singh refused. So bitter were the troops at this that they began plotting to murder him, says their chronicler, Sohan Lal Souri.

At about half past twelve a cloud of dust heralded Littler's approach. He rode into Gough's camp about 1 pm, and soon after, his two cavalry regiments, six infantry battalions and twenty-one guns were united near Misreewalla with Gough's army — at a position rather more than three thousand yards south-west of the south-west corner of the Sikh entrenchments. Littler had left his camp standing at Ferozepore to trick Tej Singh into believing he hadn't moved, but whether the Sikh commander was really taken in, in view of his later treachery, is doubtful.

Counter-marching, and the deployment of this army with a strength now of eighteen thousand men, two heavy howitzers and sixty-three light guns in the new position meant more delay, but refusing suggestions that he should attack forthwith,

Gough moved his force properly into place for an attack on the south and west lines of the Sikh entrenchments. On the extreme left was Littler's division, one and a half batteries of nine-pounders and two troops of horse-artillery six-pounders, with his six battalions of infantry led by Brigadiers Ashburnham and Reed between, and his cavalry divided on either flank. In the centre, under the command of General Hardinge, came Brigadier Wallace's division of four battalions, two eight-inch howitzers and two batteries of nine-pounders; and on the right Major-General Gilbert's division of five battalions, with a troop of horse artillery on the extreme right and the 4th Light Cavalry and 3rd Light Dragoons protecting it at the rear. General Smith's reserve division of six battalions was stationed behind on either side of a troop of horse artillery six-pounders.

Gough's worst fears were now realized. Sir Henry's interference had left the army in a far less favourable position to attack, for it was too late now to march the whole force back to the eastern face. The British were to attack the Sikh western and southern positions, 'thus presenting ourselves as targets to every gun the enemy had,' General Harry Smith lamented. 'Nor,' he added, 'were generals of divisions made the least aware of how or what or where they were to attack. The army was one unwieldy battalion under a Commanding Officer who had not been granted the power of ubiquity.'

Gough was certainly hard pressed and obviously had no time for detailed discussions, but it is clear that Littler knew he must attack on the long western face; Wallace the angle of the western and southern faces and Gilbert the southern, and part of the eastern face. It was 3.30 pm before the army was in place.

The eighteen thousand men stood ready and waiting, the declining sun casting long shadows over the plain, the bloodstained regimental colours and the long scarlet and white plumes of the Dragoons drooping in the quiet air. There had been no thought of probing for weak points in the enemy lines, or reconnaissance in force expanding into a strong attack as in modern warfare. This was pitched battle. Tense and excited, praying that they might live, the men waited to advance coolly into the holocaust.

Came the clear notes of the bugles at 4 pm and the battalions began deploying into line and advancing through low trees and jungle towards the open ground three hundred yards in front of the Sikh position, about a mile away. They were met soon by a fierce cannonade. Sikh shot and shell, ripping through the trees, struck with growing sound and fury. 'Long before our artillery was in range of them, their cannon were making fearful havoc of us,' Captain John Cumming of the 80th Foot, wrote in a letter to his father, six thousand miles away in the Orkney Isles. 'The first compliment that the 80th received was an immense ball, which, passing over Captain Lewis's head, struck Major Lockhart's horse right in the breast, smashed the animal to pieces, and injured the Major severely. Fainting between two soldiers he called out "Fight on lads, I am gone".'

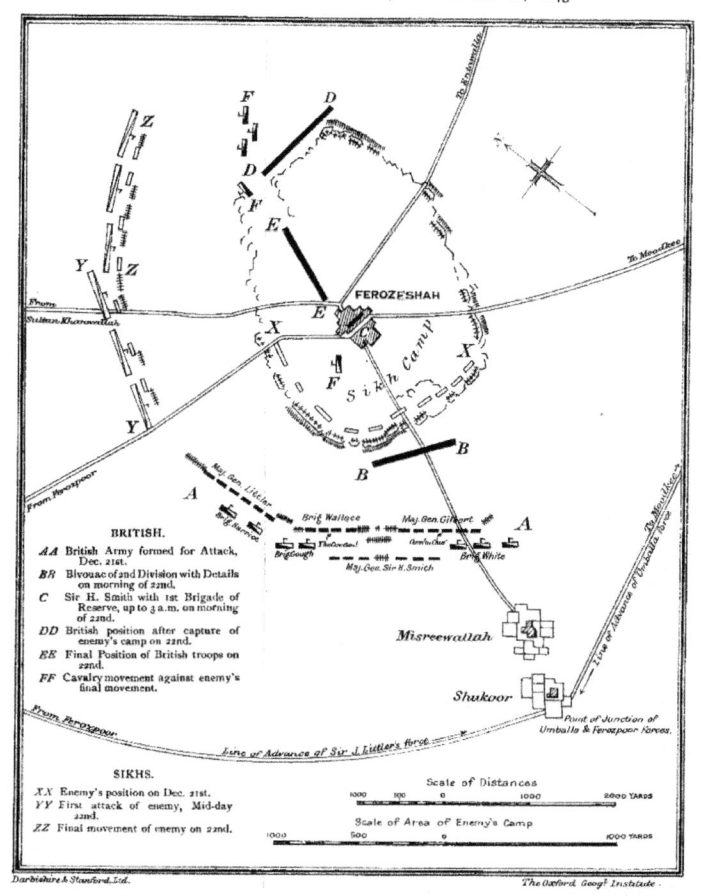

The Battle of Ferozeshur, 21 and 22 December 1845

The Sikh artillery, much heavier and more numerous, were hitting the British gunners as well. Brigadier 'Bully' Brooke, who commanded the main artillery in the centre, rode up to the commander-in-chief and shouted above the roar of the cannonade — 'Your Excellency — I must either advance or be blown out of the field.'

General Littler, on the left, had ordered his own artillery to attack the Sikh batteries facing him and the eager Colonel Huthwaite dashed forward with his two troops of horse artillery and his light field batteries. Unlimbering, firing a dozen rounds from each of his guns, limbering up, riding forward, firing again, from one position to another, for a time he drove the gunners of the opposing batteries from their guns and withdrew to make way for Littler's approaching infantry.

But already, at this vital moment, things had gone awry. Littler had ordered Brigadier Reed to station his brigade next to General Wallace's division, on his right, with Brigadier Ashburnham's brigade of Native Infantry on his left. Deployment from column into line was from the right, so that each regiment having to move to the left, must deploy in succession. Ashburnham's three regiments therefore needed longer to get into line than Reed's.

But Littler, eager for action now that his guns were silencing the Sikhs', placed himself behind Reed's brigade as soon as the men were in line and ordered the advance without waiting for Ashburnham's brigade to come up. Three disastrous consequences followed: Reed's right flank was separated from Wallace's troops by nearly four hundred yards; his left flank was exposed because Ashburnham's men had not yet been able to catch up; and the Sikh guns were able to bring down a tremendous blast of grapeshot upon these two brigades alone directly they emerged from the jungle into the open within three hundred yards of them.

Brigadier Reed, frightened for the lives of his men in this hail of shot, gave the order to charge the batteries almost at once. HM's 62nd Foot, led by Major Short, ran forward on the right, with the 12th and 14th Native Infantry on their left over the open space whistling with grape. But the two sepoy regiments hung back under the tremendous fire, the 62nd taking the brunt of it alone, and in two or three minutes seventeen out of twenty-three officers and two hundred and fifty men were killed or wounded. The remainder, exhausted even before they charged, refused to go on, threw themselves down near the enemy batteries and began ineffectually firing. Lieutenants Gubbins and Kelly ran forward to the batteries but were cut down. Reed, Short and the remaining three officers made desperate efforts, pointing out the short distance the men had to go to drive the Sikhs off their guns and win the day, but in vain. 'Unable to urge them on,' Reed reported, 'they declaring they would stay there as long as I wished, but had not the strength to charge (which was true), seeing the fire to which they were exposed, I took the responsibility of ordering them to retire, which they did in perfect order.'

Brigadier Ashburnham's three regiments of sepoys had during these several disastrous minutes given almost no support to Reed's brigade. Where they deployed, unfortunately, they came upon a well, and 'no power', says Ashburnham candidly, 'could restrain the thirsty sepoys from running out to drink. What with these and many who positively fell from the ranks from exhaustion or funk I did not take two-thirds of my brigade into action.' The grapeshot began hissing among them; they couldn't take any more and retreated by sixes and sevens.

When 'Bully' Brooke had pleaded with Gough to be able to loose his horse artillery at the powerful Sikh batteries, there came the crash of Littler's musketry above the noise of the Sikh cannonade. 'Littler will be in the (Sikh) trenches unsupported,' Gough exclaimed and gave orders for a general attack to support him, even though some of the units were still deploying into line. General Harry Smith, his division correctly placed in reserve, rode forward to look at the enemy's position, and met General Hardinge, who asked him which troops were firing alone on the left. 'I galloped forward to ascertain,' Smith says, 'and reported that they were of Littler's force, that his attack appeared to me one of no weight from its formation, and that, if the enemy behaved as expected it would fail.' Hardinge said, 'Then bring up your division.' Smith had in fact then two British regiments, the 50th and the 31st, and four sepoy regiments with one troop of Horse Artillery, and these he quickly ordered up to the left of Gilbert's division, in place of Littler's.

Of the British artillery, only the two howitzers were having the slightest effect upon the Sikh batteries. 'Bully' Brooke's Horse Artillery were ordered to ride to within two hundred yards of them to attack. 'Our major, evidently with the object of ascertaining how close it would be necessary for him to advance, laid one of the guns himself, ordering it to be fired,' noted the six foot three inches Trooper Bancroft.

> He stepped aside to note the result, which must have disappointed him, as he was observed to stamp his foot impatiently. He turned round in search of his horse, and not seeing it he said — his last words, alas! — 'Bancroft, where is my horse?' Pointing to the direction in which the animal was standing, the writer answered: 'There he is sir!' The words were scarcely uttered when he saw the gallant major lying at a little distance from his horse — headless! The shot must have struck him full in the face, for there was no trace or vestige of his features to be seen.

For the British, the fighting was going badly. The triumphant shouts of the Sikhs at the repulse of the British infantry and the outgunning of their artillery were heard now above the roar of the battle as the divisions of Generals Gilbert (on the right) led by Gough, and Wallace (on the left), by Hardinge, both in echelon of brigades, assaulted the Sikh trenches. Taylor's brigade, consisting of the 29th and 80th Foot, led the way, and, noted Captain John Cumming of the 80th:

> We advanced against a hailstorm of round-shot, shells, grape and musketry. To heighten the destruction mines had been dug before the trenches and sprung under our feet: the slaughter was terrible. Yet our fellows pressed nobly on with the charge, and with the bayonet alone rushed over the entrenchments and captured the guns in front of us. The Sikhs flinched not an inch, but fought till they died to a man at their guns. Our further advance was checked by the bursting mines setting their camp on fire, and we retired a short distance to be clear of it.

Maclaren's Brigade moved forward on their left, led by the 1st European Light Infantry commanded by Major Birrell, in the centre, Captain Box, second-in-command, on the right, Captain Douglas Seaton on the left and Ensigns F. O. Salusbury and P. Moxon bearing the Colours. Fire from the Sikh batteries redoubled in violence, round-shot and grape splintering trees, tearing gaps in the ranks, leaving a trail of maimed and dying men. Here, recalls Ensign Innes, Captain Box received the shot he had foretold 'right slap in the face' and fell dead from his horse. Captain Kendall, leading 6 Company and Captain Clark 1 Company, were both mortally wounded in this maelstrom. Ensign Salusbury, a boy of eighteen, fell under the Queen's Colour, the bone of his right arm exposed from shoulder to elbow. Ensign Innes seized the Colour just as the regiments brought their bayonets down and charged the Sikh guns. 'We were in a few minutes right under the enemy batteries, but the air was so filled with fire and smoke that it seemed to be as dark as night.'

Through the branches and leaves hiding the ditch in front of their positions the British, blaspheming and cursing, tumbled and fell on top of each other, then slinging their muskets, clambered out, sprang up the ten feet to the sloping bank upon which the guns were mounted, and charged the yellow-turbaned Sikh gunners, in their unmistakable white tunics and black trousers. Heavy *tulwars* whirling and slashing, the Sikhs fought back desperately, but they were overwhelmed by the fury of the British attack and bayoneted to a man.

Quickly reforming, and mounting the few remaining feet to the top of the plateau, the two brigades suddenly faced a murderous volley from unexpected Sikh infantry drawn up in line before their tents in camp-streets behind the guns. During the fight for the guns they had held their fire to avoid hitting their comrades intermingled with the British in the hand-to-hand struggle. Now, after their first galling volley they threw down their muskets, drew their *tulwars* and rushed at the charging, cheering British. Along the whole line of Gilbert's division, controlled by Gough himself, the two armies fought hand-to-hand. Soon the ditch below and the plateau, were covered with heaps of dead and dying Sikh, sepoy and British, until the Sikhs gave way, retreated to their tent lines and began knocking the British down with volleys of musketry.

Sir Walter Gilbert's division, having so far succeeded in penetrating the Sikh positions, bayoneting the gunners and driving back the infantry, were now threatened by a mass of Sikh cavalry. But suddenly, the 3rd Light Dragoons, led by Brigadier White and accompanied by a troop of Horse Artillery, charging through a furious hail of musketry and grape from batteries still in Sikh hands, dashed with irresistible force against the enemy cavalry, clove their way through the dense column, overthrowing horse and man, and put them to flight.

They then attacked a strong defensive position, but met such heavy fire that they had to retreat, leaving many dead behind. A brilliant and victorious charge, it probably saved the day.

All this time, Wallace's division on Gilbert's left had continued to advance both against the western Sikh positions, from which Littler's men had retreated, and against the southern positions. Black smoke and dust formed a dark screen in the late afternoon haze which hid the enemy guns, and when they emerged before the muzzles the Sikhs mowed them down with grapeshot. Colonel Taylor, many junior officers and men were killed, and part of the long red line fell back in confusion. Captain Borton rallied them, the right battalions pressed on and captured the batteries facing them. General Harry Smith, advancing with Colonel Ryan's brigade in response to the earlier order of Hardinge, had difficulty in establishing himself on the front line, owing to the broken masses of troops falling back on him.

> Scarcely was I firmly established, when Major Broadfoot, the political agent, rode up and said, 'Be prepared, General, four battalions of Avitabile's Brigade are close upon you in advance. I have it from correct information — a man in my pay has just left them.' The smoke and dirt rendered everything at the moment invisible. I saw, however, that to resist this attack, which was made to take advantage of our check, and penetrate our line between Littler's right and Wallace's left, I must bring up the right of my brigade. I endeavoured to do so, and with HM's 50th Regiment I partially succeeded under a storm of musketry and cannon which I have rarely, if ever, seen exceeded.

This was not surprising, for Smith was advancing in the dust and smoke at once on the Sikh western and southern positions. He was caught in that most killing thing, a crossfire. Captain

Abbott's horse was shot from under him. When he got up from beneath the struggling animal he was struck down at once by one bullet in the right shoulder and one in the left arm. Galloping forward, Broadfoot called to him to get up and Abbott, to his surprise, as he later recalled, found that he could.

Broadfoot, slightly behind Smith's advancing brigade, with Hardinge, and those of his aides still alive, rode with them through the smoke towards the right and the south face. Here it was his turn. He was hit in the thigh and his horse threw him at the same moment. He remounted and shortly afterwards was killed advancing with the troops against a battery in front, shot through the heart and the arm.

General Smith at this moment, noted that officers and men were falling fast:

> I saw there was nothing for it but a charge of bayonets to restore the waning fight. I, Colonel Petit and Colonel Ryan put ourselves at the head of the 50th and most gallantly did we charge into the enemy's trenches, where such a hand-to-hand conflict followed as I have ever witnessed. The enemy was repulsed at this point, his works and cannon carried and he precipitately retreated.

Smith pressed on furiously with Ryan's brigade to the western part of the Sikh tented camp where he saw the enemy-occupied village of Ferozeshur some four hundred yards away. By this time he had been joined by stragglers from the left of Wallace's division on his right, but none from Littler's on his left, and, uncertain whether Avitabile's battalion had been repulsed, or even where they were, he became nervous about an attack on his exposed left flank and set about taking the village to make himself more secure.

Sir Walter Gilbert's division, on the right of the line, where it was controlled by Gough in the attack on the right of the southern face, had, as we know, taken the guns and driven the Sikh infantry back into their tents. Maclaren's brigade, with the 1st European Light Infantry leading, were then ordered to charge along the Sikhs' centre camp-street and take the village of Ferozeshur, towards which Sir Harry Smith was then leading his men about half a mile away on the left. 'The soldiers gallantly carried out these orders,' noted Ensign Innes, a teenager who was in the thick of it.

> But they had not proceeded more than two hundred yards when there was heard beneath their feet a frightful roar; the ground heaved and the men in the vicinity were blown away amongst the tents, the air being filled with fire, and a dense smoke arising, which, as it cleared away, exposed to view a horrible and appalling scene, numbers of our men having fallen frightfully burnt and mutilated, and in some instances their pouches ignited, causing terrible wounds, agony and loss of life.

This explosion of a Sikh powder magazine deadened all noise of the twilight battle. Flames spread, dump after dump of powder exploded, regiments scattered, reformed in the flickering gloom. Captain Seaton led about one hundred and fifty men through the dead and dying in the camp and joined Smith's force in the attack on Ferozeshur itself. 'I continued,' Smith wrote,

> to advance in line in perfect order until impeded by the enemy's tents, when the whole broke and, a mass of undaunted British soldiers, pell mell, rushed forward, bore everything before them, until we reached the mud-walled village of Ferozeshur, where the enemy attempted to rally, and

compelled me to collect my troops. I speedily seized this village, filled with infantry, cavalry and horses… I planted one of the colours of HM's 50th on the mud walls. A scene of awful slaughter here ensued, as the enemy would not lay down their arms. The village was full of richly caparisoned horses and there were camels innumerable around it. By this time, many detachments belonging to the regiments composing the left of the main attack had joined me…

Noting, in the twilight, that on the right, where Gough commanded, victory seemed complete, Smith resolved to push forward again to consolidate the advance. He succeeded in seizing the enemy camp half a mile beyond the village, where, after being joined by more stragglers, his force amounted to some three thousand men. In the darkness, he found that far from being defeated, the Sikhs faced him in force on his right, and in front, and that his position was critical: he had pushed the enemy back far beyond the ground held by the army on his right.

He managed to form a defensive semi-circle in front of the Sikh camp with the men of 50th Foot, the 9th Foot under Major Barwell, the 1st European Light Infantry under Captain Seaton, the 24th Native Infantry under Major Bird and the 19th, 23rd, 28th and 73rd Native Infantry. But the Sikhs soon discovered how weak and isolated was his force and attacked his right, where the sepoys of the 24th gave way. Smith contracted the circle and managed to hold it, but the Sikhs closed in, keeping up a destructive fire and calling out in French, English and Hindustani that the attackers were all doomed. Dead tired, officers and men were killed while falling asleep, yet aware of the importance of his advance, Smith — although he could hear nothing of Gilbert's division or see any camp fires — resolved to try to maintain himself.

But every moment his losses became heavier and when the enemy began firing grapeshot from behind, Smith saw that he would have to retire. While the Sikhs, shouting and cheering, began attacking on all sides, he made a feint attack, opened fire and retreated by regiments under cover of darkness, until he had passed through the village.

It was pitch dark. While Smith was retreating, two or three miles off, Gough took stock of the general situation. His army had driven the Sikhs from most, though not all, of their defensive positions, occupied different parts of their camp and, except for Littler's first repulse, had nowhere failed despite a tough and courageous resistance. Gough had then no means of knowing that Smith had advanced so far — in the excitement of the battle that general had failed to send messengers to tell him. But he did know that there was now a danger that the scattered British troops might fire upon each other.

To prevent this danger Gough had the buglers sound the retire.

The Bengal European Regiment at this time still attacked the Sikhs in their camp-streets amongst the red and white tents. Behind a barricade a group of Sikhs had brought their fire to bear upon a well, around which the parched troops had gathered. 'Several of our men had fallen,' Ensign Percy Innes noted, 'others... were pressing forward and seizing the tin pots from their wounded comrades, preferring the immediate prospect of death to the fearful torture of thirst.'

It was found the regimental colours had disappeared. Innes ran up to the barricade they had just attacked and found Ensign Philip Moxon's dead body where he had fallen on the colours and saturated them with blood. Under fire, he seized them and brought them back safely. Led by Lieutenant Greville, the troops then assaulted the barricade, drove the

Sikhs off and cleared the main camp-street leading to the village from the south-east.

Thus the village and the camp were in British hands.

An aide-de-camp then arrived with orders from General Gough to retire to the plain outside; every bugler inside and outside the entrenchments began sounding his regimental call amid shooting and shouting. Greville led his men back across the entrenchments which had been taken with so much loss of life, groped his way at their head to where he heard their own regimental call.

The Sikhs at once re-occupied the camp and entrenchments. Lieutenant Robertson of the 31st, recalling the confusion that followed the withdrawal, wrote of a large Sikh gun that he saw in the light of the blazing tents with not a living man beside it.

> The Sikhs had retired and we had possession of this part of their camp; but instead of holding on to what we had got with so much loss, we were ordered to retire for the night. We then went back in a sort of mob, men of all regiments being mixed together, and every officer shouting for his company or regiment. One man would say, 'Where is the 80th?' 'Here it is,' would say another. 'No, this is the 31st,' would say a third, and so on. The colours of two or three regiments were all together, and everyone would have it that he was right. I ran up against Law, who was crying out, 'Where is Paul and the colours?' and at last seeing him he held on and called out, 'Here is the 31st; this way 31st, etc.,' until we got into some sort of order. But there was no firing in front of us then and we thought the battle was over. We formed at quarter-distance column, and lay down on the cold sand. It was then that we began to feel the most frightful thirst, and not a drop of anything was to be had. I had a little drop of gin in a flask, and took a pull at it, giving the rest to the men with me. But

this only made us the worse, and the cold was so intense that we were quite frozen.

The Sikhs now held their entire position again. There had been a large and fruitless loss of life on the British side. Even one more hour of daylight would have enabled them to consolidate and drive the Sikhs out completely, for the British infantry had proved their superiority. Tragically, the daylight had been thrown away on the Governor-General's orders to wait for Littler, whose infantry, after their first repulse, had ironically, taken no further part in the fighting.

The battle could go to either side when fought afresh next day — some British officers were already counselling a retreat to Ferozepore. Sir Harry Smith, marching his three thousand men back in the direction from which he had advanced, guided by the line of dead soldiers, reached a fire around which were grouped men of Littler's 62nd who had earlier retreated. Some of these officers urged him to retreat. Smith says he answered: 'The commander-in-chief with his army is not far from us, meditating an attack as soon as it is daylight, and find him I will if in hell, where I will join him, rather than make one retrograde step.' A large flare mounted up at that moment, as if someone were lighting a fire. 'There's my point,' Smith exclaimed — 'friend or foe!'

Thirty minutes stumbling in the dark brought Smith and his men to the fire, where he found two or three thousand stragglers of every regiment with some Horse Artillery and a brigade of cavalry. Smith halted his men, and procured enough rum to issue a swig to all his British troops. Now occurred an extraordinary incident. Captain Lumley, Assistant Adjutant-General of the Army and during the sickness of his father, General Lumley, acting Adjutant-General, rode up to Smith, who, believing he came direct from Gough, recalls that he was delighted to see him, but not for long.

According to Smith, Lumley said: 'Sir Harry Smith, you are the very man I am looking for. As senior officer of the Adjutant-General's department, I order you to collect every soldier and march to Ferozepore.'

Smith, characteristically, replied: 'Do you come direct from the commander-in-chief with *such an orders*? If you do, I can find him, for, by God, I'll take no such order from any man on earth but from his own mouth. Where is he?'

'I don't know, but these in my official position are the orders.'

'Damn the orders, if not the commander-in-chief's,' Smith growled. 'I'll give my own orders and take none of that retrograde sort from any Staff Officer on earth. But why to Ferozepore? What's the matter?'

'Oh, the army has been beaten, but we can buy the Sikh soldiers.'

'What! Have we taken no guns?'

'Oh yes, fifty or sixty.'

'Thank you. I see my way and want no orders.'

Captain Christie, who commanded a regiment of irregular cavalry, stepped forward and offered to guide Smith to the commander-in-chief. Smith sent an officer forward to report that he was on his way with several thousand men, then had them formed up and marched off with him and Christie leading. Lumley however, next ordered the 8th Light Cavalry to Ferozepore, and the officer commanding, being neither of Smith's metal nor rank, did as he was ordered, set out on the road to Ferozepore and so weakened the already depleted army.

Gough and Hardinge all this time were trying to re-establish order and control. They ordered the confused regiments and mixed detachments to be formed into squares ready to repel any enemy cavalry or infantry charges. Men and officers, exhausted, hungry, parched with thirst, bitterly cold, without greatcoats or shelter and unable to light fires without bringing down Sikh grapeshot on themselves, knew that back again now in their trenches the Sikhs had half-won a victory already. If the British were to do no better next day, with their weakened forces, they faced defeat. Some senior officers with the commander-in-chief now urged a retreat to Ferozepore.

> Were I to have taken, [Sir Hugh Gough wrote to his son later] the strenuous representations of officers, some of rank and in important situations, my honour and my Army would have been lost... Two said they came from the Governor-General. I spurned the supposition, as I knew it could not be well-founded. My answer was, 'Well, I shall go to the Governor-General, but my determination is taken rather to leave my bones to bleach honourably at Ferozeshah than that they should rot dishonourably at Ferozepore'.

With shell bursting all around, Gough and Hardinge discussed this grim situation by the light of a lantern in a small hut which the commander-in-chief had made his headquarters. Both agreed that retreat was not to be considered and that they must attack again at daylight, yet both knew that their exhausted men could not face another ordeal as severe as that which they had undergone. The likelihood of defeat was even considered, and with this in mind the Governor-General sent Prince Waldemar of Prussia, who had been present as an observer throughout the battle, back to Mudki with other non-combatants, taking with them Napoleon's sword, presented to Hardinge in 1816 by Wellington on the plains of Sedan, and messages to Robert Cust, and to Frederick Currie, his political secretary, to destroy all state papers. 'News came that our attack had failed,' Cust wrote in his diary, 'and that Mr Currie was to destroy papers of State… Affairs appeared to be very gloomy indeed, and though the news was kept quite secret, we were concerting measures to make our unconditional surrender, to save the wounded in the fort.'

All this time the Sikhs fired continually into the troops huddled on the open ground between two and three hundred yards from their batteries until it was covered with dead and wounded. To Lieutenant Bellars of the 50th Regiment the night was one of horrifying uncertainty:

> A burning camp on one side of the village, mines and ammunition wagons exploding in every direction, the loud orders given to extinguish the fires as the sepoys lighted them, the volleys given should the Sikhs venture too near, the booming of the monster guns, the incessant firing of the smaller ones, the continued whistling noise of the shell, grape and round-shot, the bugles sounding, the drums beating, and the yelling of the enemy, together with intense thirst, fatigue and cold, and not knowing whether the rest of the army were the conquerors or conquered — all contributed to make this night awful in the extreme.

Captain John Cumming felt the terror of the Sikh shot whistling and hissing among them — the trampling of men and horses among the dead, the groans of the wounded, and noted the strange contrasts in behaviour of men under the threat of death:

> Many a gallant fellow was lying in the square silent, though severely wounded, some of them bleeding to death without a murmur. In the 80th square a grapeshot struck a man in the

shoulder, producing a rather severe flesh wound. The foolish fellow wanted to get out of the square: where he intended going I know not, but if he had got his wish he would probably have been cut to pieces. He would not be quiet, but kept telling everyone that he was wounded, as if his wound was of more consequence than that of anyone else. Being refused by a sergeant of his company, he went to the Colour-Sergeant saying, 'Sergeant, I am badly wounded, let me get out of the square to go to the surgeon.' The Colour-Sergeant replied, 'Lie down where you are man, look at me' — lifting up a leg without a foot. But he was determined to gain his point, and came to Lieutenant Bythesea, who commanded his company, and was lying next me. 'Oh Sir, I wish you would give orders to let me out of the square: I am wounded.' 'So am I,' coolly answered Mr Bythesea, putting round his right arm, and lifting up his left hand which hung shattered from the wrist. Though he was not near me I did not know till then that he had been hurt. But the man persevered and came now to Colonel Bunbury, who commanded the regiment, and was still on horseback. He was about two yards from where I lay. 'Sir,' cried the man, 'I am wounded, please give orders for me to go and have it dressed.' 'So you're wounded, my good man,' said the Colonel. 'Yes Sir.' 'So am I' — I then perceived that the colonel was wounded just below the knee, and the blood had filled his boot, and was trickling from the heel to the ground. The assistant-sergeant-major had been watching this man, and, becoming angry at the annoyance he was causing, determined to stop it. He ran up and seized him, saying 'Damn —,' but before any more was out of his mouth a cannon ball carried away his head, and a part of the unfortunate private's, killing both at once.

Gough and Hardinge spent the night moving from square to square and line to line in this cataclysm, cheering on the men. 'Eightieth, you have behaved nobly today!' Hardinge told the men of this regiment, who had borne the brunt of so much of the fighting. 'We shall have a royal day tomorrow — glory, plenty to eat and drink, and a good time to rest ourselves after.' He lay down and rested among them for some time, the shot whistling low overhead, and asked Colonel Bunbury why he didn't dismount and lie down. Bunbury shrugged coolly and said he thought he was as safe one way as the other.

Not long afterwards the Sikhs increased their hail of fire with a very heavy gun, thought to be a 48-pounder, backed by a battery of smaller ones, double charges of grapeshot from which killed and wounded many. Hardinge shouted: 'Take that battery!' Colonel Bunbury at once led a detachment of the 80th and Major Birrell one of the Bengal European Light Infantry, in two lines, at the double, firing volleys. The Sikhs in reply sent out an infantry detachment, and two lines of fire blazed in the darkness. The British infantry met the Sikhs in a rush forward, bayonet and sabre clashed together, pistol shots, shouts, curses and groans intermingled. They won through to the guns to hammer iron spikes into the vents to make them unserviceable. They then returned with some losses to the lines.

It grew bitterly cold. 'I paced up and down,' wrote Brigadier Thomas Ashburnham, of Littler's division, 'occasionally venting my spite by kicking the blackguard sepoys who kept firing away into the air, to keep up their courage, but what was more likely to bring down the enemy's fire or cavalry... Forgetting myself, I thought how the very fate of the British Empire seemed hanging on a thread...'

In the early hours, General Harry Smith brought in his men. Soon after, when the first white streaks of dawn showed in the sky and ended this, the most desperate night ever spent in India by a commander-in-chief, the troops were quietly formed up in order, guns in front, infantry in two lines behind. Morning broke with a thick mist, which the hot sun dispelled and the Sikhs were there — holding positions from which they had been driven the day before.

Gough took one look at the lines of glittering bayonets, then gave the order to attack again.

Captain Mills raised his sword and three troops of horse artillery galloped forward, unlimbered and opened up on the enemy batteries with the first British shots in the second day of the battle. The Sikhs answered accurately — their fire blew up three of the British ammunition wagons, but soon it began to die away. The reason can only have been that the Sikhs lacked the staying power of the British; and discipline had partially collapsed in their camp, the Akalis, the religious fanatics, having mutinied and pillaged Lal Singh's headquarter tents before they were thrown back at gun-point. Moreover Lal Singh and his generals had failed the Khalsa, giving no leadership or encouragement. So when the Sikh soldiers heard the drums beating and saw the banners and the long lines of the army they thought beaten, their morale collapsed too.

Gough now led the right wing and Hardinge the left, the 'advance' shrilled over the plain and the infantry charged as a flight of rockets soared up and crashed down into the Sikh positions. The trenches were taken at the bayonet point, lost in some places then re-taken during three hours' fighting. Lieutenant Robertson of the 31st, noted that Major Spence, his commanding officer, ordered the regiment to the right, so as to avoid casualties:

> We advanced very quietly upon a strong battery, on the left of the Sikh camp and just at the angle; they did not see us till we were right upon them, and they had only time to fire one or two rounds when we gave them a volley and charged right

into them. Spence was on foot in front and was one of the first over the ditch. We bayoneted a great many artillerymen and infantry who stood to the last; we also took a standard, and then charged on through the camp, polishing off all we could get at.

Having carried the trenches on the southern and eastern faces, the British cavalry and infantry drove the Sikhs out of Ferozeshur and their camp, wheeled to the left and swept through all the defences and gun positions. John Cumming noted: 'By one o'clock we had... driven the enemy clear out. The camp and all its guns and stores were ours. As the line now stood, the Governor-General and the commander-in-chief rode along it: we presented arms to them as at a review, and then cheered, with a heartfelt pride, our noble commanders as they passed our ranks.'

The Sikhs, many of whom had deserted during the night, fled through the jungles north of Ferozeshur towards the Sutlej. A regiment of cavalry rode north to observe their retreat while parties searched for water and food. Sir Henry's promise of plenty came to next to nothing: only a small quantity of oranges, a supply of grain and dried peas and some sugar were found in the enemy camp, a diet that supports the view that the Sikh oligarchy was using every possible method to destroy the Khalsa, including starvation.

But more than food, the parched British needed water. Lieutenant Robertson found a well without bucket or line. Having found a bucket he cut and tied tent ropes together for a time and brought up the water. Cumming noted that it was bloodstained — the Sikhs had thrown numbers of dead in it 'but it was eagerly drunk by both officers and men' from the one single bucket, the mob of troops almost fighting for it. Sir

Hugh Gough came up and waited with one or two of his staff, but it was some time before he got any water. 'The men were too mad with thirst to pass it even to the commander-in-chief.'

A feeling of relief at survival, buoyed by the hope that the Sikhs had been beaten arose now in the army. Parties set out to bring in the wounded and bury the dead, the army began reorganizing itself. Then suddenly, cavalrymen tore into the village to report that the regiment sent to watch the retreat had been checked by a big Sikh force advancing from Ferozepore. A heavy cloud of dust obscured the horizon in the direction indicated.

Battered and disorganized, Gough's troops now faced another attack by Tej Singh's fresh army from Ferozepore. Only a miracle could save them, for they were quite without the strength to fight again.

9: Treason

Even Gough's indomitable spirits fell. His men were exhausted, the cavalry horses so tired and hungry that they could barely gallop; worst of all, his artillery ammunition was almost finished. Yet advancing upon him, great red and gold banners streaming, was another Sikh army, ready and eager for a battle which he could not avoid. 'The only time I felt a doubt,' he wrote in a letter to his son, 'was towards the evening of the 22nd when the fresh enemy advanced, with heavy columns of cavalry, infantry and guns, and our cavalry horses were thoroughly done up... But it was only for a moment and Hugh Gough was himself again'.

It was a strange encounter. The respective positions of British and Sikhs were changed. The British were formed up in a defensive square round Ferozeshur, following the earlier line of the enemy trenches; and out on the plain were the Sikhs, the attacking force.

The exhausted Horse Artillery staggered into action, two troops under Colonel Huthwaite trotting through the jungle, opening up upon Tej Singh's force from the left of the village. The Sikhs answered furiously. Major Brind, in command of two more troops, then attacked and he in his turn was pummelled by some thirty Sikh guns. Colonel Geddes, with another two troops, joined the fray and he too met a heavy answering fire. The British were outgunned. Colonel Huthwaite retired when he had no more than about a dozen rounds left, Major Brind was driven back by fierce enfilading fire; Colonel Geddes gave up the unequal contest when his ammunition was finished, and fell back to the infantry square around the village.

The long line of Sikh infantry, red jackets, black crossbelts and blue trousers reflecting British influence, advanced steadily. Brind's five six-pounders and three of Huthwaite's opened up on them with a ragged salvo. Once more the Sikhs responded with a furious cannonade from some forty guns, the heavy shot whistling through the air, hitting the British infantry and artillery severely for twenty minutes. The fire ceased as masses of Sikh cavalry emerged from the jungles skirting the plain and formed up ready to charge.

Now it looked as if the British would be slaughtered.

It was about 2 pm Gough suddenly ordered the infantry to change front, facing them to the north in echelon of regiments formed into squares four deep to oppose the enemy cavalry charges — with almost no ammunition. The Sikh cavalry were now about two hundred yards in front, trotting forward hesitantly, awaiting the order to charge, their long bamboo lances lowered, heavy *tulwars* flashing. But while they hesitated, a rush of horsemen was suddenly heard to the rear of the British infantry. The 3rd Dragoons — 'terribly reduced in number, but not in courage,' in the words of Ensign Percy Innes — were charging to the rescue at full gallop, supported by two regiments of Native Cavalry. Colonel White, at their head, was bravely, though rashly, joined by General Gilbert, commanding the Second Division, as they dashed past and on with a furious shock into the Sikh cavalry, with their full force and weight. A fierce hand-to-hand combat followed, but the Sikhs failed to recover and gradually gave way. The infantry waited, passive spectators, as scores of riderless horses trotted around the dismounted riders fighting on foot.

Part of the Sikh cavalry now retired and the surviving Dragoons withdrew to regroup, but their horses were unlikely to be equal to another such effort. The enemy artillery poured in another furious cannonade, the heavy round-shot whistling and thudding in among the British. It was a murderous affair. The redcoats fell in swathes. Gough's feelings as he watched the fate of these men who had fought so bravely for the last thirty-six hours were all at once too much for him. Suddenly, his white fighting coat flying behind, he rode forward out in front of the line, accompanied by one aide, Captain Sackville-West, utterly disdaining the storm of shot, 'to draw a portion of the artillery fire upon us from our hard-pressed infantry,' as he told his son later. 'We, thank God, succeeded, and saved many unhurt, my gallant horse being a conspicuous mark — unheeding the thunder of shot (both round and grape) — ploughing up the earth around him.'

Gough knew his men and the courage this magnificent act — coolly attracting enemy fire upon him for their sake — would inspire. But it brought only a temporary respite; where they had wavered they now stood firm, but all believed the day was lost. To Captain Cumming the fate of India 'seemed to hang upon a single hair. I believe that there were few among us... who did not feel that the field would be their burial ground.'

But the strange denouement of this battle was now at hand, undreamt of by anyone, and the upshot was to be stranger still.

The entire force of British cavalry and artillery all at once reformed column and began to canter off the field towards Ferozepore. Gough, Hardinge, the men of the infantry, all gazed incredulous, hardly able to believe their eyes. Messengers were sent galloping to recall them, but in vain; the long line of horses disappeared over the horizon. Gough's observations unfortunately were not recorded. But the stern-faced infantry, seeing guns and cavalry vanish in a cloud of dust, coolly braced themselves for the end. Their last hour, it seemed, had come.

Then, for the second time the totally unexpected happened, what one can only call the miracle. Tej Singh's infantry had begun to advance, his cavalry had reformed for their long-expected charge. The drums were beating. Victory was within their grasp. All at once their bugles blared the *retreat*, again and again, the *retreat*. Infantry and cavalry both hesitated, turned about and in front of the astonished British, moved off as fast as their legs could carry them towards the Sutlej.

Soon the plain where they were arrayed in their thousands was empty of all but the dead and wounded, scattered where they fell.

Thus, at 4 pm on 22 December 1845 in this strange and unexpected way ended the bloody battle of Ferozeshur. The light faded, the blue dusk softened the bloody carnage. Left on the field, with five thousand of enemy dead and hundreds of their own killed and wounded, the British infantry leant on their muskets, looked at each other with almost empty eyes and raised a ragged cheer. Pursuit was not even considered. Gough's men were weak, disordered, lacking ammunition, guns and cavalry. Tej Singh's retreat was a providential gift. There can have been few who wished then to risk another clash.

The British had taken seventy-five Sikh guns, but at a cost of 2,415 casualties, about a seventh of their entire force, 694 of whom were killed. Sir Hugh Gough's horse, at some unstated time during the fighting, was killed under him. Five of the Governor-General's staff were killed and two wounded. Brigadier Wallace was killed, Brigadiers Harriott, Taylor and White wounded.

It was accounted a victory, but of course, only Sikh treachery and a mad British officer saved an appalling disaster. What was the explanation then, first of the British cavalry and artillery riding off; and secondly, of the Sikh retreat in the face of victory? The answers are linked, but the first can only be understood in the light of nepotism that then prevailed in the British army. Captain Lumley, the half-crazy acting Adjutant-General, was, incredibly, still at his post, doing mischief. Falsely, he had used the commander-in-chief's authority to order the artillery to retire to Ferozepore to refill their ammunition boxes; and, the cavalry to accompany them. The Governor-General offered him resignation as an alternative to court martial, which he accepted. He may have been a Sikh sympathizer, but he was generally assumed to be mad; yet he was not lacking an ironic sense of humour. When next day he appeared before the Governor-General and was asked why he still wore pyjamas, he answered that his uniform had been so riddled with shot that it had fallen off him.

What of the Sikh retreat? Colonel Gardner, who a few days later met some of the Khalsa generals at Lahore, quotes them as saying that Tej Singh, desperately anxious not to fight the British, had proclaimed, when he saw their cavalry and artillery retreating, that they were about to attack from the rear. He had good reason for an order to retreat, one which didn't end till his army had crossed the Sutlej.

Thus by accident, Captain Lumley rescued the British from certain defeat.

Meantime, on the field, as many men as possible had been sent out to bring in the wounded. Some of them were housed at Ferozeshur, where quantities of bedding for the Sikh army had been found, and others in the fort at Mudki. Facilities were hopelessly inadequate, largely because Sir Henry Hardinge, allowing his optimism or caution to override his humanity, had countermanded Gough's orders for transport for the field hospital. Dr W. L. McGregor, surgeon in the field with the 1st Bengal European Light Infantry, condemned the situation outright:

> During the night of the 21st many a poor wounded European soldier found his way to the rear in search of medical aid; but the arrangements for affording it were very incomplete excepting through the efforts of the regimental surgeons, who did everything in their power with the means at their command. As for the field hospital, it had no existence, so confidently had the opinion been entertained that the Sikhs would not offer resistance, that it was deemed unnecessary to make any arrangements for a field hospital. There were no medical stores or instruments in the field, except those attached to regiment hospitals and the hurry of the movements prevented any sufficient supply from being obtained without great delay.

Robert Cust, the political official, had been ordered to stay behind at Mudki, during the fighting, together with a sanctimonious clergyman, the Reverend J. J. Coley, who complained bitterly in his journal how the wounded soldiers — 'men hardened in iniquity, their neck an iron sinew and their brow brass' — disdained the comforts of religion on their deathbeds. 'They have need rather to be persuaded by the terrors of the Lord to flee from the wrath to come.' Little wonder that the wounded had no time for Coley; no spark of sympathy for them did he show. While they were dying, he complained of the dust and the dangers of standing too near their graves:

> To stand outside one's tent is to be smothered with dust. The bottom of the graves in the burial ground is as fine and impalpable dust as the top, however deep they are dug; and they fall in almost as fast as they are made: it is quite dangerous to stand near them... It is nothing but dust wherever one goes; and the whole country round seems a desert of dust. It is not sandy dust, which would be heavier, but pulverized alluvial soil... They say it penetrates the works of watches.

In sharp contrast to this triviality, this indifference, was Cust's sympathy for the wounded and dying. Aged twenty-two, a sensitive and highly educated man, who had never before seen death, though it was no part of his duty, he voluntarily spent the two days at Mudki with them. He wandered into the deserted village, the sole tenants of which, apart from hundreds of wounded, were the wife of an officer, who had taken possession of a house, the commissariat officer who had installed himself in a shop, and the surgeon 'busy amputating limbs in the street — a ghastly spectacle... The cries of the sufferers were dreadful to hear.' Cust found the camp full to overflowing with wounded.

> Every corner was occupied... I found the still warm though lifeless body of Sir Robert Sale, who had expired from the severity of his wounds... Nothing can describe the painfulness of the scene around me — friends or at least countrymen, or men, suffering from various kinds of torments, groaning and in pain. In one corner I fell in with a ghastly crew — poor Munis the ADC, settled in his bed yellow in death — Hillier, ADC, by his side three officers of the Dragoons and one of the Bodyguard with their faces so slashed with sword cuts as to have scarcely a semblance of their former features...

He spent much of the 21st while the battle raged with a school friend, Captain Dashwood, whose leg had been shattered and who had been told by the surgeons that he would not live for more than a few hours.

> He put his hand into mine and said good-bye and told me he was growing much weaker... The room was dark. I called for a light. He had just breathed his last as the clock struck eleven... I closed his eyes and fastened a handkerchief round his head and then went to Coley's tent to pass the night there. Never shall I forget the complicated horrors of these two days at Mudki. I make no mention of the discomforts and the dirt — the vast mass of men and beasts crowded in a confined spot. This was not all — it was the accumulation of suffering of which I was the spectator on all sides.
>
> In the tent next to where I slept... was a poor wounded officer who was crying out — 'For God Almighty's sake spare me this torture — spare me — I cannot bear it!' There was the wounded sepoy exclaiming — 'Mercy colonel — kill me, kill me!' There were the mangled bodies of those killed in action lying outside. There was the even more painful sight inside; the useless heaps of clothes in the dhooly ready to be conveyed to the grave — all that remained of a gallant officer and a valued friend. Death indeed became familiar. Those were days in the chapter of misery never to be forgotten.

With these feelings in his heart, Robert Cust entered the tent where lay the body of his friend Major George Broadfoot, chief of the Punjab intelligence and diplomatic service. The sight wrung the truth from him.

> There stretched before me, laid low by a violent death, the mortal remains of one whose ambition was boundless, whose talents were of the highest order, and who was gifted with energy and fertility of resource which no circumstances could

overpower. There lay he — *the prime weaver, the cause of the war now commencing* — the man most hated by the enemy whom we were opposing, and most feared.

Broadfoot had received a dusty answer to his quest for power and glory. Cust's words, written at white-heat, are startling confirmation that he, more than anyone else, with all the possibilities for good and ill that he had in his hands, was responsible for the final outbreak of war between British and Sikh.

Night fell on the field. Shivering, exhausted men huddled round blazing fires. Wandering cattle were slaughtered, crudely grilled in the flames, devoured ravenously. Camels loaded with the canteen stores now arrived, ending their long slow march from Ambala. The troops ate their fill, then while sentries patrolled, slept on the ground the thankful contented sleep of men who have held their fives in their hands and lived. In Captain John Cummings's memory the bitter cold of the night stayed and the grim early morning sight of the battlefield where many wounded still lay:

> I awoke as the reveille was sounding on the morning of the 23rd to find myself stiff with cold, my clothes covered with hoarfrost and my limbs so benumbed that I could not rise. After my servant had chafed and squeezed them I got on my legs. A walk was necessary to bring me round and I staggered through the entrenched camp — a horrible sight: death was there in its most hideous forms, and men dying in all the most excruciating agonies. Walking about was still dangerous, for the Sikhs' mines were every now and then exploding as fire happened to reach them.
>
> I wandered along in a confused way in search of something. I hardly knew what it was that I wanted. At length behind a curtain in a Sikh tent, I saw a large earthen vessel full of pure

cold water. This is what I had been looking for! I flew upon it, and plunged my head and arms into it, clothes and all. I drank till I could drink no more, then stood up and drank again and again.

Dr McGregor's resources were almost overcome by the wounded who began flooding into Ferozepore, eight miles away from the battlefield. At first all were put in the camp while elephants and carts were requisitioned and sent back for more. 'During the whole night of the 22nd, the wounded were being brought in, or found their way on foot in a state of dreadful exhaustion from pain, loss of blood and want of food and water. Every available place... was filled with wounded men calling loudly for assistance...' At McGregor's insistence the entire barracks of the 62nd Regiment there were made over as a hospital, with blankets and beds.

Among the wounded was Trooper Bancroft, who had been hit in the arm and lost much blood. He recalls Sir Henry Hardinge visiting the hospital with 'jocative' remarks for the wounded, among whom was Bancroft's own comrade. ('A soldier was nobody in those days unless he had a comrade, no matter where he was or what he was doing.') Bancroft's comrade had been brought in badly wounded, having been accidentally blown away from his own gun during the night, left for dead on the field for twenty-four hours, then picked up with all his clothes burnt away, his left hand shattered to fragments, his left eye gone and his body badly burned. His arm had been amputated just below the elbow and, noted Bancroft, as Sir Henry neared his bed he pointed to his own empty sleeve, as much as to say — 'There's a pair of us, as the devil said to his knee-buckles.'

Sir Henry's bedside manner was, inevitably, bluff and hearty, as if he must say something, no matter what. Beside Bancroft was another young soldier, wounded by a grapeshot which had passed through both cheeks. Sir Henry, Bancroft noted, remarked: 'Well, my lad, I see you have two beauty spots on your face to take home to your sweetheart.' The lad abruptly said: 'I have no sweetheart!' 'That's quare,' Bancroft recalls the Governor-General saying. 'I thought soldiers and sailors had sweethearts wherever they went. But never mind, my boy, if you haven't you will have, and that's some consolation. You won't be the worse thought of though for having a little less cheek than usual.'

At Lahore, meanwhile, first reports had said that the British had been defeated. The Maharani and her council, though they doubted this, were, says Alexander Gardner, 'afraid that their own army might in the end be successful. They well knew that it would return to Lahore and that anarchy and bloodshed would once again be the order of the day:

> They therefore sent congratulatory messages to the troops, and counselled an immediate advance southwards by way of Bhawulpore. By this means, they said, the British army could be taken in flank, and Delhi captured. The only duty imposed on me was to protect Maharani Jindan and her child, and to get the dread Khalsa army destroyed somehow. 'Don't come back gallant men of the 'Guruji', said we, 'without at all events seeing Delhi'.

But, says Gardner, Lal Singh ran back to Lahore after the first encounter at Mudki, 'preferring the embraces of Venus to the triumphs of Mars', only to find that instead of welcoming him to her bed, the Rani jeered at him for running away, and the court followed her example. Soon however, she once again succumbed to his sexual prowess and issued orders that there were to be no more jokes at his expense.

Tej Singh, still in command of the army which he had rushed back across the Sutlej, sent pleas to Lahore for more troops, guns and provisions. He had in mind the promises of aid which Gulab Singh, Raja of Jammu, had promised earlier, amounting to some forty thousand men. But Gulab was playing a tricky double game with British and Sikhs. If he would lead in the field, the Khalsa had offered to kill Lal Singh and Tej Singh and make him Maharajah. But luckily, British prestige still counted with Gulab. He remembered the treachery he and his family had suffered at the hands of the Sikhs, decided to stay put for the time being at Jammu (Kashmir), yet pretended great loyalty to the Sikh army and, observed Gardner, welcomed any messengers from the Khalsa, 'whether he was bathing or eating, as if his whole heart was with the Sikhs.'

> He got all the wheat-carriers in the country (noted Gardner), loaded them with immense display with about one-fourth of what they could carry, put placards in *Gurmukhi* on their necks to the effect that they were carrying supplies from Gulab Singh, and told them, under pain of mutilation, not to go two abreast, in order that the army and the country might imagine that incessant and enormous supplies were being forwarded to the stalwart and devoted Khalsa by their loyal and affectionate friend. 'I'm not going empty-handed to the great campaign that is to end at Calcutta,' gave out Gulab Singh. 'When all is ready for campaigning, off I start. This will be a long war. It's a race to the capital, and devil catch the hindmost.'

Thus he temporized. But he held the power, and would have used it (if Dhyan Singh had been alive, or if he himself had been a Sikh) to create an insurrection which would have shaken the British power more even than the mutiny of 1857.

All the protected Sikhs States in Malwa — Nagha, Jhind and Patiala — were ready to envelop the British army in case of a reverse.'

And so it was. Gough meanwhile, camped in a strongly fortified position ten miles north of Ferozeshur, while Hardinge went on to Ferozepore with General Littler's division. Reinforcements of men, heavy artillery and ammunition were urgently ordered from Delhi, Meerut and Cawnpore. Gough and Hardinge jointly decided not to oppose the Sikhs without these reinforcements if they crossed the Sutlej; and, if they attacked Ludhiana, to hold only the fort, Hardinge declaring that 'he who defends everything, defends nothing'; and saying he would willingly take the responsibility if the town were plundered or burnt. Brigadier Godby with a regiment of cavalry and three native regiments was sent to defend Ludhiana fort. Gulab Singh, playing his double game with skill, sent an agent to negotiate terms for helping the British by withholding aid to the Khalsa. Hardinge, at the same time issued a proclamation ordering all sepoys in the Khalsa to desert on pain of forfeiture of property in India, with the promise of British protection if they did. And so the British made ready for the next battle.

10: Aliwal

Curiously high was the morale of the Sikh army, camped just north of the Sutlej, after their untimely retreat from the field of Ferozeshur, for they were convinced that their leaders' treachery, not military inferiority and defeat in open battle, was the cause of their reverse. Certainly, they had suffered heavy losses in men, guns, ammunition and supplies, but believing they had shattered the myth of British invincibility they resolved to go on with the fight, if possible with new leaders. Under pressure from the military *panchayats* work was begun on a bridge of boats across the Sutlej at Sobraon, and a bridgehead was established on the left bank. But provisions were the most urgent Sikh need for, observed the American Colonel Gardner, they were literally starved for want of rations:

> They sent a deputation of five hundred picked Sikhs to Lahore to urge the dire necessities of the army — for three days they had lived upon grain and raw carrots. The Rani at first would not allow the deputation to enter Lahore. She justly feared for her personal safety at the hands of these desperate men. I therefore placed four battalions of infantry in guard over the queen, and she at last consented to hold a durbar and receive a deputation. They were told to come armed with swords only. Under the pretence of this being a State occasion, I turned out a very large personal guard for the queen, who waited behind a screen...
>
> I was standing close to the Rani and could see the gesticulations and movements of the deputation. In answer to the urgent and loud complaints of the sacrifice to which the army was exposed, she said that Gulab Singh had forwarded vast supplies. 'No, he has not,' roared the deputation, 'we

know the old fox: he has not sent breakfast for a bird, (*chiria-ki-haziri*).' Further parley ensued, the tempers of both parties waxing wroth. At last the deputation said, 'Give us powder and shot.' At this I saw some movements behind the *purdah* (the little Dhulip was sitting in front of it). I could detect that the Rani was shifting her petticoat; I could see that she stepped out of it and then rolling it up rapidly into a ball, flung it over the screen at the heads of the angry envoys, crying out, 'Wear that you cowards! I'll go in trousers and fight myself!' The effect was electric. After a moment's pause, during which the deputation seemed stunned, a unanimous shout arose, 'Dhulip Singh Maharaja, we will go and die for his kingdom and the Khalsaji!' And breaking up tumultuously and highly excited, this dangerous deputation dispersed, and rejoined the army. The courage and intuition displayed by this extraordinary woman under such critical circumstances filled us all with as much amazement as admiration.

No doubt secretly more afraid of the Khalsa after this challenging meeting, the Rani saw to it that guns, powder, ammunition and even provisions were supplied quickly; but more than ever she hoped for its destruction. Meantime, at Sobraon, where there was a bend in the Sutlej and a ford, the Sikhs had completed a bridge of boats, led over their whole army and entrenched themselves on the south bank, 'a movement,' said General Sir Harry Smith, rather too boldly, 'unparalleled in the history of war from time immemorial.'

So cleverly chosen was the site of the crossing, where the north banks of the bend were high and commanded the south banks, that the British, still awaiting their heavy guns, simply could not oppose it. Had they advanced into this salient they would have faced attack from three sides. So the crossing was unmolested, the Sikhs dug trenches, built fortifications, thrust outposts forward, brought over heavy guns fresh from the foundries of Lahore.

Gough, having meantime been reinforced by some ten thousand men[8] under Sir John Grey, who had left Meerut in mid-December, moved eastwards in reply so that his centre faced Sobraon. On his left, Sir John Grey's division maintained communication with Ferozepore; Sir Harry Smith's division and Brigadier Cureton's cavalry brigade were posted ten miles east facing the ford at Hurreke; Sir Walter Gilbert's division stood at the centre, and on the left Sir Robert Dick's.

The Sikhs continued unceasingly active. At Sobraon their outposts forced the British defensive troops back two or three miles, and at Dharamkot, a fort crammed with guns, a garrison of Afghan and Rohilla mercenaries threatened trouble. Worse still, near Philour, eighty miles east, General Runjur Singh crossed the Sutlej and with a force of some eight thousand men and seventy guns imperilled both Ludhiana and communications with India. It was time for counter-action.

On 16 January 1846 Sir Hugh Gough sent for General Sir Harry Smith and told him that both Dharamkot and another smaller fortress of Futteyghur nearby were to be taken — under their cover the Sikhs were drawing supplies from the north bank. Smith recalled Gough saying: 'A brigade will be sufficient to send, the 3rd Light Cavalry and some Irregular Horse, but who will you send?'

Much to Gough's delight Smith answered that he would rather go himself. 'When will you march?' Gough asked. 'There is no hurry.' Smith's answer — 'Soon after this time tomorrow I shall be writing my report that I have reduced them both,'

---

[8] 9th Lancers, 16th Lancers, 3rd Bengal Light Cavalry, 4th Irregular Cavalry, two Batteries of Artillery, the 10th Foot, three regiments of Native Infantry, one company of sappers.

surprised even Gough, for he laughed and said: 'Why, the distance to Dharamkot is twenty-six miles from your right.' Smith, the intrepid, said with that pugnacious ebullience that distinguished his whole career: 'I know that. Still, what I say shall be, provided that the Engineers supply me in time with the powder I want to blow in the gates in the case of necessity.' (He recalled saying to himself, 'Powder or no powder, I march'.)

Smith collected all the provisions and elephant transport he could lay hands on and marched two hours before daylight, when the red streaks of dawn had not yet appeared. The defenders of Futteyghur fled at his approach and he pushed on to Dharamkot, reaching it at 2 pm, and finding it occupied, 'but without any gun deserving the name of cannon,' he noted.

> I invested it immediately with the 3rd Light Cavalry and Irregulars (the infantry not being yet up), and summoned the garrison to surrender... The leader or *killadar* came out and made a variety of stipulations, which I cut short by saying, 'You may march out with your arms, ground them on the glacis, and I will endeavour to secure all hands six weeks' pay. Go back to the fort. I give you twenty minutes to consider, after which I shall make no terms, but open my cannon upon you.'
>
> I waited twenty-five minutes, and no communication being made, although I rode close to the works myself and beckoned to them, I ordered our 9-pounders and a howitzer to open a few shots. The Sikh flag was then hauled down, and a white one hoisted. I allowed the garrison to march out and lay down their arms as prisoners of war, and as the infantry arrived, I immediately occupied the fortress and commenced improving its defences. I was thus able to report, as I had promised, to my commander-in-chief.

While Smith was thus happily engaged, news reached Gough that scouts from Runjur Singh's force had before Brigadier Godby reached Ludhiana, attacked and burned down the British cantonment there. 'This was to be expected,' the Governor-General wrote to the commander-in-chief, 'and is of no importance. This great feat may excite them to be impudent in your neighbourhood.' It was a strangely complacent remark, for clearly Runjur Singh could now, if not driven back, take the fort at Ludhiana and go on to attack the great twenty-mile-long British convoy of ammunition, heavy guns, treasure, supplies and men coming up from Delhi. Gough therefore ordered Harry Smith, then at Dharamkot, to advance by Jogruon towards Ludhiana, strengthening him with the 16th Lancers, the 3rd Light Cavalry, a troop of Horse Artillery and HM's 53rd Foot, then at Bussean.

Smith believed that Runjur Singh's force was still at Bara Hara, some twenty miles west of Ludhiana, on the road to Ferozepore, and that the Sikhs had a small garrison and a few hundred cavalry in the fort of Budhowal, and more cavalry and guns in the strong fortress of Gangrana, eight miles to the south. He marched with the infantry from Dharamkot on the 19th to Kohari, halfway to Jogruon, where next day he was joined by the 16th Lancers, the guns and the 53rd Foot. Leaving his wheeled transport and heavy baggage with two companies of Native Infantry to ward off robbers, he marched by moonlight half an hour after midnight on the 21st. By sunrise he had covered eighteen miles to within two miles of Budhowal, intending to march north of it so as to avoid the chance of being attacked from Gangrana to the south, as well. Every two hours he sent orders to Brigadier Godby to join him with the strongest force possible at Suneth, a strong position midway between Budhowal and Ludhiana.

A fortunate message now saved him from a trap — Godby's spies had discovered that Runjur Singh had marched from Bara Hara and was encamped around Budhowal with his whole force, about ten thousand strong. Smith had two alternatives: to march on and force his passage in a battle with Runjur Singh; or to make a detour towards Gangrana, leaving Budhowal on his left. He wisely chose the second. During the night march Smith saw the enemy's signal rockets and at daybreak found him deploying to attack on the new line of march. Afterwards he discovered that the Sikhs had assembled more than forty guns on the direct route by Budhowal.

Smith's men now had to march in order of battle over ploughed fields of deep sandy soil as the Sikh force moved parallel through a line of villages linked by roads. The head of the Sikh column, a large body of cavalry, outflanked Smith's force by about a mile and his rear of guns and infantry equally so.

> With great celerity (wrote Smith) he brought to bear on my troops a considerable number of guns of very heavy metal. The cavalry moved parallel to the enemy, protected from the fire of his guns by a low ridge of sandhills. My eighteen guns I kept together close in rear of the cavalry, in order to open a heavy fire on the enemy and to check his advance… This fire, which I continued for some ten minutes, had a most auxiliary effect, creating slaughter and confusion in the enemy's ranks. The enemy's cannonade upon the column of infantry had been previous to this furious. As the column moved on under this cannonade, which was especially furious upon the rear of the infantry, the enemy, with a dexterity and quickness not to be exceeded, formed a line of seven battalions directly across my rear, with guns in the intervals of battalions, for the purpose of attacking *my* column with *his* line. This was a very able and well executed move, which rendered my position

critical and demanded nerve and decision to evade the coming storm.

In the swirling sand and dust, Smith formed up part of the 31st Regiment to begin an attack on this line, but so tired were his men and so deep was the sand that he was forced to abandon the idea.

> I therefore under this fierce cannonade, changed front on the centre of the 31st Regiment and of the 53rd, by what is a difficult move on parade, even — a countermarch on the centre by wings. Then became conspicuous the majesty of discipline and bravery. This move was executed as accurately as at a review... I now directed the infantry to march on Ludhiana in echelon of battalions, ready to receive the word 'Halt, Front!' (when they would thus confront the enemy's line if he advanced), and the cavalry to move in echelon of squadrons, the two arms mutually supporting, the guns in rear of the cavalry... The movement was so steady that the enemy, notwithstanding his overwhelming force, did not attack, but stood amazed, as it were, fearing to quit his stronghold of Budhowal, and aware that the junction of my force with that of Ludhiana was about to be accomplished.

And so this was done, Smith camping in front of Ludhiana, rather than in a waterless position near to the Sikh force, but he established outposts close upon them and ordered frequent strong patrols up to their position, 'intending if he dared interrupt our line of communication via Bussean... to move on... and attack under any circumstances.'

The day's action was costly, more than two hundred men being lost in a purely defensive action, but Smith showed a superb sense of generalship, realizing that the relief of Godby, and of Ludhiana, not the dissipation of his strength in an attack on the Sikhs, was imperative for the security of Gough's army, of his own, and of British India.

Remarking that the vital British convoy was then not ten miles away from Ludhiana, Smith wrote:

> Had I adopted any other course at Budhowal on the 21st of January than I pursued, had I not pushed the war entrusted to my conduct with vigour, and effected a junction with the troops at Ludhiana, they and the city would have fallen, and next our treasure, battering train, ammunition, etc., would have been captured or scattered and lost to the army; had I sustained a serious reverse, all India would have been in a blaze. I steered the course invariably pursued by my great master the Duke, never needlessly to risk your troops or fight a battle without an object.

Smith rested his men next day in readiness for the attack he intended to make on Runjur Singh at Budhowal as soon as reinforcements of guns and troops arrived, but the Sikh commander prudently retreated northwards towards the river to link up with his own reinforcements — four thousand troops trained by General Avitabile, twelve heavy guns and additional cavalry. The commander-in-chief, meantime, had ordered Brigadier Wheeler's brigade of the 50th Foot, the 48th Native Infantry and the Sirmoor Gurkhas, of Smith's own division to join him. He also received reinforcements of a battery of eighteen 14-pounders, each drawn by an elephant, and twenty-five bullock-drawn wagons of ammunition. The regiments of infantry and the gunners still coming up from Delhi marched on through fertile country, 'through forests of magnificent trees with the Jumna murmuring its way through the middle of them and the peafowl and paroquets trying to outdo each other in screaming,' Tom Pierce, an eighteen-year-old junior ensign noted.

'While marching up,' said Pierce, 'they were busy getting perfect with the new percussion drill. The men like them much better than the flintlock ones. They never took a bold aim with them, as they were afraid of a piece of flint flying into their eyes.' The old Brown Bess had at last been replaced in some, if not all, regiments in India with the Baker musket. It should have given the British a decided advantage over the Sikh infantry, armed with replicas of the Bess.

At a leisurely pace considering the danger to British power in India, the convoy moved up from Delhi, marching from about 3 am until ten, breakfasting, then resting in the heat of the day until 3 pm drilling for two hours, dining at sunset, and in due course turning in. 'No women were allowed on the march,' Pierce confided in a letter home, 'but one of our soldiers' wives was detected this morning in a suit of her husband's regimentals, and they say that she is not the only one… I suppose there will be a general inspection this afternoon.'

General Smith marched his force back to Budhowal on January 23, and three days later Brigadier Wheeler and his brigade joined him. Smith's force was now twelve thousand strong with twenty-eight field guns and two 8-inch howitzers, organized into two brigades of cavalry and four of infantry, two of which however, were of only two battalions.[9] Smith was now ready to take the offensive. His spies reported that

---

[9] CAVALRY: Brigadier-General Cureton. Brigadier Macdowell's Brigade: 16th Lancers, 3rd Bengal Light Cavalry, 4th Irregular Cavalry. Brigadier Stedman's Brigade: Governor-General's Bodyguard, 1st & 5th Bengal Light Cavalry, Shekawati Cavalry. Horse Artillery, Three Batteries (Major Laurenson). INFANTRY: 1st Brigade (Brigadier Hicks): 31st Foot, 24th NI, 36th NI, 2nd Brigade (Brigadier Wheeler): 50th Foot, 48th NI Sirmoor Gurkha Battalion: 3rd Brigade (Brigadier Wilson): 53rd Foot, 30th NI, Shekawati Battalion: 4th Brigade (Brigadier Godby): 47th NI, Nisiri Battalion of Gurkhas. Two Field Batteries, two 8-inch howitzers.

Runjur, with an army of about twenty thousand, would at dawn on 28 January attack either Budhowal or Ludhiana. Never one to stand and wait, Smith therefore marched northwest that day with the cavalry leading in line of squadron columns and two horse artillery batteries in the centre. Behind came the redcoats in continuous columns of brigades at intervals of deploying distance, artillery in the intervals, followed by the two 8-inch elephant-drawn howitzers. Cavalry patrols under Major Bradford and Captain Waugh were well out in front.

After some six miles a spy came in to report a massive advance towards Jograon. Smith, unperturbed, continued another four miles to the village of Poorein, where from the roof of a house he saw their army in the distance, 'directly opposite my front, on a ridge, of which the village of Aliwal may be regarded as the centre... I immediately deployed the cavalry into line and moved on.'

A level grassy plain two miles long and a mile wide lay below the ridge upon which Smith stood, leading to a slight rise upon which were two villages, Aliwal, slightly fortified, facing his right, and Bhundri, to his left, covered by a thin groove of trees, both of them linked by a curved line of three miles of trenches.

The Sikhs still marched, but when the red, blue and gold lines of Smith's cavalry topped the ridge they halted, occupied the trenches, and the rising land. The Sutlej was barely a mile behind. Runjur Singh, with his back to it, had little room to manoeuvre, a sight which must have brought joy to Smith's heart.

There was no dust; it was early morning and the sun shone brightly. Tom Pierce, in his first battle, remembered: 'We reached the summit of a high hill and came to an extensive level plain… and about eighteen hundred yards ahead was the Sikh army in battle array, drawn up in line, guns in front, drums beating… Our troops had only just time to deploy in line before they boomed forth their murderous fire.'

Harry Smith had ordered his eager cavalry brigades to wheel off to left and right, and had deployed his infantry into a long line on the hard springy turf facing the enemy. Wheeler's brigade was on the right and Wilson's on the left in the front line; Godby's brigade was echeloned to the rear of them on the right, with the Shekawati brigade on the left, Stedman's cavalry brigade on the right, Macdowell's on the left, the guns massed on right, centre and left. Observing that the Sikh position outflanked his left, Smith took ground to his left, then wheeled to his front again, movements the twelve thousand men carried out with the precision of a grand review, swords and bayonets glittering in the bright sunshine.

The line had advanced barely a hundred and fifty yards when the Sikh artillery, about seven hundred yards away, opened a fierce cannonade with a roar of angry sound that rent the blue vault of the sky. At first, the shot fell short, but soon reached the ranks as they marched forward. 'The first man that was killed stood only a few yards from me,' Tom Pierce noted. 'A 9-pound shot took his head from his body. I felt rather sick at seeing the men fall by threes and fours around me.'

Smith halted the advance for a few moments, now that he could for the first time see the enemy's position clearly. His sharp eye instantly saw what needed to be done. The village of Aliwal on the right was the weakest spot, by carrying which he would be able to make a general attack on the left and centre. He therefore brought up Brigadier Godby's brigade of sepoys and Gurkhas up quickly; with the 1st brigade of the 31st Foot and two more sepoy regiments they made what Smith called 'a rapid and noble charge,' carrying the village and two guns of large calibre with only slight losses. He now ordered a general attack upon the Sikh centre and left where wreaths of black smoke belched from the guns. The battle became general. 'Whiz! Whiz! came the cannon balls over our heads at intervals of two seconds.' Pierce wrote. 'Forward and lie down!' came the word of command.

> Forward we went by about forty yards at a time, then lay down on the ground, allowing the balls to pass over us... Then when his fire became slack, forward again for another fifty yards and so on... our artillery on the right blazing away as hard as they could... On and on we went in this manner for about an hour. By this time we were eight hundred yards from their battery and could see, through the clouds of smoke, their infantry and horse drawn up in rear of their guns. They now began to flay us with grape and chain shot, which at first thinned our ranks a little.

The hot air thudded and shook as the Sikh cannonade mounted. Major Lawrenson, commanding the Horse Artillery, seeing his men and horses falling, raised his sword high and without waiting for orders, galloped his brigade of guns thunderingly to within two hundred yards of the Sikh batteries — wheeled round, unlimbered, and with a sharp blast of fire drove the Sikhs from their guns for a time. Tom Pierce noted their hesitation under 'our severe cannonading, which by this time had greatly silenced them. All of a sudden the whole of our line from right to left gave a wild hurrah and rushed forward, the enemy flying like chaff before the wind, leaving their guns upon the field, which were at once spiked by us.'

But, in fact, only the Sikh left had given way, and realizing at this point that it was a danger, a large mass of cavalry dashed forward to try to re-establish the position. The Sikh infantry, after a four or five hundred yards retreat, halted and formed squares and triangle formations, while the Sikh gunners opened up with their remaining guns. But before the enemy cavalry could reach the lines, Smith ordered up the British cavalry, 'who, in the most gallant manner dashed in among them and drove them back upon their infantry.'

On the summit of the high ground, Smith now saw the enemy's camp for the first time — it was packed with infantry. He ordered Brigadier Godby's brigade to change front to attack their left front and their rear. The Gurkhas and sepoys now charged the Sikh infantry drove them out of their camp and captured some more guns.

The entire Sikh army was now falling back in confusion. Realizing that retreat across the river was endangered, the Sikhs tried to retrieve the situation by wheeling their infantry upon their left and re-forming their line at right-angles to the river, using Bhundri village as a pivot and strongly occupying it. They supported this manoeuvre by bringing forward a mass of cavalry, but Brigadier Macdowell countered with a squadron of the 3rd Bengal Light Cavalry and another of the 16th Lancers.

The 16th Lancers charged first and led by Captain Bere and Captain Fyler, tore into the Sikh cavalry and scattered them. At the same time, General Smith ordered the other two squadrons of the 16th against an entrenched battery. 'Away we went,' wrote Captain Knight, in a letter home that tells something of the perils and delights of a cavalry charge, 'and as we cleared the trenches with a bound, the enemy were lanced by our men at their guns.'

> We suddenly found ourselves in the midst of a fearfully large square of the enemy's infantry, firing at us right and left and completely surrounding us. The moment that I felt my horse leap the ditch in which their battery was placed and found

myself charging into the square… a proud sensation of delight came over me… everything seemed charged into a thrill of ecstasy; and how we all escaped the deadly shower of musketry that was poured into us on all sides is wonderful.

One fellow discharged his gun right across my face and for the moment I was quite blinded by the gunpowder, and my face so blackened no one knew me, and the bullet from another matchlock grazed my fingers and killed the man on my left. Meick, who commanded our squadron, was attacked by a Seikh who put his musket to his side, and would have discharged it through him, but luckily Meick gave it a push and the ball went through the neck of his horse. Everyone who charged with the 16th must have had narrow escapes, for the bullets hissed over our heads like hail. Here poor Swetenham was killed almost close to me, and our brave leader Major Smyth terribly wounded by a musket shot in the thigh. Pottle was also shot in the cheek and only just escaped losing an eye… Our brave fellows fell very thickly here, and every man whose horse was killed was to a certainty slain also, for the moment those savages saw any one on the ground they rushed at him and never ceased hacking at them, till they had literally severed them to pieces with their tulwars, which were like razors. All of us that escaped owe their lives, under God, to our horses, for no one escaped who once came to the ground. After having charged through this mass of infantry we rallied and pursued the stragglers to the very banks of the river. Poor Williams fell, mortally wounded. Orme was also bayoneted in the stomach and, we fear, may not survive. Captain Fyler is also severely wounded and is likely to lose a leg, and Captain Bere and Lieutenant Yule are both much cut up and bruised.

The 53rd Regiment of infantry now followed up the cavalry to seize the village — brilliant masses of scarlet in the burning sun, against the sepia of the mud walls. Black smoke swirled in the narrow streets, bayonet and *tulwar* clashed, men and horses screamed, until with a roar of frenzied triumph, the sweating well-disciplined ranks of the 53rd emerged with the village of Bhundri in their hands. Major Lawrenson's Horse Artillery now dashed among the flying Sikh infantry and blasted them with grape.

Then came a setback. About a thousand Sikhs hidden in the hollow of a ravine just outside the village, suddenly opened a heavy fire with their long matchlocks and mowed down the British. 'Here our regiment suffered most,' Tom Pierce noted. 'Now we longed for some cavalry to cut them up.' They were scattered eventually, by a flanking charge of the 30th Native Infantry, ordered by Smith himself. 'This native corps nobly obeyed my orders,' he reported, 'and rushed among the Avitabile troops, driving them from under the bank and exposing them once more to a deadly fire of twelve guns within three hundred yards. The destruction was very great… from guns served as these were.'

The whole Sikh force, completely hemmed in, were now running away to the ford by their camp, throwing themselves in disorderly masses into the water and the boats, the eight-inch British howitzers firing shell that burst among them murderously. The Sikh artillery commander had unlimbered nine guns to cover his retreat by the ford, but the gunners fired them once only before they were cut down or ran off; two more were stuck in the mud, two were seen to sink in the quicksands and two were dragged across. What Smith called the 'debris' of the Sikh army tried to form a line upon the opposite and higher bank of the Sutlej, but they were scattered after the first salvo from some twenty British guns lashed them with shrapnel. The gunners then fired over the water in their direction for another two hours to stop the Sikhs regrouping.

So ended the battle of Aliwal, at 5.20 in the evening. The Sikhs lost sixty-seven guns, their tented camp, their supplies, animals and three thousand men. British losses were one hundred and fifty-one killed, four hundred and thirteen wounded and twenty-five missing, a total of five hundred and eighty. The 16th Lancers, whose intrepid charges against guns and well-trained Sikh infantry did so much to help win the day, suffered most, with fifty-nine killed — more than a third of the total — and eighty-three wounded.

Gough at Sobraon, some fifty miles west, first knew of the battle through the sound of the cannonade. An officer who was with him recalled asking what he thought of it. 'Think of it!' the white-haired old General replied. 'Why, that 'tis the most glorious thing I ever heard. I know by the sound of the guns that Smith has carried the position and silenced their artillery.'

When the news of Smith's win came through, Gough was said to be nearly 'frantic with joy'. Trooper Eaton, 16th Lancers, said of this in a letter home: 'As soon as the commander-in-chief received the dispatches, which he did on horseback while reconnoitring, he leaped from his horse and gave three cheers, a salute of eighteen guns was fired, and the line gave three hearty cheers for us, their gallant comrades, as they called us.'

Sir Harry Smith, never one to underrate his own achievements, wrote boastfully to his sister:

> I have gained... one of the most glorious battles ever fought in India, driving the enemy over the Sutlej double my numbers, posted in an entrenched camp with seventy-five guns, fifty-two of which are at my tent door, the others lost in the passage of the river, or spiked in its bed... And oh, the fearful sight the river presents! the bodies, having swollen,

float, of men, horses, camels, bullocks, etc. Thousands must have perished, many threw away their arms and fled headlong into the broad river and difficult ford... Never was victory more complete, and never was one fought under more happy circumstances, literally with the pomp of a field day; and right well did all behave.

Smith later referred to Runjur Singh's move in throwing himself between his own advance from Budhowal to Ludhiana as bold, most able and energetic. 'It is the most scientific move made during the war... and had he known how to profit by the position he had so judiciously occupied, he would have obtained wonderful success,' he wrote.

> He should have attacked me with the vigour his French tutors would have displayed and destroyed me, for his force compared to mine was *overwhelming*; then turned about on the troops at Ludhiana, beaten them, and sacked and burnt the city — when the gaze I speak of in India would have been one of general revolt! Does the world which argues on my affair at Budhowal suppose I was asleep, and had not in clear perspective a full view of the effect such success of the enemy would have had upon the general features and character of the war?

But Runjur Singh, like all the Sikh oligarchy, hoped for the destruction of the unruly, democratic Khalsa, which was trying to take over the state, so he had little heart for the battle. Likely it is that the move Smith praised was in fact initiated by the *panchayats* and thrown away by Runjur Singh. At all events, according to Captain J. D. Cunningham, then of the North-West Frontier political intelligence, he ran away at Aliwal after Smith's first charge and left his army to its own resources.

Major Mackeson, also of North-West Frontier Intelligence, substantiates this in a letter to Frederick Currie, government secretary, with the remark: 'However well a force without leaders may defend itself in its trenches, when required to move or manoeuvre in the plain without a directing head, it will be completely helpless and at our mercy.'

And so it was, for even Tej Singh, the Sikh commander-in-chief, had no heart for the war. 'I, Teja Singh, do not wish to fight, and will not,' he wrote to Sir Harry Smith shortly before the battle at Aliwal, according to the official Punjab Intelligence Report, 'but will be willing to come to terms, but the men don't obey my orders.'

It was Tej Singh who at Ferozepore saved the exhausted British by marching his own troops off the field and across the Sutlej on the pretext that he feared an attack from the rear. His predicament was difficult. As commander-in-chief he had to make a show of leading the army for whose destruction he hoped, yet believing the British would win he ensured his future by double-dealing, secret negotiations and deserting his troops — leaving them to their own resources when in action.

Great indeed however was the moral effect of Aliwal, on both sides. The British felt themselves to have partly restored the legend of their military superiority. The Sikhs, while still attributing their defeat to treason, believed they had destroyed this legend and, though saddened at the sight of the bodies of so many of their comrades floating down the Sutlej with the dead bullocks and horses, were ready to fight again and take revenge at Sobraon, their only remaining outpost on the south side of the river. Here, against a strongly fortified position, they believed the British would destroy themselves in bloody, but useless assaults.

11: Sobraon

Desperately the Sikhs spent day and night with spade and pick strengthening their defences at Sobraon. Gough and his engineer and artillery officers had 'repeatedly reconnoitred' and knew that they faced 'in a position covered with formidable entrenchments no fewer than thirty thousand men... with seventy pieces of cannon.'

Gough had now an army of twenty thousand, but no artillery heavy enough to smash the Sikh defences; these, the 24-pounders, were still lumbering and clattering behind the teams of elephants and bullocks on the road up from Delhi. Nevertheless, Gough wanted to attack immediately without waiting for Smith's force to rejoin him at Sobraon, from Aliwal, relying on infantry and cavalry backed by light artillery. Every day that he waited the Sikh defences would be harder to overcome and his troops in this wet season be weakened by sickness.

Again he clashed with Hardinge, who flatly refused to authorize an attack until the arrival of the heavy guns. 'Gough was then so extremely anxious to storm the entrenched camp at Sobraon, with eighty or ninety guns and a force varying from forty to fifty thousand men, that I went back to camp rather than give way to his request,' he wrote to the Duke of Wellington.

In fact Hardinge's wish to have his way as supremo had caused the delay in the arrival of the heavy artillery. Early in January 1846 Gough had sent him a report he had obtained from his chief engineer, Brigadier E. Smith, outlining the heavy guns and ammunition necessary to take Sobraon and other fortified cities across the Sutlej.

On 4 January Hardinge turned down the requirements on the ground that they were excessive, would take too long to bring up and would mean postponing the campaign. (As early as August 1844 he had refused to agree to Gough's request to bring forward the artillery magazine and park from Delhi to Ambala, because he wanted to avoid giving offence to the Sikhs). As a result, on 5 January Brigadier Smith went to see him and with the full weight of his professional knowledge reiterated what he had asked for in the report.

For the proud and obstinate Hardinge this was still not enough. He called a conference of all his senior engineer and artillery officers on 8 January and asked for their opinion on Brigadier Smith's requirements, which his commander-in-chief supported. All confirmed Smith's view; Hardinge had then no alternative but to agree and the next day he sent orders for the weapons to start at once. He said in a letter to Gough dated 13 January 1896 that he had authorized thirteen 24-pounders, five 18-pounders, six 10-inch howitzers, one 8-inch howitzer and about five hundred charges of ammunition per gun, plus twenty-seven thousand rounds for six and nine-pounders. He confirmed his order that 'no movement across the Sutlej towards Lahore can be made before the arrival of these guns' and emphasized once more that 'the existence of the Sikh army on its present Republican system cannot be permitted to remain as it is.'

Hardinge was, of course, saying that unless this republican army was totally destroyed in a decisive victory, British prestige in India, after the Afghan debacle three years earlier, would face a collapse that could encourage a general uprising.

Meantime, while the Sikhs paraded daily outside their defences to taunt the British, and cavalry officers fond of pig-sticking chased boars within musket range of the Sikhs, who sportingly held their fire, politically, events took a strange, though perhaps not unexpected turn.

Ostensibly to lead the Khalsa, Gulab Singh was persuaded to return from Jammu to Lahore and on 27 January he became vizier, or prime minister. The next day the Sikhs were defeated at Aliwal. The representatives of the Khalsa implored the Raja, whose military skill was considerable, to lead them against the enemy, but, according to the British spies at the court, Gulab merely taunted them with their stupidity in fighting allies to whom Ranjit Singh had been loyal for more than a quarter of a century. 'I refrained from joining you against the English when you first crossed the Sutlej,' he told them. 'Why should I help you now when you face certain defeat?' When they offered to murder Lal Singh and Tej Singh and make him commander-in-chief instead, he merely laughed at them.

At the same time he secretly sent his personal physician, a Hindu named Bunsee Dar Ghose, to negotiate on his behalf with the British. Not very adroitly, his messenger gave this secret letter to Lieutenant Edward Lake, a junior political assistant at Ludhiana, rather than to his chief, Broadfoot's successor, Major Henry Lawrence, a long lean man with a van Dyck beard destined to play an important role in the history of British India.

Gulab Singh wrote that he would help the British in their campaign with all the means in his power if they would: (1) confirm him and his family for ever in possession of their present estates and lands: (2) leave him also in possession of all the territories[10] then under his rule, 'contenting yourselves with

---

[10] The territories ruled by Gulab Singh included the state today called

a tribute of four annas in every rupee of revenue.' The inexperienced Lake, who only a few weeks before had transferred from the army, must have felt himself suddenly at the very pinnacle of power, with issues of peace and war in his hands. He wrote an answer, which he sent off to Gulab without the authority of the Governor-General, Lawrence, or anyone else. Naively, the letter said: 'He who wishes to climb the summit of a lofty mountain must start at daybreak. Should he delay night may close over him 'ere he has gained the desire of his heart. The Treasure which is buried in the depths of the mountain will become the prize of that man who is the first to reach its summit.'

Foolishly, Lake then sent a copy of this reply not to his chief, Major Lawrence, but to the all-powerful Government Secretary, Frederick Currie, with a covering note describing it as 'ambiguous', not realizing that, especially when translated into Persian, it would have a very inviting meaning indeed. He was at once reprimanded for having made any reply at all and ordered to make clear to one of Gulab Singh's messengers, who remained with him, that the Governor-General did not approve of his reply.

Hardinge was by no means displeased that the Lahore government, in the person of Gulab Singh, was ready to negotiate. Captain J. D. Cunningham, who was then employed in the political intelligence department and aware of what was happening, says that the prudent Hardinge felt that to defeat the Sikhs at Sobraon, cross the Sutlej, lay siege to Lahore, Amritsar, Multan and Peshawar was a task full of grave risks, especially in the approaching hot weather. Involvement in such a protracted campaign might also disturb India's political calm. Moreover, the Sikh force at Sobraon could not be destroyed by

---

Kashmir.

one defeat; and Gulab Singh might well become a leader of all the desperate chiefs in the Punjab.

Negotiations with Gulab were therefore opened. It was made clear to him that provided the Khalsa was disbanded or greatly reduced in strength Sikh sovereignty in Lahore would still be acknowledged. Gulab Singh, according to *Punjab Intelligence*, then ordered the Khalsa at Sobraon to withdraw north across the Sutlej into Lahore territory. His order caused much uncertainty and low morale, and it was not obeyed. So Gulab Singh let the British know he could not control the Khalsa. It was therefore agreed that the Sikhs should be attacked and beaten by the British, who would then cross the Sutlej and advance on Lahore without opposition, the Khalsa being refused arms and ordered to stay where it was at Sobraon, more or less disowned by its government. A few days later what were said to be plans of the Sikh defences around Sobraon found their way into the hands of Major Lawrence. 'It was under such circumstances of discreet policy and shameless treason that the battle of Sobraon was fought,' Captain J. D. Cunningham wrote.

Meanwhile, disappointed at the convoy's slow progress, the British, waiting for weeks facing the Sikhs without firing a shot, were almost sick with frustration. 'The army,' remarked Lieutenant Herbert Edwardes, aide-de-camp to General Gough, 'was sickening for want of a battle; a malignant fever of epidemic horrors must have broken out at Sobraon had it been delayed another week.'

Eventually, heavy guns rattling, the first part of the convoy lumbered into the British camp on 7 February — bringing the wagons of reserve ammunition and all the heavy guns except the vital 24-pounders, which had fallen behind. It was a setback, but Sir Harry Smith marched his victorious little army into the camp the next day; and on the day following, despite the absence of the heavy guns, Gough summoned his senior officers to his great glass-windowed tent to hear details of his plan of attack and the Sikh defences.

A Spanish officer named Huerba had directed their construction, and the position was formidable. On the south side of a bend in the river, where the northern banks were highest and the Sutlej four hundred yards wide, strong earthworks twelve feet high with deep ditches below, stretched from bank to bank in a semi-circle some three miles long, within which lay two concentric lines of trenches with parapets. Behind these across the river stretched the bridge of boats, linked to batteries and trenches sited so that fire could enfilade both the eastern and western fronts and the northern egress from the bridge. Most of the twenty thousand Sikh infantry, and seventy guns, were placed in the defences on the south side; reserves, with more guns were arrayed on the north side. Weakest point of the defences was the Sikh right, where loose sand prevented the construction of high parapets. Irregular troops manning a line of some two hundred zambureks, or swivel guns, defended here, while the best infantry, the disciplined, French-trained battalions, held the centre and left.

Cunningham, whose spies told him what the Sikhs were doing, reported that, as in the earlier battles, the soldiers did everything and the leaders nothing. 'Hearts to dare and hands to execute were numerous; but there was no mind to guide and animate the whole: each inferior commander defended his front according to his skill and means…' The position allowed the Sikhs no room to manoeuvre; and should they have to retreat, the river behind them was a danger, despite the boat-bridge. But against massed artillery and the accurate Sikh marksmen it was a formidable position to attack.

Sir Henry Hardinge now intervened and strongly urged a plan of ferrying over secretly, at night, a force of twelve thousand infantry and forty to fifty guns in boats already assembled at Ferozepore in case of need. This force should move swiftly down the northern bank, make a surprise attack on the Sikh position there, occupy the commanding ground and so force the enemy out of the outwork on the south bank. At first glance it seemed a good idea, but Gough objected that surprise, owing to the known Sikh vigilance, would be impossible; and that such a move would lay open the whole of the country between Ferozepore and Ludhiana, leading into India, as well as the British lines of communication, to attack by masses of Sikh cavalry.

He held that the only practicable method was an artillery bombardment, followed by a direct attack on the Sikh entrenchments. The Governor-General agreed to this provided the senior artillery and engineer officers said that destruction of the Sikh defences was feasible, at the same time pressing his own plan. Something akin to a comedy of errors now followed. Hardinge first consulted Colonel Brooke of the artillery and Captain Baker of the engineers. Both agreed that after a heavy cannonade the defences should fall to infantry assault. Hardinge sent Colonel Benson, his military secretary, to report this to General Gough, who had already satisfied himself that this was the only way.

But Brigadier Smith, chief engineer, after another reconnaissance of the Sikh entrenchments, told the Governor-General that he was, after all, uncertain of the success of Gough's plan — two hours' shelling with thirty heavy howitzers and five 18-pounders followed by an infantry assault;

and Hardinge sent him to explain his objections to Gough, who fumed and exploded over the vacillation at this critical stage. Gough assembled the artillery and engineer officers at his headquarters on 9 February, where they again opposed his plan. The Governor-General was omnipotent, and human nature being what it is, Hardinge was able in effect to command support for his plan by influencing these officers against Gough's one. In despair, Gough left the decision to Hardinge, who looking for more support, consulted Major Henry Lawrence, the political agent, also an artillery officer, and Major Abbott of the Engineers. Both, especially the independent-minded Lawrence, argued that after such an artillery bombardment the attack should succeed. In face of this, Hardinge now wrote guardedly to Gough: 'Upon the fullest consideration of this question, if the artillery can be brought into play, I recommend you to attack. If it cannot and you anticipate a heavy loss, I would recommend you not to undertake it.' He then withdrew his own plan for a flank attack, and the arrangements for Gough's frontal attack went forward.

Gough commanded an army of some twenty thousand men with three divisions of infantry.[11] He decided to attack on the

---

[11] CAVALRY: Major-General Sir Joseph Thackwell. 1st Brigade: (Scott) HM. 3rd Light Dragoons; 4th and 5th Bengal Light Cavalry; 9th Irregular Cavalry. 2nd Brigade: (Campbell) HM's 9th Lancers; 2nd Irregular Cavalry. 3rd Brigade: Governor-General's Bodyguard. 4th Brigade: (Cureton's) HM's 16th Lancers; 3rd Bengal Light Cavalry; 4th Irregular Cavalry. ARTILLERY: 9 Horse Artillery Batteries; 3 Field artillery 9-pounder batteries: 2 field artillery 12-pounder batteries: six 18-pounders: 18 heavy howitzers and mtr. INFANTRY: 1st Division, Sir Harry Smith: 1st Brigade (Hicks's) HM's 31st: 47th Bengal Light Infantry, 2nd Brigade (Penny) HM's 50th Foot: 42nd Bengal Light Infantry, Nasiri Battalion. 2nd DIVISION (Gilbert): 3rd Brigade (Taylor). HM's 29th, 41st and 68th Bengal Native Infantry. 4th Brigade (Maclaren) 1st Bengal Europeans

western front, corresponding to the Sikh right, where the defences were known to be weakest. There, after an artillery bombardment of two to three hours, Sir Robert Dick's division on the extreme left of the British line, would storm. General Gilbert's division in the centre and Sir Harry Smith's on the left, were at the same time to make feint attacks to divert the enemy from Dick's real attack. Brigadier Cureton, with a brigade of cavalry and a troop of horse artillery, was to threaten a ford at Huriki, about a mile from the eastern corner of the Sikh entrenchments, on the opposite bank of which were the enemy cavalry.

Heavy rain fell during the night of the ninth, followed by a heavy mist. Gough massed three batteries of heavy guns facing the enemy's right front — six 18-pounders commanded by Lieutenant-Colonel Lawrenson — six 10-inch howitzers under Brigadier Dennis — and eight 8-inch howitzers under Lieutenant-Colonel Huthwaite. To the left of them, slightly forward, were the rocket batteries under Lieutenant-Colonel Geddes. The heavy guns were sited about thirteen hundred yards from the Sikh defences, instead of in batteries about half that distance. It was a basic error for which the British would pay dearly. Moreover, that skilled tactician Sir Harry Smith observed the deployment of his own division, on the left, with grave doubts as to the correctness of Gough's plan.

> In my own mind (he wrote) I very much disagreed with my gallant commander-in-chief as to the place of his attack being

---

(102nd): 16th Native Infantry, Sirmur Battalion. 3rd DIVISION (Dick): 5th Brigade (Ashburnham) HM's 9th: HM's 62nd: 26th Native Infantry. 6th Brigade (Wilkinson) HM's 80th: 33rd and 63rd Native Infantry: 7th Brigade (Stacy) HM's 10th; HM's 53rd; 43rd and 59th Native Infantry. DETACHED BRIGADE: 4th, 5th and 73rd Native Infantry.

the most eligible one. I saw at once that the fundamental principle of 'being superior to your enemy on the point of attack was lost sight of, and the whole of our army, with the exception of my division, which was reduced to 2,400 bayonets, was held in reserve just out of reach of the enemy's cannon.

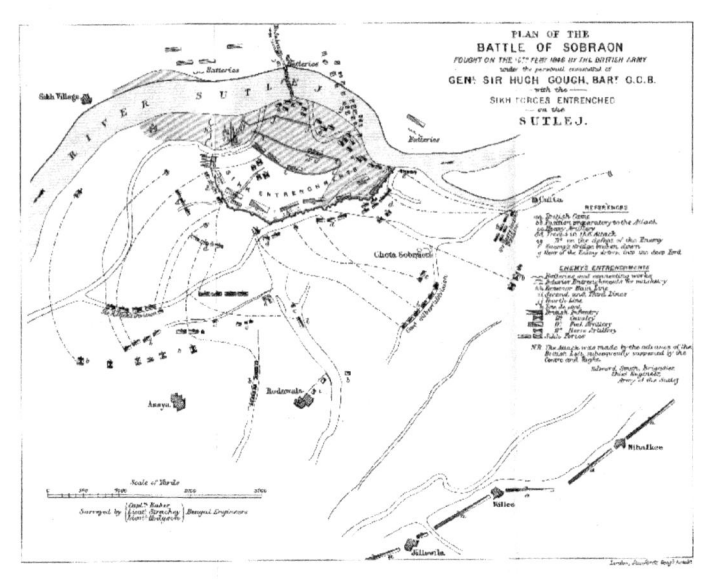

The Battle of Sobraon, 10 February 1846

It was first intended that the cannonade on the Sikh defences should begin at dawn, but a thick grey mist over plain and river prevented it. Then the gunners with the heavy guns lost their way and not till long after the appointed time were they in position and ready to open fire. 'Had the morning been clear it would have been serious for us,' wrote Ensign (later Major-General) Newall, in action for the first time.

But the same veil of heavy mist which so hampered us hung over the hostile camp, and concealed from the view of the enemy the formidable peak of heavy cannon being aligned on the prolongation of his bastion faces and flanks. On that day, when I first smelt powder, I served with the heavy howitzers and can never forget the moment when old Gough (who was there present in person) sent the order to 'open fire.' No 1 fire! No 2, 3, 4, 5, 6. Six 10-inch shells hurtled through the mist just lifting, and could be seen in the still dark morning light, bursting in the enemy's camp and entrenchments. A minute's pause, and then the hum of the surprised camp like a vast hive, followed by the drums beating to arms, and the trumpets of the Sikh hosts sounding the alarm.

The air thudded and shook as every gun on the British side now opened up — tongues of orange flame and wreaths of black smoke belched from them. A storm of missiles hissed and hurtled through the air into the Sikh trenches. Bancroft, who was serving with a rocket battery, recalled seeing a body of enemy cavalry with banners waving charging his battery. 'We immediately gave them a salvo of rockets, followed by single doses; the hissing noise of the long destructive shafts and the shells bursting unerringly among them suddenly threw their ranks into the utmost confusion and they were driven back in a whirlwind of defeat, leaving hundreds slain upon the field.'

The plain reverberated with the crash of the heavy guns on both sides. The British mortar shells burst in the air, their fuses being too short; and the 18-pounders were too far off to do much damage. The Sikhs stood to their guns unafraid, returning shot for shot, round for round; louder than anything heard in India before were the ear-splitting detonations of over a hundred guns for the next two hours.

Gough, with his white coat trailing behind him, then rode through the whistling shot and the black sulphurous smoke that now lay like a cloud in the valley, reluctantly to tell the Governor-General that the bombardment was having little effect; but they agreed that the attack should go on as planned. Gough's anxiety to attack had undoubtedly caused this setback, for the artillery officers had wanted to site the guns overnight behind parapets six hundred yards nearer, but fearing delay he refused, contenting himself with placing them on the open plain out of range of the Sikh guns.

Sir Harry Smith noted that the guns fired with 'apparent success… but to our astonishment, at the very moment of this success our fire slackened and soon ceased altogether, when it was ascertained that the ammunition was expended, the officer in command of the Artillery not having brought half the quota into the field which was ordered by the Governor-General and the commander-in-chief. Thus there was no time to be lost.'

Four rounds only per gun were left — this was reported to the commander-in-chief a little after half past eight. Gough ordered his nephew, Colonel J. B. Gough, Quartermaster-General, to order General Sir Robert Dick to launch an attack at once on the Sikh right front. Gough's determination, in face of this alarming news, which reversed his plans, threatened the lives of thousands of his troops and put the outcome of the battle in doubt, spread to the men, for reports agree that a rumour ran like lightning among the waiting redcoats, 'that old Gough had been told that there were only four rounds left per gun, and says, "Thank God! then I'll be at them with the bayonet".'

These words have been used to denigrate Gough, evidence that he was a fire-eater with a contempt for artillery, faith only in the bayonet. Gough was, of course, expressing his relief that, at last, after waiting a month for the heavy guns — after being involved in a time-wasting squabble as to their power to knock down the Sikh defences — and after witnessing their failure and their lack of preparedness, he was at last free, as he said later, to bring the battle 'to the arbitrament of musketry and the bayonet.'

Now came an incident which shows how the fortune of war then depended so much on the unexpected human factor. Colonel Benson, one of Hardinge's staff officers, rode furiously through the smoke to Gough with a message to the effect that if Gough did not feel confident of success without great loss, he had better withdraw Sir Robert Dick's attack and instead work up to the enemy's defences by regular approaches — in an effect a suggestion that he should retreat and then try to stalk up to the enemy as best he could, bit by bit.

Major Patrick Grant (later Field-Marshal Sir Patrick) who was present, says that Gough answered: 'Loss there will be, of course. Look at those works bristling with guns, and defended as they will be; but by God's blessing, I feel confident of success.' Benson nevertheless repeated the message and received the same answer. When he foolishly gave it a third time, Gough shouted: 'What! withdraw the troops after the action has commenced, and when I feel confident of success. Indeed I will not. Tell Sir Robert Dick to move on, in the name of God!'

Later evidence showed that Benson had misinterpreted Hardinge's message. What Hardinge had in fact said was that, if Sir Hugh doubted the issue he might exercise his discretion, but if he only apprehended a severe loss, to go on.

Sir Robert Dick had already given the word to go.

12: Victory

Brigadier Stacy's brigade led the attack on the Sikh right, walking into murderous volleys of musketry and hissing grapeshot, for which, deployed in line, they made an easy target. On their flanks tore up Colonel Lane's troops of horse artillery and Captains Horsford's and Fordyce's field batteries, unlimbering, firing and galloping on to within three hundred yards of the enemy's heavy gun emplacements, and briefly driving back the gunners. Many of the 53rd Foot fell to fire from an enfilading Sikh battery on the north bank, but the line pressed on doggedly, stormed the Sikh right with the bayonet and drove the defenders from their guns to the inner trenches.

Generals Gilbert and Smith had meantime launched their feint attacks on the enemy's left, but these failed to distract the Sikhs, who realizing where the real danger lay, rushed masses of troops over to their right to repel Stacy's first thrust with a strong counter-attack. The British hung on, in desperate hand-to-hand fighting, hoping, amid the black sulphurous smoke and the frenzied cries, that the men of the two remaining brigades of their division would come up to their aid in time. Here, Sir Robert Dick, the old and fearless divisional commander, was shot dead; and under the weight of the massed Sikh infantry, firing volley after disciplined volley, the exhausted British slowly fell back step by step, out of the trenches they had gained at such cost.

Gough's first attack had failed.

Already he had ordered Smith and Gilbert to transform their feints into storming attacks and these divisions moved forward in line — but against ramparts, noted Captain J. D.

Cunningham, 'higher and more continuous than the barriers which had foiled 185 the first efforts of their comrades.'

On Smith's front, the enemy's extreme left, the men of Brigadier Penny's brigade, followed by those of Hicks, stumbled over rough ground in a killing fire. Faced then by a desperate struggle to climb the high ramparts, they gave way and fell back exhausted, leaving many dead and wounded on the field. For a moment, amid the crash of musketry, the boom of the heavy guns and the drifting smoke, it seemed as if Penny's exhausted men might cause confusion among the advancing redcoats of the following brigade, but with impressive discipline, Hicks's men opened their ranks while advancing so that these shattered units could fall back to reform.

The British now hurled themselves desperately at the ramparts, while the black-bearded Sikhs fired down at them and inflicted great gaping wounds on their heads and arms with razor-sharp swords. Hicks's men, too, were repulsed, fell back, took what shelter from the storm of fire they could get in a dried up gulley while they made ready to attack again.

In the interval they saw the Sikhs rush down from their defences and with merciless sword blows hack to pieces their wounded comrades lying below.

Furious at this butchering they attacked again, backed by the men of the 31st (East Surrey Regiment) from Penny's Brigade, scaling the ramparts by climbing on each other's shoulders. At the height of the attack Lieutenant Tritton, carrying the Queen's colours, was shot through the head and Ensign Jones, a mere boy, who carried the regimental colour, was killed as well. Lieutenant Noel seized the Queen's colours; seeing the regimental colour fall to the ground Sergeant Bernard McCabe rushed forward, took it up, leaped across the ditch and planted it high on the Sikh ramparts as a rallying point. With a roar of frenzied triumph the British surged in and drove the Sikhs before them.

By no means the work of a mere moment was this achievement, and amid the ceaseless groans of wounded men, the shrieks of animals, the crash of musketry, fighting had been intense all along the front. In the centre, just as Gilbert's division had begun to advance in response to Gough's order, the Sikhs, having repulsed the first attack, on their right, rushed up to deal with this new threat. Watching their movement, Gough shouted, 'Good God! They'll be annihilated.' The centre was indeed the strongest part of the Sikh defences — the entrenchments were apparently too high to be scaled without scaling ladders. 'The fire from the enemy's heavy guns in their centre batteries, their zambureks and musketry fire was terrific,' noted Ensign Innes of the Bengal European Regiment.

> The air, charged with sulphur, was stifling and so heated that it was almost unbearable. Now on rushed the Bengal European Regiment with a determination which promised to carry everything before it; soon reaching the ditch which formed the outer defence, and springing into it, they found themselves confronted by the massive walls, which in the distance had appeared less formidable, for they now found these works too high to escalade without ladders. To retire again was to encounter the storm of fire through which they had just passed, to remain in their present position was annihilation; therefore, the Regiment, mortified and chagrined, was forced to seek shelter under cover of the bank of the dry river which it had left but a short time before.

Officers and men alike suffered great losses. Ensign Percy Innes, who wrote the above words, being among the wounded.

Smith's division, which had entered on the Sikh left, was also now hard put to hold on, 'By dint of the hardest fighting I ever saw, I carried the entrenchments,' Smith wrote.

> Such a hand-to-hand conflict ensued, for twenty-five minutes I could barely hold my own. Mixed together, swords and targets against bayonets, and a fire on both sides... We were at it against four times my numbers, sometimes receding (never turning round, though) sometimes advancing. The old 31st and 50th laid on like devils... This last was a brutal bulldog fight...

Uncertain still was the outcome of the battle, for Smith's hold was weak and if the Sikhs reinforced their left he could be repelled too. But Gough's original plan now at last bore fruit, for the defenders, in repelling the attacks elsewhere, had weakened their right. Sir Robert Dick was dead, but the men of his division attacked again, penetrated the defences once more and struck down the Sikh gunners. At the same time, Gilbert's division rallied and attacked a little towards the left of the centre where the defences were not so high. But a second time the men failed to scale the ramparts. General Gilbert was wounded, Brigadier McLaren killed. A third time they charged, and now, facing heavy losses, the men climbing on to each other's shoulders, they at last surged into the entrenchments, bayoneted the Sikhs at their guns, spiked them and drove back the infantry. Brigadier Taylor died here, shot in the head after being wounded by a sword cut in the face.

But right, centre and left, the British were now inside the defences and before the enemy infantry could regroup and counter-attack, Gough called on the cavalry under General Sir Joseph Thackwell to sweep the enemy's entire camp. The engineers made a small gap in the defences, where they were lowest on the Sikh right. General Thackwell led the dark blue-jacketed Third Light Dragoons through in single file. Long red and white plumes streaming they tore triumphantly down the interior of the Sikh defences, cutting the gunners down at the batteries and scattering the infantry where they tried to form squares. But the Sikhs yielded only stubbornly.

A shower of hissing grapeshot from a Sikh battery one hundred and fifty yards away halted the first squadron of the Dragoons. Aided by the 4th and 5th Bengal Light Cavalry, brilliant in white jodhpurs, blue turbans and tunics, with red cummerbunds, the Dragoons rallied, charged and cut down the dogged Sikh gunners. Barely a moment later, in the smoke and confusion several of them were wounded by grapeshot fired over the outer Sikh defences by the Horse Artillery.

But more redcoats and blue-jacketed horse artillerymen were now pouring in through gaps and bridges across the Sikh defences made by the sappers. Still, the turbaned Sikhs fought fiercely for every inch of ground, even though Tej Singh, the treacherous commander-in-chief, had fled early in the battle, leaving his subordinates to cope as best they could; and by accident or design, had sunk one vital boat at the centre of the four hundred yards long bridge to the northern shore, so that it was useless. Sham Singh, the revered and ancient leader who had fought with Ranjit Singh, now remembered a vow he had made to conquer or die, and noted Captain Cunningham, who was present:

> Calling on all around to fight for the Guru, who had promised everlasting bliss to the brave, he repeatedly rallied his shattered ranks, and at last fell a martyr on a heap of his slain countrymen. Others might be seen standing on the ramparts and amid a shower of balls, waving defiance with their swords, or telling the gunners where the fair-haired English

> pressed thickest together... The parapets were sprinkled with blood from end to end; the trenches were filled with the dead and the dying. Amid the deafening roar of cannon, and the multitudinous fire of musketry, shouts of triumph or of scorn were yet heard, and the flashing of innumerable swords was yet visible; or from time to time exploding magazines of powder threw bursting shells and beams of wood and banks of earth high above the agitated sea of smoke and flame which enveloped the host of combatants...

More and more guns of the Horse Artillery were heaved through the gaps and the final onslaught began. Lashed by a merciless fire, attacked by cavalry and infantry on three sides, the Sikhs only stubbornly yielded, fighting bitterly to the death, until at last they could take no more. First a few, then all gave way, until a retreat became a rout and finally a desperate stampede. Soon they were hemmed in a mass at the head of the bridge, there to be shot down or hurled into the river below, which the heavy rains had made no longer formidable. 'Happening to be an eyewitness of what then occurred,' wrote the Governor-General's son, Arthur Hardinge.

> I saw the bridge at that moment overcrowded with guns, horses, and soldiers of all arms, swaying to and fro, till at last with a crash it disappeared in the running waters, carrying with it all those who had vainly hoped to reach the opposite shore. The river seemed alive with a struggling mass of men. The artillery, now brought down to the water's edge, completed the slaughter. Few escaped; none, it may be said, surrendered.

All was over before noon. The British had won a total victory. The Sikh losses were estimated at ten thousand, together with sixty-seven guns, more than two hundred zambureks and vast quantities of powder and ammunition. Not since the battle of Buxar in 1764, when the dead of Mir Kasim's Shuja u'd daulah's forces formed a mole over which the defeated survivors escaped, had there been such slaughter in India.

Lal and Tej Singh and the Rani had schemed the destruction of the troublesome Khalsa and they seemed to have succeeded.

Why hadn't the British shown more mercy to a defeated foe? There were two reasons; first, they had seen the Sikhs butcher and mangle every wounded comrade whom the fortune of war left at their mercy, which had put the men in a grim, revengeful mood; secondly, Sir Hugh Gough, who allowed, if not ordered the artillery to shoot down the enemy floundering through the river, sought the total destruction of the Khalsa.

The Governor-General called the victory 'one of the most daring ever achieved, by which, in open day, a triple line of breastworks, flanked by formidable redoubts, bristling with artillery, manned by thirty-two regular regiments of infantry was assaulted and carried'. But a heavy price was paid. In those few hours three hundred and twenty officers and men were killed, two thousand and sixty-three were wounded — perhaps a surprisingly small number for the amount of shooting, though of the wounded, it is not known how many subsequently died. Certainly, it was a bloody battlefield. 'The stream was choked with the dead and dying — the sandbanks were covered with bodies floating leisurely down,' wrote Robert Cust.

> It was an awful scene, a fearful carnage. The dead Sikh lay inside his trenches — the dead European marked too distinctly the line each regiment had taken, the advance. The living Europeans remarked that nought could resist the bayonet... As the place was becoming dangerous from the explosion of mines I passed out of the trenches, and rode

along the dry nullah that surrounds it and marked the strong defences which the enemy had thrown up... Our loss was heavy and the ground was here and there strewn with the slain, among whom I recognized a fine and handsome lad whom I had well known, young Hamilton, brother of Alistair Stewart. There he lay, his auburn hair weltering in his blood, his forehead fearfully gashed, his fingers cut off. Still warm, but quite dead. Flames were spreading over the Sikh camp, igniting the powder beside each gun and the air was rent with terrific explosions. The guns were now nearly all removed and our dead were being buried. We rode slowly home.

Gough wasted little time after the battle. He organized the river crossing at once and by early evening on the same day the first units had stepped on to the northern shore. Most of the force crossed two days later at Ferozepore, where Cust wrote of watching the camels cross over for three days without interruption. 'Our camp followers alone must have amounted to one hundred thousand — beasts of burden, elephants, camels, horses, bullocks, mules, etc., to an amount frightful and incalculable.'

On the night of 12 February the advanced guard camped among the ruined domes and fallen arches of the old town of Kasur, about twelve miles north-west of Ferozepore, and the next day the rest of the force moved up. Hardinge had meanwhile sent a note to Gulab Singh, now the Sikh vizier, advising him that it was imperative to present himself for negotiations at once if Ranjit Singh's kingdom was to survive as an independent state. Gulab arrived promptly the next day, accompanied by numerous chiefs — 'a stout heavy-looking man,' Cust observed, 'who had passed the prime of life, with naught of bearing or dignity — no spark of Rajput nobility to distinguish him from the common herd.'

But Gulab was the most astute and powerful man in the Punjab. He had kept aloof from what he had always regarded as a suicidal war, though for his own purposes he had secretly encouraged it. Now this Machiavellian leader was about to reap the reward for which he had long hoped.

Gulab left the bearded chiefs sitting upon their elephants near the British camp and went alone into the Governor-General's durbar tent to hear the surrender terms. Occasionally he came out to confer, but it was not until after midnight on a long hot day that he finally agreed to them.

Hardinge had decided not to annexe the Punjab, because it would be very hard to do. The Khalsa had been decisively beaten, but ten thousand Sikh soldiers had escaped, taking with them twenty-five heavy guns from the north bank; moreover, another twenty-five thousand of the Khalsa with about fifty more guns were distributed around Amritsar and Lahore, with many thousands more at Peshawar and Multan. Complete subjugation, a prerequisite of annexation, would mean a lengthy war of sieges with a doubtful outcome. Instead, it was thought more expedient to weaken the Sikh state militarily and territorially while letting it remain independent with a friendly government supervised by a British Resident.

The terms that Gulab Singh accepted were, accordingly: (1) cession to the British of the Jullundar Doab between the rivers Sutlej and Beas, thus advancing by a hundred miles the borders of British India; (2) payment of one-and-a-half crores of rupees (one and a half million pounds) as indemnity for the expenses of the war; (3) the reduction of the Sikh army to twenty thousand infantry and twelve thousand cavalry and the surrender of the twenty-five guns used on the north bank at Sobraon; (5) the British to have complete control of both banks of the Sutlej.

But the treasury at Lahore was almost empty and the indemnity could not be paid; so the Lahore government agreed instead to hand over all the hill territories between the Indus and the Beas, including Hazara and Kashmir. This, the British then sold to Gulab Singh, as an independent principality, for the trifling sum of £750,000. Hardinge justified this fateful and somewhat sordid transaction in a verbose letter to the Secret Committee in London on 4 March 1846:

> While the severance of this frontier line from the Lahore possessions materially weakens that state and deprives it, in the eyes of other Asiatic powers, of much of its pride of position, its possession by us enables us at once to mark our sense of Raja Gulab Singh's conduct during the later operations, by regarding him in the mode most in accordance with his ambitious desires; to shew forth, as an example to the other chiefs of Asia, the benefits which accrue from an adherence to British interests; to create a strong and friendly power in a position to threaten an attack, should it be necessary to do so, the Lahore territories in their most vulnerable point; and at the same time to secure to ourselves that indemnification for the expense of the campaign...

When on 18 February 1846 Gulab Singh had accepted these terms on behalf of the Rani and the Maharajah, Lord Hardinge directed that this boy, Duleep Singh, aged nine, should be brought to his camp. Cust described him as 'a child of an intelligent and not unpleasing appearance The usual salutes and ceremonies of present offering were at first studiously ignored by Hardinge, but when the innocent boy asked pardon for the offences done by the Khalsa, agreed to accept the British terms and begged that he might be restored to the friendship of the Governor-General, harmony was restored and the presents were accepted.

Cust describes the intense confusion and turmoil, the absence of all order and dignity in the Governor-General's tent, where hundreds of officers pushed and heaved in the sweltering heat. He compares it with the Governor-General's return visit to Duleep Singh's camp:

> a beautiful scene, of which the two chief characteristics were order and magnificence. Shawls and cashmere carpets on the floor. The Maharajah sat on a silver chair with his ministers and nobles standing behind him. There was no crowding, no confusion, all were handsomely dressed — the carpets most beautiful and one side of the tent being thrown open admitted air and light... On the whole it presented as mortifying a contrast to our durbar as can be imagined.

The British, it seems, had yet to learn the art and importance of well-ordered ceremony.

The Maharajah later accompanied Sir Henry Hardinge and Sir Hugh Gough and their staffs, escorted by four cavalry regiments and artillery under the bewhiskered Brigadier Cureton, to the fine city of old Lahore, all on elephants. A mile from the city Gulab Singh and the Sikh sirdars awaited them on their elephants. Salutes were fired, the elephants threatened to stampede, but were calmed; and the procession paraded past the lofty minarets and the great ruined pillars and arches of the former Muhammadan kings, 'the colours of the dresses, the line of elephants, contrasting with the display of troops, were a sight not easily to be effaced from our recollections'.

With the Governor-General's approval, the two traitors, Lal Singh and Tej Singh, were appointed respectively vizier (chief minister) of the Lahore government and commander-in-chief of the reduced Khalsa. But these two knew well that their lives, as well as that of the Rani, would be in danger directly the

British left. They therefore asked for a protecting force at the capital, and the British, who wanted a weak, dependent government, agreed. So on 8 March, when the Treaty of Lahore was signed in Major Lawrence's tent, a letter from Maharajah Duleep Singh was read aloud asking for this force. On the 9th, when the Treaty was ratified, it contained a clause to the effect that at the Maharajah's earnest request, the Governor-General had consented to occupy the town and citadel of Lahore with British troops until the end of the year, so that the Sikh government, acting through a Council of Regency headed by Lal Singh, could reorganize its army according to the Treaty.

The little prince Duleep Singh, glittering with jewellery and with the Sikh aigrette shining in his brilliant blue turban, attended as ruler-to-be and descendant of the great Ranjit. But one jewel would no longer be his. By the terms of the Treaty the priceless Kho-i-noor diamond — the 'mountain of light' which Ranjit had procured from Shah Shujah — was in due course to be surrendered to Queen Victoria. Hardinge whispered to Frederick Currie, his foreign secretary, that it should be shown for their inspection. At last, 'a small tin box enveloped in a shabby cloth was brought in, containing the diamond...'

Hardinge ended the speech he made on this occasion with these words to the assembled Sikhs: 'Success or failure is in your own hands; my co-operation shall not be wanting; but if you neglect this opportunity, no aid on the part of the British Government can save the State.'

And on this ringing note of apparent sincerity ended the first attempt at conquest of the Punjab, commonly known as the First Sikh War. Hardinge was rewarded with a viscounty; Gough a barony, and each a generous pension.

The kingdom founded by Maharajah Ranjit Singh was thus broken up, the Sikh territories on the south bank of the Sutlej were confiscated; the rich and fertile Jullundar Doab was ceded to the British, Kashmir detached and sold to Gulab Singh as a separate, independent state. Outside the Punjab, from Cape Cormorin to Kabul, the moral effect of these arrangements was great. British military prestige was re-established and neighbouring peoples felt themselves subject to a power which could guarantee them peace, security and justice.

But within the Punjab things were more complex. At Lahore there was a government with a king, a prime minister and an army, all of whom depended upon a foreign power, whose soldiers were lent to keep up the pretence of peace and order. 'The British Government,' Hardinge told the assembled chiefs when the Treaty was signed, 'desires to see a Sikh government reestablished, which may be able to control its army, protect its subjects, and willing to respect the rights of its neighbours.'

Hardinge no doubt believed these words. But it would have been strange indeed if the Sikhs could at this time have been made to believe that they had a king and an independent government of their own. They showed little allegiance to the Queen Mother or the boy king before crossing the Sutlej. How much were they likely to show now that these two were puppets of the British under a treaty that parcelled out the kingdom? How far, with a prime minister and a commander-in-chief, Lal Singh and Tej Singh, who were hated as traitors, did the king's power extend? The truth was that without a British escort, neither he nor his mother could set foot outside the fortress of Lahore and not risk being murdered.

The Khalsa had through its defeats learned a lesson and been humiliated, but both those who fought and those who did not, still believed that treason had lost them these battles. And although they were disbanded, the profession of arms was the only one they knew; besides, the profession had a religious foundation. So they were unlikely to exchange the sword for the ploughshare, and their livelihood must therefore depend on the sword. Yet, if the government was powerless to maintain them thus, where could they turn as soldiers of fortune — the British had not in 1846 seriously considered absorbing them in the Indian Army — but against each other, as they did before Ranjit Singh unified them; or, against the public enemy, the British occupiers?

So to all but Hardinge and his entourage, this peace was a mirage.

First sign of trouble came when the Sikh governor of Kashmir refused to hand the territory over to Gulab Singh until a mixed force of his troops backed up by British and Sikhs under the Resident, Henry Lawrence, marched against him. He then surrendered without firing a shot and produced evidence showing that he had held out on the orders of Lal Singh, the prime minister. After trial, when he was found guilty, Lal Singh was deposed from the Regency Council and exiled.

Colonel Gardner, whose personal enemy, Lal Singh, had some weeks earlier ordered him to leave the Punjab because he had found out that the American was Gulab Singh's special agent in Lahore, had returned to the country from British India to take part in the operations. Once Gulab was seated on the throne of Kashmir, Gardner received his reward — command of a regiment of infantry and all of the Kashmir artillery as well as the revenue from a number of villages. He was thus enabled to live in style for the rest of his long life, in peaceful Kashmir.

Meantime, Lal Singh's actions had made it clear that the removal of the British force from the Punjab at the end of the year would lose all the gains won in a hard-fought war. Hardinge therefore offered the Sikh chiefs two alternatives: first (which he doubtless knew they would not accept) that the British should quit Lahore entirely and leave government to the chiefs: second, that a British Protectorate should be established in the Punjab until the Maharajah came of age.

Unanimously, the fifty-two chiefs entitled to vote called for a protectorate and the arrangements, set down in the Treaty of Bhyrowal, 16 December 1846, were: there would be a Council of Regency of eight — Tej Singh, Shere Singh (the Maharajah's brother-in-law), Runjoor Singh, the Dewan Dina Nath, Fakir Nur-ud-din, Utter Singh, Shumser Singh and Bhae Nidham Singh. The Council was to act 'under the control and guidance of the British Resident' who was Lieutenant-Colonel Henry Lawrence. 'The power of the Resident,' it was added, 'extends over every department, and to any extent.' Twenty-two lakhs of rupees (£220,000) were agreed as an annual payment to the British during the protectorate. In addition: 'A military force may be placed in such forts and posts, and off such strength, within the Lahore territory, as the Governor-General may determine. These terms give the British Resident unlimited authority in all matters of internal administration and external relation…'

Stiff as these terms were, for twelve months the system worked well. Hardinge was confident enough to write to the Secret Committee in April 1847: 'The Sikh authorities composing the Durbar appear to be carrying on the Government of the country, under the British Resident, with a sincere desire to insure a successful result.' And a few days later, 'Everything is perfectly quiet, and nothing has occurred worthy of remark.'

Hardinge now believed that he had solved the problem of the Punjab. But Henry Lawrence, who he had appointed as Resident at Lahore, had virtually to recreate government there, a task to which he brought his own rare and exceptional character. To his subordinates — his own two brothers, John and George; John Nicholson, Major Abbott, Harry Lumsden, John Beecher, Reynel Taylor and Herbert Edwardes, among others — Lawrence allowed complete freedom of action in the various districts, the guiding principle being briefly summed up in the words, 'Settle the country, make the people happy and take care there are no rows'. In practice this meant less taxation, curbing the powers of the chiefs, dismantling practically all fortifications but those needed by the government and, above all, setting an example in honesty and orderly conduct. These measures certainly added to the prestige of the British among the peasantry, but they had little effect upon the feelings of the Khalsa and the sirdars.

Alive to the military needs of the Resident Hardinge had felt obliged to increase British forces in the Punjab. To the occupying force at Lahore under Sir John Littler — one British, eight sepoy infantry battalions, two field batteries, one horse-battery and a wing of irregular cavalry — he had added an infantry brigade with twenty guns organized as a mobile column, and a mobile column of similar strength at Jallundar, forty miles north of Ludhiana, and at Ferozepore — a total of fifty thousand men and sixty guns.

But the exchequer was low — the cost of first the Afghan War and now the Sikh War had left India hugely in debt. Anxious to make the books look more satisfactory before going home, Hardinge now decided, in spite of Gough's objections, to reduce the Indian Army by fifty thousand men, cutting down sepoy battalion establishments from a thousand to eight hundred each and Indian cavalry regiments from five hundred to four hundred and twenty. He also made reductions in the artillery. Gough had no alternative but to accept these reductions, imposed as they were despite his arguments against them. Hardinge was convinced that no shot would be fired in anger in India for years to come and that the cuts were justifiable. Events were soon to prove him wrong, though certainly 1847 seemed a year of promise, except for a plot to kill Henry Lawrence and the members of the Regency Council, in which the Rani was said to have been involved, and for which she was sent to semi-confinement at Sheikapur.

Late in 1847, Hardinge resigned and went home, leaving his successor, James, Earl of Dahousie, a young aristocrat and politician, aged 35, who had been President of the Board of Trade in Sir Robert Peel's government, to carry on. For nearly three months, nothing occurred, as Hardinge would have said, worthy of remark, then came an incident, quite fortuitous and not directly concerned with the Sikhs, which released their pent-up warlike feelings, and had the most far-reaching effect upon the destinies of British India and the Punjab.

Part Two: The Second Anglo-Sikh War, 1848-9

13: Rebellion

Henry Lawrence had fallen sick in the Punjab's withering summer heat and at the end of 1847, he left for England, with Lord Hardinge. His district commissioners continued trying to force equitable government and just administration on the Sikh provincial governors. Of them, only Sultan Mohammed, a seasoned Afghan intriguer, and Chutter Singh, father of Shere Singh, and of a daughter betrothed to Maharajah Duleep Singh, were then suspect. Major George Lawrence at Peshawar, and Major James Abbott, in Hazara, next door to Kashmir, kept a watchful eye on their movements. Lieutenant Herbert Edwardes was settling the Derajat district, which lay between Dera Ishmael Khan and Dera Ghazi Khan, on the west bank of the great swift-flowing Indus, and separated from Multan by the river Chenab and thirty-five miles of sparse country.

Multan, formerly an outpost of the Afghan monarchy, had been torn away from it in 1819 by Ranjit Singh. The city, as distinct from the province, teemed with Hindu merchants busy trading with Afghanistan and Central Asia. Multan was one of the main gateways to India; the passes from Ghazni and Kandahar led to it and had, indeed, opened the door to the great invasions of India. The Diwan, or Muslim governor of Multan province, Mulraj, farmed its revenue in the traditional oriental fashion, paying as little as possible to the central government and keeping the rest for himself, as his father had with equal success done before him. When however, late in 1847, he was asked to give an account of certain items, he decided that the time had come for him to retire.

Magnanimously, he agreed to stay in office until March 1848, by which time he was asked to have ready the accounts of his last three years of office for his successor, a Sikh, Sirdar Khan Singh, with whom to Multan went Mr Vans Agnew, of the Civil Service, and Lieutenant Anderson, of the Bombay European Regiment, to see that all was in order. An escort, fourteen hundred Sikh soldiers of the reformed Khalsa, a Gurkha regiment, about seven hundred cavalry and a hundred artillerymen with six guns went by land, while the new Diwan and the two officers whom they were escorting went by water, a much more pleasant route. Thus the troops and their commanders — Vans Agnew, and Anderson, with the Diwan — met for the first time on 18 April, in a spacious Muslim building, the Eedgah, within cannon-shot of the north face of Multan's impregnable fort and about half a mile from Mulraj's own residence, a garden house outside the fort called the Am Khas.

Complete strangers thus were Vans Agnew and Anderson to their escorts, lacking that rapport so essential to military action — a fatal mistake as things turned out.

Mulraj paid a courtesy call on their arrival and early next day, before the sweltering sun was too high, the two British officers and Sirdar Khan Singh, escorted by a company of Gurkhas, accompanied him into the fort, still in the hands of Mulraj's own garrison. Its seventy-feet-high walls, very thick, and many tall towers made the fort one of the strongest in Asia when forts were still expressions of military strength. The Englishmen studied it closely, Mulraj only demurring at one heavily barred door, leading to a room called *Muztaffa's Kutcheree*, which, he explained, was unsuitable for inspection — it was kept for recalcitrant prisoners. He then handed them the keys to the fort, Lieutenant Anderson placed his Gurkha sentries at their posts and the party prepared to leave. But Mulraj's own garrison loitered sullenly around, fingering their sword hilts, angry at the prospect of unemployment. Anderson promised them service in the future, then the three officers, Mulraj and his bodyguard, rode towards the bridge over the moat, upon which stood two of Mulraj's soldiers, staring morosely at the foreigners who presumed to take over their great fortress. One of them impetuously jabbed Vans Agnew with his spear and knocked him off his horse. Agnew jumped up and hit the man with his stick. His attacker then struck and wounded Agnew twice with his sword and probably would have killed him had not one of the escorting horsemen knocked the attacker into the moat.

Mulraj, riding beside Vans Agnew, made no attempt to rescue him, but spurred his horse and rode off to his house, followed by his mounted escort. A number of these suddenly turned about and cut down Lieutenant Anderson, too. Sirdar Khan Singh, protected by Rung Ram, Mulraj's brother-in-law, had meantime rescued Vans Agnew from the mob, helped him up on to an elephant and rode off to the camp, binding up Agnew's bleeding wounds as they went. Passing Mulraj's residence, they saw a puff of black smoke and a cannon-shot whistled over their heads. They reached the Eedgah safely. Later, badly wounded, Anderson was brought in by a party of Gurkhas. Nothing linked this Muslim incident with the Sikhs, or the Lahore Regency Council, or pointed to it being so far more than a storm in a teacup. Nevertheless, after a Gurkha doctor had dressed his wounds, Vans Agnew, at 11 am reported the affair in a letter to Sir Frederick Currie, acting Lahore Resident, in Lawrence's absence, and also wrote to Mulraj, generously declaring he did not believe him guilty of ordering the attack, but asking him to prove this by seizing the guilty and coming himself to see him. At 2 pm when Mulraj had still not come, he prudently wrote for help to General Van Courtlandt, a soldier of fortune serving some eighty miles away in the reformed Khalsa, sending it through Lieutenant Herbert Edwardes, a political officer seventy-five miles away at Dera Ishmael Khan. The letter, a copy of which Vans Agnew sent to Sir Frederick Currie, Resident at Lahore, said:

> Dear Sir — you have been ordered by Sir F. Currie to send one regiment here. Pray let it march instantly, or hasten it top-speed. If you can spare another pray send it also. I am responsible for the measure. I am cut up a little, and on my back. Lieutenant Anderson is much worse. He has five sword wounds, I have two in my left arm from warding sabre cuts, and a poke in the ribs from a spear. I don't think Mulraj has anything to do with it. I was riding with him when we were attacked. He rode off, but is now said to be in the hands of the soldiery.

The two officers nursed these painful wounds and hoped that they were faced merely with a riot and not a rebellion. But it was a vain hope. At 4 pm Mulraj sent an official to say that he could neither give up the guilty nor come himself, having been stopped by the soldiers when he tried to do so, for all the garrison, Sikh, Hindu and Muslim, had rebelled, and the British officers had better look to their own safety. Vans Agnew pointed out how grave the matter was and how absolutely necessary it was for Mulraj to call on him if he wished to be thought innocent. The official returned with the admonition, but Mulraj never came. He was presiding over the excited council of war — the Pathans of the garrison were setting their seals to an oath of allegiance on the Koran, the Hindus on their sacred Shastras and the Sikhs had fastened on Mulraj one of their iron war-bracelets.

That night the British officers' transport animals grazing nearby — horses, elephants, camels, bullocks — were driven away. Flight was cut off.

Anderson being too sick and weak, Vans Agnew ordered their six guns to be suitably placed and the soldiers and camp followers to prepare to repel an attack. Next morning, in a last effort to prevent a conflict, he sent to Mulraj's officials the personal decrees of Maharajah Dhulip Singh ordering them to obey Mr Agnew's orders and to hand over the fort to Sirdar Khan Singh. The messengers found Mulraj preparing proclamations to the people to rise and join the rebellion against the British, and on reading the Maharajah's letters the chiefs with him replied that Mulraj was their master and him only would they obey. Agnew, thoroughly alarmed at this, sent an urgent letter to Peer Ibrahim Khan, British Agent in the Muslim state of Bahawalpore, eighty miles south across the Sutlej, to hurry troops to his aid, intending meantime to hold out.

The rebels, or, as they felt they were in reality, patriots defending their homeland against foreign occupiers, finally went the whole hog and began shelling the Eedgah both from the fort and from Mulraj's residence nearby. Agnew gave the order to return fire. One shot only was fired. The Lahore artillerymen then refused to serve the guns. They had, after all, few reasons to do so and many reasons not to.

Perhaps sensing where their loyalty lay, Mulraj sent messengers offering a big increase of pay to every soldier who deserted the British and joined him. Led by the commandant of the Sikh cavalry, whom Mulraj decorated with gold necklaces and bracelets, they went in twos and threes, until by the evening all had gone. Only the new governor, Sirdar Khan Singh, and the personal servants of the two officers stayed.

Vans Agnew dealt his last card and sent messengers to Mulraj asking for terms. The Diwan conferred with his chiefs and, so it was stated at his trial later, agreed that the officers were to quit the country and that the attack upon them was to cease. But it was too late — the insurgent army, thronging from all quarters of the city in the hot dark evening, clamoured for blood.

A yelling crowd of a thousand or more surged round the Eedgah, burst into the main hall brandishing swords, lances and muskets and surrounded the two wounded men where they sat beneath the lofty dome. Agnew was sitting on Anderson's bedside holding his hand and talking as they said good-bye. Sirdhar Khan Singh was made prisoner, the servants were driven off with musket butts. Goodhur Singh, an old soldier among the insurgents, so scarred with wounds that he was said at Mulraj's trial to look more like an imp than a man, struck Vans Agnew three blows on the neck, and cut off his head. The mob hacked Anderson to death and the two bodies were dragged outside, mutilated, subjected to various oriental indignities, and left lying in the courtyard.

All the insurgents now joined Mulraj. He strengthened the fort and sent the fiery cross of revolt through the surrounding districts, calling upon all to rise against the British 'who are treating the Maharajah and our proper rulers as prisoners'.

At Lahore, Sir Frederick Currie, on learning of the attack on his envoys, ordered General Whish to march on Multan with the British mobile column stationed at Lahore, and General Van Courtlandt, an old Sikh European officer, to march down from Dera Ishmael Khan with two battalions of Muslim troops, a regiment of cavalry and a troop of horse artillery. But when news of the actual murders reached Lahore later, Currie felt that nothing could be done now to help the two officers and the question had become one of policy. He therefore countermanded his orders for the British troops and applied to Lord Gough for instructions. 'The fort of Multan is very strong,' he wrote, 'and full of heavy cannon of large calibre. This cannot be taken possession of by direct attack. Except the Multan garrison, Mulraj has not many troops, and only five or six field guns. He is very unpopular both with the army and the people.'

Lord Gough opposed an immediate large-scale advance because he was certain it would provoke the next Sikh War that he anticipated. And after Hardinge's reductions, British forces were far from ready for it. The weather was getting very hot too and would certainly bring heavy casualties. Sending British troops against Mulraj was therefore postponed. 'I am very confident,' wrote Lord Dalhousie, the Governor-General, to Gough, on 15 May, 'that Your Excellency has exercised a most sound discretion in counselling the postponement of operations until after the rains.'

Gough told Dalhousie that for an invasion of the Punjab, should it become necessary, a force of twenty-four thousand men and seventy-eight guns from Ferozepore, co-operating with another five to six thousand from Sind would be vital and that the trained soldiers disbanded by Lord Hardinge should be reenlisted. 'If we do not enlist them, those opposed to us will exert every nerve to get them.' Dalhousie said then that he could not recommend to the Board of Directors the reversal of the economy policy begun by Hardinge, to which Gough answered that Hardinge would at once have abandoned this policy 'could he have anticipated that the army of the Power we have engaged to uphold were ready, to a man, to turn against the present Government.'

But while these questions of high policy were being argued that gallant and high-spirited young officer, Lieutenant Herbert Edwardes, was fighting a campaign against Mulraj on his own account.

The letter Vans Agnew had written to General Courtlandt after the first attack reached him while he was in camp at Dera Fateh Khan. Having read it, he decided without hesitation to march against Mulraj with all the troops of the British-supported Lahore government that he could assemble — a mere two guns, twenty zambureks, three hundred and fifty cavalrymen and twelve companies of infantry. He also wrote to Lieutenant Reynel Taylor, who was with General Courtlandt at Dera Ishmael Khan, asking him to send to Leia, a town on the Punjab side of the Indus, a regiment of infantry and four guns, 'sharp', but no other troops. 'I felt certain,' he wrote later, 'though I had never seen Multan, that if there was to be a war, and that fortress was to be reduced, the emergency must be met from Lahore. I went myself, not so much to fight Mulraj as to help my countrymen.'

He began crossing his very mixed force over the Indus with three boats — 'a grand river at all seasons, but at this it was mighty and terrible. Each trip of the boats was a little voyage and occupied between two and three hours.' Mulraj had ordered one of his subordinates to raise three thousand soldiers, seize the town of Leia and hold it, but when Edwardes and his force crossed and approached it, this man fled to Multan.

Edwardes had already made a clever move in occupying Leia, a large brick-built, tree-lined city trading in furs, skin and wool with Kabul, for it swarmed with mercenary soldiers looking for service. He enlisted them for the double purpose of holding

Leia and stopping them joining Mulraj. He expected, he said in a letter to Currie at Lahore,

> that you will have sent off our field brigade on the 24th of April, and that it will reach Multan in ten days, but trust that will only be the vanguard of a regular army, for the reduction of Multan will be no child's play... At present I am very much like a Scotch terrier barking at a tiger. If a week only passes over, I shall have got enough men together to hold on. If not, we are in God's hands, and could not be better placed.

Daring and resourceful, Edwardes was aided by a Muslim chief named Faujdar Khan, a Pathan, and a clever soldier, upon whom he had already learned to rely. Faujdar Khan's knowledge of the province of Multan, its people and local resources proved invaluable, while his suave oriental manners softened a capacity for acute criticism. He usually accepted Edwardes's proposals with unconcealed admiration — 'they were all that could be desired; were, in fact, exactly the right thing — *but*' — and he would suggest that there was one slight improvement to be made and just another small defect to be got rid of until, usually, the impetuous plan put forward by Edwardes was torn to pieces and another much more effective one was in its place.

Faujdar Khan knew every soldier on the banks of the Indus and with his aid Edwardes gathered a force of three thousand Pathan and Baluchi mercenaries. Then on 29 April he learned that Mulraj had sent across the Chenab from Multan four thousand men and eight heavy guns to attack him at Leia by 1 May. Of the various courses open to him before the advance of this superior force — such as entrenching himself before Leia, or marching north-east to Munkera, a strong fort thirty-five miles north-east — he prudently chose to recross the

Indus and await the arrival of General Courtlandt's reinforcements.

He marched on 30 April to the east bank of the Indus, about ten miles north of Leia, facing Dera Fateh Khan, and there awaited news of the arrival of Mulraj's heavy guns before actually crossing, meanwhile sending his cavalry under Faujdar Khan to Leia to reconnoitre and cover his retreat. He formed his infantry and guns in a protective crescent and ferried across the river all his baggage and cattle. At dawn the cavalry returned with the news that the enemy were approaching Leia. Leaving his infantry in position, Edwardes next sent his cavalry and guns across and finally finished this smooth withdrawal by taking his infantry over at 8 am just when Mulraj's heavy guns were clattering into Leia.

So doubtful was Edwardes of the loyalty of the Sikhs in his force during this move that he would not trust them to cross either first or last, 'lest in one case they should keep the boats on the right bank, and in the other go over to the enemy on the left; so that I was at last obliged to march every company into a boat of its own, at one sound of the bugle, and cross them all in a body, along with me.'

Edwardes was balanced on a razor's edge of loyalty and treason. He knew that the Sikhs in his force had already sold him to Mulraj and were, therefore, against retreating across the Indus, but his loyal Pathans scared them into obedience. The price was twelve thousand rupees (£1,200) to the Sikh regiment for joining the rebels at Leia, and twelve thousand more if they brought over Edwardes's head with them. But Edwardes's anxieties were somewhat allayed when early next morning General Courtlandt arrived with reinforcements of a twelve hundred strong Muslim regiment and six horse-artillery guns in a fleet of twenty-six boats.

Mulraj now heard a rumour of the advance of troops from Lahore against him and on 7 May ordered his brother, in command of the troops at Leia, to retreat at once and 'to make Multan in two marches.' They retreated so swiftly over those seventy miles that all discipline was lost in their army.

Reacting quickly, Edwardes sent over a small force of one hundred cavalrymen to enter Leia and report back to him. Mulraj's governor fled and they took peaceful possession of the city. Edwardes was about to cross the Indus once more, occupy Leia and advance on Multan itself, when he received orders from Sir Frederick Currie at Lahore to stay on the west bank. He was given a part to play as one of five columns which were to confine the rebellion in a circle of fifty miles diameter. Three of these columns were made up of Sikhs under Sikh commanders, chief of whom was Raja Shere Singh; the fourth was Edwardes, Van Courtlandt and their troops; and the fifth to be those of Bahawal Khan, the Muslim ruler of the province of Bahawalpur, south of the Sutlej. The fortress of Multan itself was to be attacked, in due course, by a force of British troops.

But the plan went awry. The Sikh columns loitered on the road and failed to arrive. Edwardes, and later Bahawal Khan, were left alone to occupy the Lower Dejerat, made up of the two districts of Singurh and Dera Ghazi Khan. Singurh was commanded by the fort of Mungrota, then held by Mulraj's troops, which Edwardes took possession of by guilefully enticing the chief there to quit it, so that it fell easily into his hands.

Edwardes was now about to cross the Indus and advance on Leia, still held by the small body of cavalry he had sent there. But the day before he heard that Mulraj had taken fresh heart at the failure of the Sikh columns to co-operate and, crossing the Chenab with an army of six thousand men and fifteen guns was marching towards Leia and the Indus with the object of destroying Van Courtlandt's small force and isolating that of Edwardes himself, who was then at Dera Futteh Khan. The forces under Edwardes and Van Courtlandt were still much weaker than those of Mulraj. In face of this new threat, Edwardes sent an urgent appeal to Sir Frederick Currie at Lahore, that Bahawal Khan's troops should cross the Sutlej from Bahawalpur and move north towards Multan as a diversion. The one hundred troops he had left in Leia had orders to retire before a superior force without waiting for further orders from him. He received word from them that five hundred men with artillery were within a march of them at Leia. Knowing that his brave fellows at Leia were unlikely to retreat Edwardes sent two hundred swordsmen to back them up.

Mulraj's force opened fire outside Leia with zambureks, across a shallow river. 'Our men, finding this annoying, plunged into the nullah, forded it in the face of the fire and attacked the enemy on the further side,' Edwardes reported. A short struggle followed, ending in the total defeat of the Mulraj rebels, who were pursued for about two miles beyond Leia, losing all their zambureks and twelve men killed.

It was an encouraging minor success but Mulraj, not yet having been attacked by the strong British force he expected, was growing daily in confidence, having at his call six thousand men, fifteen guns and a fleet of boats to transport them across the Indus. Van Courtlandt had six guns and two regiments, one of which was permanently occupied in keeping the other from deserting to the enemy. Edwardes had four guns, fourteen zambureks, and less than two thousand men. 'If therefore, General Courtlandt and I were to unite,' Edwardes wrote to Currie,

> our strength would be little more than half that of the enemy's on the other bank, which the enemy may cross tomorrow by a skilful choice of a ferry. The consequences of a defeat on this frontier would be so extensive and disastrous that, plainly as they stare me in the face, I have deemed the responsibility of not acting on my own judgement greater than that of acting without authority. Supposing that no British force is likely to take the field till after the rains, the only move which can save this frontier, is, in my opinion, the advance of Bahawal Khan's army across the Sutlej, so as to threaten Multan and oblige Mulraj to recall his frontier expeditions. I have, therefore, this evening, addressed a letter to that Prince, stating my position, and recommending him to cross at once…

In a spirit of desperation now, Edwardes joined forces with Van Courtlandt near Mungrota, fifteen miles south of Dera Futteh Khan and there faced the whole of Mulraj's force on the opposite bank. 'Our "iqbal" is once more in the ascendant,' this spirited young man then wrote to Currie. 'If they had not the heart to cross, when General Courtlandt was alone, they are little likely to do so now; and, for the time, I consider our position most materially improved since I last wrote.'

Edwardes's enthusiasm rose even more next day. He received the news that in the south his Beluchi partisans had captured the fortress of Dera Ghazi Khan from Mulraj's allies. This small but significant victory, with that of Leia earlier, caused another few hundred mercenary fighters to join him rather than Mulraj. On 31 May, Currie, faced with the failure of the three Sikh columns to join the operations against Muraj, agreed to Edwardes crossing the Indus again and joining forces with Bahawal Khan's forces, the Daudpatras, or 'Sons of David' as the Bahawalpore race was called. Edwardes was, moreover, given full discretion to act as he thought fit, subject to confining the area of the rebellion.

He was not chafing to cross the Indus and with Bahawal Khan's force drive Mulraj back into Multan. Nothing had been heard of the three Sikh columns who were supposed to have cooperated. 'Would it not be better, therefore,' Edwardes wrote to Currie on 30 May,

> to let Bahawal Khan co-operate with those who will exert themselves at this crisis? General Courtlandt and I are quite prepared to force the passage of the Indus, whenever you give the word; and to unite with the troops of Bahawal Khan. In a few words, my request is, that the task of driving in the rebels be confined to this force, and Bahawal Khan's, leaving us at liberty to adopt our plan of operations. Undoubtedly, there can be no feeling of security for the empire, during the next four months, if the enemy is not confined to the fort at Multan; and I am willing to be responsible for reducing him to that condition, if Bahawal Khan's assistance is put at my disposal.

Edwardes, a lieutenant in his twenties, was asking for *carte blanche* in a war upon the outcome of which the security of British India largely depended.

And on 10 June he received Currie's authorization. He was to confine the area of the rebellion as much as he could and to force Mulraj back into Multan until siege could be laid to it. 'I must leave much to your discretion, to act as you think best, as circumstances may arise,' Currie wrote.

At last, Edwardes noted joyfully in his diary, 'were matters brought to the point I had so long and ardently desired.'

Bahawal Khan had already early in June crossed his force of ten thousand over the Sutlej and had advanced north. On 10 June, having assembled a small fleet of boats, Edwardes safely transported two thousand five hundred of his Pathan troops over the thirteen-miles-wide stretch of the Indus at Dera Ghazi Khan. By the 14th his entire force were across. He marched at once with the vanguard of his force towards the Chenab, intending to cross it at Kineyree and join forces with Bahawal Khan's Daudputras, then fifteen miles south of Shujabad, about thirty miles north. But on the evening of 15 June a spy brought in the information that Mulraj's troops, three miles south of Shujabad, under his brother-in-law, Rung Ram, were marching hot foot with orders to defeat Bahawal Khan's army before the arrival of Edwardes, and in any case before 17 June. Edwardes at once sent orders to Bahawal Khan's commander, through the British agent Peer Ibrahim Khan, to dig trenches and avoid a battle until his arrival, and another letter to Rung Ram, Mulraj's commander, inviting him to come over, as he was aware of his secret feelings of loyalty to the British. At the same time he set every possible man to the task of building bridges across the Chenab strong enough for his guns. But at dawn next day the distant boom of artillery rolled across the river like thunder and Edwardes believed that the unfortunate Daudputras were already under fire. Two hours later it stopped, and soon a messenger reported that it was merely their *feu de joie* to greet the approach of aid.

On the evening of 17 June Peer Ibrahim Khan reported that Rung Ram intended to camp that night at the village of Bukree, within easy marching distance of the ferry where Edwardes's force was to cross. He suggested that the Daudputras, under General Futteh Muhammed, should march at once down to Kineyree, secure the ferry and cover the disembarkation. Peer

Ibrahim Khan, according to Edwardes, was one of those men found only on frontiers 'as the chamois is found only amid snows. On one side of his girdle was a pen, and on the other a sword; and he had a head, a hand and a heart, ready to wield either with vigour.'

Edwardes sent immediate orders for the Daudputras to march the fifteen miles to the ferry at Kineyree 'at whatever hour of the day or night this letter reaches you…' He then packed his small fleet of about thirty boats with a picked force of three thousand infantry and dismounted cavalry, and sent them across under the command of Faujdar Khan in the early hours. He slept until shortly before dawn on the west bank, intending to take over a second division as soon as the fleet came back, but at six o'clock on the 18th there was no fleet to be seen. Commandeering two small ferry boats, and leaving General Courtlandt to bring over the rest of the force as best he could, he embarked on these with his own horse, a few cavalrymen and his personal servants.

A hundred yards from the shore there was a sudden burst of artillery about a mile away. Two tall columns of white smoke rose out of the surrounding jungle. 'Gazing at this unmistakable symbol of the fight below, I could scarcely forbear smiling at the different speculations of my companions in the boat,' Edwardes noted. 'The servants, men of peace, declared and hoped it was only "a salute", fired by the Daudputras in honour of the allies who had joined them; but the horsemen knit their brows, and devoutly cried "Al-lah! Al-lah!" at every shot, with an emphasis like pain on the last syllable. They quite *felt* there was a fight going on.'

Edwardes thought then of his own situation. He had seen but one campaign before and now he was about to take command, in the middle of a battle, of one force whose courage he had never tried, of another which he had never even seen, to oppose a third of uncertain strength, knowing that defeat would extend immeasurably the rebellion he had undertaken to suppress and embarrass gravely the government he was serving. 'Yet, in that great extreme,' he recalled, 'I doubted only for a moment — one of those long moments to which some angel seems to hold a microscope and show millions of things within it. It came and went between the stirrup and the saddle. It brought with it difficulties, dangers, responsibilities, and possible consequences terrible to face; but it left none behind.'

With the smoke and roar of the battlefield as a guide he rode ahead, wondering how to tell friend from foe and how not to ride into the hands of the enemy. By luck he met soon a horseman sent by Faujdar Khan to lead him to the field. He gathered that Rung Ram had marched before dawn for the ferry, had found the approaches to it occupied by the Pathans and the Daudpatras, and had withdrawn to the hills nearby to open gun fire at troops below.

Rung Ram commanded a force of eight to ten thousand horse and foot and ten good guns. Bahawal Khan's Daudpatras, led by General Futteh Muhammed Khan, were eight thousand five hundred horse and foot, eleven almost useless guns and thirty zambureks. Edwardes commanded five thousand Muslim irregulars, horse and foot — only one half of whom had crossed the Indus — plus another fifteen hundred men and ten guns led by General Courtlandt, still on the other side of the river.

It was a strange encounter. When Rung Ram's guns began firing, the Daudpatras had shouted Bahawal Khan's name with one great cry, then rushed forward tumultuously with camels, baggage, artillery, and bullock carts all mixed up with them in a confused mass. The six-pounder shot and shell that lashed them now was so different from the matchlocks of their own border warfare that they wavered, staggered, stopped and finally fell back in ever greater confusion. It was at this moment that Edwardes came upon the scene, a plain covered with low jungle, through which heavily loaded camels were stumbling to the rear out of the range of the guns, while detachments of warriors with hair and beards dyed red with henna were being urged to take up a line of defence.

From among the milling crowd of Asians in brilliant robes and turbans a solitary white man in a red coatee rushed up to Edwardes, mopping his forehead, and sadly exclaiming: 'Oh, Sir, our army is disorganized!' His name was Macpherson, he said, and, asked where his General was, he laughed and pointed to a large peepul-tree, under the shade of which a crowd of officers and chiefs was gathered, while the shot from the enemy's artillery whistled overhead. Edwardes rode among them and over the soldiers' turbans saw a little old man in dirty robes with a black skull-cap on his head sitting under the tree telling the beads of a rosary. Peevishly and helplessly, he was muttering '*Ulhumdoolillah*! *Ulhumdoolillah*!' (God be praised! God be praised!) quite oblivious of the six-pounder shot tearing through the branches above — of his officers begging for orders — or of an efficient army of eight or nine thousand drawn up ready to destroy the troops of which he was the General. 'He had,' Edwardes noted, 'to be shaken by his people before he could comprehend that I had arrived; and as he rose and tottered forward, looking vacantly into my face, I saw that excitement had completed the imbecility of his years, and that I might as well talk to a post.'

Edwardes turned away to Peer Ibrahim Khan and the General's officers, heard from them the main facts of their situation and came out there and then with a plan for holding out.

> Nothing, (he told them bluntly), can be done with an army so disorganized as this, or with guns such as Peer Ibrahim describes yours to be. The enemy has taken up a strong position and will probably prefer being attacked. It is not likely that he will attack us until he thinks we don't mean to attack him. We have therefore got all day before us. I will write to General Courtlandt on the other side of the river to send us over some guns that are better than the enemy's, and not a move must be made till they come. In the meanwhile, occupy yourselves with recovering the order of your force; make the whole lie down in line in the jungle; keep them as much under cover as possible, and let your artillery play away as hard as they can on the enemy's guns. Above all, stand fast, and be patient.

Edwardes received cheerful promises of obedience from the assembled officers and then rode off through the confusion to where his own three thousand men had planted their standards in well chosen ground and were lying down in line between them. He dismounted and asked without much hope if anyone had a pen and paper.

'Sahib!' said a well-known voice. Turning, he saw his *moonshee* (clerk) taking out a Kashmir pen box and some paper from his girdle, as quietly and simply as if he was in the office. He had no weapon and was perfectly calm with the guns booming on all sides and men's heads occasionally flying off before his eyes.

'What are you doing here, Sudda Sookh?' Edwardes asked in surprise. The *moonshee*, says Edwardes, answered, 'My place is with my master! I live by his service; and when he dies, I die!'

Accepting the situation as normal, Edwardes dictated two notes to General Courtlandt on the far side of the river, telling him that the position was critical, but that he believed he could hold out until 3 pm, by which time he must send guns, or they would be overrun. He sent the two notes by two different horsemen with an interval of half an hour between them, and the second reached the General first. It was then 8 am. He had somehow to stave off Mulraj's army for seven hours with no artillery of any use and all but his own two thousand men completely lacking useful firearms and military discipline.

Were he to live seven centuries, Edwardes wrote later, he would never forget those seven hours.

The enemy's guns, probably made by European experts in the Sikh Lahore arsenal, hammered away at the Daudputras and Edwardes's own men. The shell often burst overhead and the Pathans were hit so much more than they had ever before been used to in their own petty warfare, that the survivors were continually leaping up furiously and demanding to charge the guns. 'Look here — and there — and there,' they roared, pointing to men as they were hit. 'Are we to be all killed without a blow? What sort of war do you call this, where there is iron on one side, and only flesh and blood on the other? Lead us on, and let us strike a blow for our lives! If we are to die, let us die, but let us kill somebody first!'

Then the officers crowded round, everyone convinced he was a general — 'If only you would listen to me,' — tugging at his sleeve to interrupt his rebuke to someone else — 'the battle would be yours.' None of them counselled retreat. Every voice was for attack, but only Faujdar Khan and one or two others supported his plan to wait for General Courtlandt's guns before moving. Happily, Edwardes had no doubt or misgivings and patiently strove hour after hour to calm the angry and excited Pathans, promising them that when the moment came he himself would lead them to victory.

So, Edwardes recalled, he waited, with only a bush for shelter under a June sun in the Punjab, a temperature of over a hundred degrees in the shade in which the landscape quivered and danced, and not a drop of water or a breath of air.

After six hours, when there was still no attack, his spirits began to rise. Then the occasional shot from the Daudputra guns stopped altogether and the skull-capped General Futteh Muhammed withdrew his troops without saying a word and began falling back to the river. The enemy saw what was going on, followed up their advantage with cavalry reconnaissance and the white-robed horsemen bore down on Edwardes's line.

Edwardes and his two thousand men faced an enemy with artillery and a four to one superiority. Faujdar Khan had brought their ten zambureks, one-pounder long-barrelled guns, across the Chenab. Edwardes had refused to let these be fired for fear of betraying his position, but he now gave the word and the ragged salvo rent the air and thinned out the reconnoitring yellow-turbaned cavalry, who hastily fell back with the intelligence they had gained.

It was about 3 pm. The enemy turned their whole fire from the fleeing Daudputras to the newly-found Pathans crouching in the low jungle on the left. The shot tore through their ranks and ploughed up the dusty ground. If they had been hard to control before, they were now almost beyond it. When the guns ceased and squadrons of enemy cavalrymen whirling tulwars galloped across the plain towards them Edwardes played his last desperate card to stave off a battle.

Imploring his Pathan infantry to lie still a little longer, he ordered Faujdar Khan and all the chiefs and officers with horses to mount, form up into a compact body, charge the enemy cavalry and try to drive them back upon their own infantry. 'Put off the fight,' he quietly told Faujdar Khan, 'or none of us will leave this field alive.'

Edwardes says that with set teeth he watched those brave men, his best officers, mount, and wondered how many of them would come back.

Drawing their swords, they dashed out of the jungle and hurled themselves into the ranks of the enemy's horse, who after a brief but savage exchange of blows turned round and fled, pursued to within a few hundred yards of their advancing lines. These halted to receive them, and though they quickly rallied and advanced again, the charge bought time.

Edwardes decided that all that was left to him now — since neither he nor his men would contemplate surrender — was a charge of the whole line, even though annihilation of all was likely. Then at that decisive moment, he heard the shrilling bugle-note of General Courtlandt's artillery in the distance.

But Mulraj's army of several thousand horse and foot were advancing. There was literally not a second to lose if the guns were not to be too late. Edwardes sent a hundred orderlies running to the rear to help them forward, then ordered his officers to their posts — 'every one to his own standard and his own men,' and, he continued (the only manoeuvre he ever tried to instil into that impatient horde):

> Let the infantry stand up, and get into as good a line as the jungle will allow; let none advance until I give the word; but when the word is given, the duty of every chief is this, to keep the standard of his own retainers in a line with the standards right and left of him. Break the line and you will be beaten; keep it, and you are sure of victory.

Away they scattered and up sprang their shouting men. Banners were seized and shaken in the wind, ranks closed, swords grasped, the slow matches of the ancient matchlocks blown and, between friend and foe, the long line waved back and forth. Still in the shelter of the jungle, the Pathans could not see their enemy, but brave as they were they must have longed powerfully for evidence that the guns would soon reach their lines.

They heard first the tramp and clatter of Mulraj's advancing host; seconds later the crack of whips, the clank of chains and the rattling of wheels of Courtlandt's artillery. Then came the foremost gun, a gleaming brass six-pounder. Amid shouts of welcome it galloped to the front. 'Oh, the thankfulness of that moment!' Edwardes wrote. 'The relief, the weight removed, the elastic bound of the heart's main-spring into its place after being pressed down for seven protracted hours of waiting for a reinforcement that might never come! Now all is clear. Our chance is nearly as good as theirs, and who asks more?'

Five more guns rattled in behind panting teams of horses, and after them, with clattering cartridge boxes, came the first ranks of two regiments of General Courtlandt's Muslim troops. So near was the enemy now that their triumphant shouts and the excited neighing of their horses could be heard. Edwardes led the artillery through the jungle to the cultivated plain. There he first saw the enemy's line. Directly in front, Mulraj's regular troops were running forward over fields of sugar cane, and between two low brick houses and walls ten horse artillery guns galloped forward.

'Action front!' came the command. Instantly Van Courtlandt's guns were unlimbered, swung round, loaded and fired at the enemy artillery. Surprise was complete, for the enemy believed that Edwardes's men had no artillery now that the Daudputras had gone. Their whole line at once threw themselves down among the long stalks of the sugar cane while officers rode up and down urging them on and the brass six-pounders banged away. 'The gunners were getting warm,' Edwardes noted calmly.

> 'Grape! Grape!' now shouted the Commandant. 'It's close enough for grape!' And the enemy thought so too, for the next round rushed over our heads like a flight of eagles. And there for the first time and the last in my short experience of war, did I see hostile artillery firing grape into each other… General Courtlandt's artillery were well trained and steady, and their aim was true. Two guns were quickly silenced, and the rest seemed slackening and firing wide. A happy charge might carry all. I gave the order to Soobhan Khan's regiment to attack, and away they went, Soobhan Khan himself, a stout heavy soldier, leading them on, and leaping over bushes like a boy. Before this regiment could reach the battery an incident characteristic of irregular troops occurred. A cluster of half a dozen horsemen dashed out from the trees behind me, and passing the regiment threw themselves on the enemy's guns. Their leader received a ball full in his face, and fell over the cannon's mouth… The regiment followed, and carried at the point of the bayonet the only gun which awaited their assault. Another gun lay dismounted on the ground.

At the same time, Courtlandt's guns lashed with grapeshot the enemy infantry hiding in the sugar cane. Hearing their own artillery retire, and having already suffered heavily, they ran back through the high crops, falling left and right, and reformed in a ragged line when they again reached their guns.

Edwardes now led his whole force forward over the contested ground, the men cheering as they passed the captured guns. Now the enemy rallied, and the artillery on both sides re-opened at short range with a crash of ear-splitting detonations in the hot air.

Edwardes saw that the time had at last come to let loose his wild Pathan infantry. One more volley from the battery and they rushed into the billowing black gunpowder smoke with a yell that had been gathering fury all day. When the smoke cleared, the artillerymen of two more of the enemy guns were dying desperately at their posts, and isolated skirmishers in brilliant uniforms slashed at each other with tulwars as the whole enemy line retreated.

Van Courtlandt's brass guns again galloped up, unlimbered and with stabs of orange flame sent grape tearing into the enemy. They tried to rally and reply, but with a roar of frenzied triumph the Pathans were upon them, hacking and thrusting. Another and another gun was abandoned. Rung Ram, the enemy commander, had long since turned tail and lumbered off to Multan on his elephant. The Daudputras now returned, burning to retrieve their reputation and poured in fresh numbers upon the enemy flanks. 'Thus,' noted Edwardes,

> without a General, without order, and without hope, the rebels were driven back upon Noonar; and having placed its sheltering heights between them and their pursuers for a moment, they threw aside shame and arms, and fled, without once halting, to Multan. Few indeed would have reached that place, had I had any cavalry to carry on the pursuit; and as it was, the cavalry of Nuwab Bahawal Khan maintained it for some miles, and brought in two more guns at nightfall.

And so on 18 June 1848 ended the battle of Kineyree, at half-past 4 pm having begun what to Edwardes seemed a lifetime ago, but was a little after 7 am. He captured eight of the enemy's ten guns and counted more than five hundred of their men dead on the field, some three hundred of his own men being wounded or killed.

Edwardes had his men spend the next three days burying the dead and dressing as best they could their comrades' wounds, for there was no British doctor to amputate smashed limbs, extract ball and sew up great sabre gashes. He visited them in the tents captured from the enemy 'and my arrival was followed by a general removal of bandages, which, for all our sakes, might better have been kept on,' he noted.

> Nourung Khan would allow nobody to dress his wounds till I came, when he requested, as a particular favour, that I would 'put my finger into the hole in his head!' On inspection however, I thought his brain had been laid open enough, and coaxed him to go to sleep. On the 19th General Courtlandt brought over a native doctor from his regular regiments, who had some English instruction; one or two Hukeems, skilled in the medicine of the country, came into camp from the neighbouring districts; and these were all the means we had of patching up our hospital for the onward march.

Significantly, the Lahore government forces had taken no part in these operations against the troops of Mulraj. Edwardes alone had achieved this with his newly-raised Pathan mercenaries, helped out by Van Courtlandt's artillery. The way to Multan was now open and in high spirits Edwardes prepared to march against it, a youthful conqueror with the world at his feet.

14: Edwardes

Edwardes let his men rest for three days while the rearguard and horde of camp followers with food, tents and equipment crossed the Chenab. On 22 June he began the thirty mile march to Shujabad, on the road to Multan. Here his spies told him that Mulraj had feverishly begun strengthening the defences of Multan fort and was now pinning his faith on the Sikh troops who had joined him, distrusting his Muslim Pathans. Already, the fighting was looking like a religious war, for Edwardes's troops were predominantly Muslim.

He now commanded a force of eighteen thousand men and thirty guns, made up of his own and General Van Courtlandt's forces with the Daudputras, in command of whom General Futteh Muhammed Khan and his rosary had been replaced by an efficient twenty-six-years-old British officer, Lieutenant Edward Lake. Flushed with success, Edwardes wanted to start the siege of Multan at once, before Mulraj could strengthen it, or more hostile Sikhs arrive to reinforce him. 'We are enough of us in all conscience, and desire nothing better than to be honoured with the commission you designed for a British army,' he wrote to Currie, at Lahore, on 22 June.

> All we require are a few heavy guns, a mortar battery, as many sappers and miners as you can spare, and Major Napier to plan our operations. That brave and able officer is, I believe, at Lahore; and the guns and mortars are, doubtless, ere this at Ferozepore, and only require to be put into boats, and floated down to Bahawalpur. Lieutenant Lake... is also an engineer, so we should not want for science, and every other material is

at hand for bringing to a rapid and honourable conclusion the rebellion at Multan.

Edwardes's proposal — to dispense altogether with British troops for his enterprise — was based also on his knowledge that Lord Gough opposed marching such an army north through the burning sun to Multan at this season; experience had taught Gough that cholera, dysentery and heat stroke would kill or incapacitate too many of them.

Sir Frederick Currie, the Lahore Resident, possessed however the delegated power to make his own military plans in an emergency. He consulted Major Napier, who said that the operations could be undertaken with every chance of success — a single brigade with guns and twenty mortars and howitzers would be enough. Currie was half inclined to agree, but the guns could not be sent without British artillerymen and Currie at first refused to take the responsibility of overruling the commander-in-chief, as well as the Governor-General, who had backed Gough on this point. He sent the request Edwardes had made on to Lord Dalhousie and Lord Gough, who had now to decide whether Edwardes's plan — to attack Multan at once — was likely enough to succeed to make a change in their own plans justifiable.

Gough, who could be prudent as well as dashing and impetuous, came down firmly against it. 'I cannot see anything in the altered position of affairs which could justify me in taking upon myself the siege of Multan at the present moment,' he wrote to Currie on 1 July 1848.

> On the contrary, the success of Lieutenant Edwardes renders it less necessary in my opinion to risk the lives of British soldiers at this season. Mulraj is shut up in his Fort — all, I take it that was contemplated by the movement of the

> Bhawalpore force, and that under Lieutenant Edwardes... The Force now proposed by Major Napier and apparently assented to by you, I consider quite inadequate... I have always understood from you that both the Sikh army and the Sikh population are disaffected and should be guarded against. I take it that these objections to weakening our Force at Lahore and on the Frontier still exist. The movement of a siege train under these contingencies, with so insufficient an escort as a Brigade, would in my mind be a most hazardous measure.

Lord Gough believed that the best Edwardes could do was merely to drive Mulraj back and not risk a general Sikh rising all over the Punjab by laying siege. He told the Governor-General so, adding that recent experience held a grave warning, for in 1826 Bhurtpore had held out for a month against twenty-five thousand men, mostly British troops with no less than one hundred and twelve heavy guns.

So Lieutenant Edwardes's high ambition was checked, though if pressed forward at once it could well have succeeded and prevented much loss of life later. But events were now to prompt Sir Frederick Currie to embark soon on a very different plan.

On 26 June Edwardes marched his army on towards Multan, seized the fort at Secunderabad, halfway there, and learned from spies that Mulraj had deployed his forces in a strong position on the banks of a canal which crossed the Multan road, and had destroyed the bridge. Edwardes therefore decided not to try to force a passage, but to cross further up, by a ferry, then turn and advance on Multan itself. A Sikh holy man and astrologer had promised Mulraj that the stars foretold that he would be invincible on 1 July; Mulraj therefore wished above all to fight on that morning.

On 30 June Edwardes was joined by the Sikh division of Imam-ud-din, one of the three columns which should have arrived at the outset of the campaign. Early on 1 July Edwardes marched his army to a plain some four miles south-west of Multan. Mulraj, learning of their move, quickly ordered his own army back from its former position to three miles in front of the city walls. Edwardes could hardly believe that Mulraj intended to force a battle at mid-day and thought he would simply prevent the British moving too close to the city; but the holy astrologer had foretold victory and for Mulraj this fact outweighed all others.

Scouts rode to Edwardes with the news that the rebel force were close at hand, advancing in line.

Edwardes's force beat to arms, formed line and advanced to meet them, with the Daudputras commanded by Lieutenant Lake on the right, General Courtlandt's two regiments and guns in the centre; Edwardes and his Pathans on the left centre, flanked by his Pathan cavalry, and on the far left Sheikh Imam-ud-din's Sikh troops. These Edwardes determined to watch closely, being uncertain of their loyalty.

Lieutenant Lake began the action by hurrying ahead to some old ruins on high ground with his Daudputras, planting his guns there and from this commanding position throwing a heavy fire on to the enemy's left. Soon the rest of the line overtook them and battle became general, all Edwardes's thirty guns firing upon the enemy, who were strongly placed in mud villages and date-tree groves. The air and ground thudded and shook; the infantry of both sides sheltered in ditches. Mulraj's guns were one after the other silenced. The action then became a series of hand-to-hand struggles in which the rebels were driven back from village to village and grove to grove. Mulraj watched behind the lines on his elephant, until a well-aimed cannon ball tore the silver howdah away and threw him violently to the ground. Despite the promises of his astrologer, this knocked all taste for war out of him for the day. Scrambling to his feet and mounting his horse, he rode desperately for the fortress, taking with him all the guns but two, which stayed to cover his retreat. 'A rush of the whole infantry and cavalry followed,' Edwardes noted, 'and the broken enemy fled in irrecoverable disorder.'

Halting his men almost under the walls of Multan, Edwardes then ordered the *retire* and the bugles shrilled and echoed over the plain. Wounded and killed, he lost two hundred and eighty-one men, while, apart from severe losses, many of the enemy were found later to have deserted and fled to their homes. Baffled, but not disheartened, Mulraj was said to have again consulted the stars. The next day too was said to be auspicious. He invited his soldiers to go again with him to fight and a number paraded, but when they heard the throbbing kettle-drums of Edwardes's cavalry, out reconnoitring, they ran back into the walled city.

Mulraj was now more or less confined to Multan, where the rebellion had started — solely owing to Edwardes's inspiration and guidance. (He was later promoted to the rank of major, appointed CB and awarded a gold medal by the Court of Directors of the East India Company.)

More than ever, after this success, he longed to attack Multan, even without siege guns. 'Up to the end of July, I am quite sure that Lieutenant Lake's force and my own could have taken the city... with the utmost facility,' he wrote in his journal.

> It was surrounded by nothing stronger than a venerable brick wall, and the rebel army was dispirited by its losses at Kineyree and Suddoosam. On this point neither Lieutenant

Lake nor myself, nor General Courtlandt (who was an older and therefore steadier soldier than either of us), had ever any doubt. The only difficulty we dreaded was the disorganization of our own army when it had once captured a city whose riches excited such cupidity, and whose rabid hostility so provoked revenge.

The news of the victory at Suddoosam reached Sir Frederick Currie at Lahore on 10 July. He now decided, despite Gough's and the Governor-General's wishes, to use his discretionary powers — not to carry out Edwardes's plan for a non-British army with suitable guns; but to launch a plan of his own, using the British troops at Lahore. General Whish was to 'take immediate measures for the dispatch of a siege-train with its establishment and a competent escort and force, for the reduction of the fort of Multan'. Reporting this important decision to Lord Dalhousie, he said he had taken the responsibility of doing so despite the remarks in the commander-in-chief's letter, 'from a conviction of its political necessity, and military practicability, at the present moment.' Dalhousie, angry and alarmed by Currie's hasty action, replied sharply: 'Since you have considered it necessary, in exercise of the powers conferred upon you, to assume this responsibility, and, in pursuance of it, have issued publicly the orders for carrying out your resolution into effect, the Government, being anxious to maintain your authority, do not withhold their confirmation of the orders you have issued.'

Currie was directed to 'proceed with vigour to carry out at all hazards the policy which you have resolved upon'. Gough, infuriated as he was by Currie's move, undertaken at the very worst time of the year, wrote tersely: 'The troops having been ordered to move upon your responsibility, I have only to assure you that every facility and aid in my power shall be freely given, so as to carry out to a successful result the operations against Multan.'

Currie justified overriding the wishes of both the Governor-General and the commander-in-chief by brandishing the spectre of 'a widespread combination and conspiracy throughout the Sikh army, to which many influential persons were parties... whereby a large portion of the Lahore garrison might be detached, which was to be the signal for a more generous insurrection for a final struggle, with a view to the re-establishment of Khalsa independence, and the expulsion of the English.' In another letter, dated 26 July, he wrote alarmingly: 'Every day brings new revelations, some of which seem to elucidate and some to mystify the whole affair.

> It is now quite certain that all last autumn and cold weather plans were forming, combinations being made, and various interests were being enlisted with a view to a grand struggle for our expulsion from the Punjab and all the territories west of Delhi... The plan was communicated to the Sikh army and to all the chiefs of the Punjab. The great hopes of the conspirators lay in the promised aid from Cabool and Cashmere. Whether either Dost Mahommed or Gulab Singh intended to keep their promises I cannot tell...

This fustian hardly satisfied a Governor-General as careful and precise as Lord Dalhousie. Nor was Dalhousie impressed by Currie's promises of mild weather. 'The consideration which mainly determined... the Government to assent to European troops not being moved till October,' Dalhousie wrote in a private letter to Currie on 4 August,

> was the imminent danger to the health and efficiency if not the very existence of such a body of troops, if moved at this season of the year and in that district... I have sought in vain

thro' the despatches for facts to show that these dangers are visionary and exaggerated. I cannot find them. I cannot even find a statement that the original representations made to Government were erroneous. Either those representations were correct or they were not. If they were correct, and *justified* a refusal to move troops before October, it is impossible for the Govt., to express an opinion that they should move now. If they were not correct, then all we can do is to regret that movement should have been so long deferred and be thankful that we have escaped the difficulties which not moving was thought likely to produce. I heartily pray God that the results may shew that the dangers of climate *have* been exaggerated and the European troops may not suffer on this service so fearfully as was anticipated.

How badly the troops did suffer, despite all Currie's optimism and Dalhousie's prayers, events were to show. But meantime, in private letters, Dalhousie challenged Currie to lay before the Government proofs of the Sikh conspiracy to expel the British, which, he said, had caused him to send the troops. 'Not a day is to be lost,' he wrote to Currie in another private letter dated 19 August 1848,

if measures of the magnitude which will become necessary are to be undertaken after the capture of Multan at the commencement of the cold weather. I must beg you, therefore, to transmit to this Government, *as soon as practicable for you to do so* after receiving this letter, a confidential report setting forth the facts or the documents on which you rely for proof of these vitally important denunciations. We cannot act on general impressions, on the supposed notoriety of such intrigues having been in progress. Prove the complicity of the Durbar, the chiefs, the officials and the army in those intrigues by reasonable evidence and I am prepared to act. I am well aware how much of your time must be occupied. But no occupation connected with the Punjab can exceed in importance an early submission to the Government of these charges and their proofs...

It was a stern demand. Currie did his best to prove his case, naming one or two chiefs who were, as always, plotting against the central government at Lahore, but he failed to satisfy the Governor-General, who a few weeks later on 16 September wrote that he was 'sorry to find that the strong statement you made of a general conspiracy does not rest on tangible proofs. I shall be very glad, however, to receive the report of the reasons which satisfied you of its existence early in the day.'

They never did materialize, but Currie had won. A British force much larger than he had first intended was on its way to Multan. Lord Gough, having been obliged to allow it, had to make it strong enough for the task. It was, therefore, increased by two brigades of infantry (each containing a British regiment), one Indian cavalry brigade, two troops of horse artillery and a siege train with foot artillery. Gough now believed that this force[12] combined with that of Edwardes, would be strong enough to overrun Multan without much difficulty, but he was to be disappointed.

It is worth notice that in the same way as Major George Broadfoot's actions largely brought about the First Sikh War, Sir Frederick Currie, by fanning the flames of a local rising,

---

[12] 1st Infantry Brigade (Brigadier Hervey) 10th Foot, 8th and 52nd Bengal Native Infantry. 2nd Cavalry Brigade (Brigadier Markham) 32nd Foot, 49th, 51st and 72nd Bengal Native Infantry. Cavalry Brigade (Brigadier Salter) 7th and 11th Irregular Cavalry, 11th Light Cavalry. Two troops of heavy Artillery: four companies of Foot Artillery: two companies of Bengal Sappers: three companies of Pioneers.

made the second one almost a certainty. Broadfoot and Currie were both appointed by Lord Hardinge.

Led by General Whish, the Multan expeditionary troops started at the end of July on the journey Dalhousie so much feared. They went part of the way in flat-bottomed boats up the river Ravi, then disembarking and marching for a week through hostile and arid territory. A young soldier from Leicester, Corporal John Ryder, aged nineteen, who three years earlier had enlisted in the 32nd Foot in search of adventure, took part in that grim journey, with typhoid, malaria and cholera raging among his comrades. Ryder, who learned to read and write in the army, described his daily experiences in a journal remarkable both for its simplicity and concreteness. 'On Sunday, the 20th, we struck camp at one o'clock,' he noted, while suffering from a bout of malaria.

> I got worse, and it was as much as I could do to keep up; and I never should have done, had I not swallowed five drams of grog, about a pint in a bottle... We marched a long way that day... One man fell dead. I arrived in camp about nine o'clock. We lay in the tents panting for breath... The heat was above one hundred degrees, and the water was very bad, on account of the wells not being used, which caused the water to be stagnant and black, and smell very offensively, so that we were obliged to stop our noses while we drank. I began to get very low-spirited and given to fret; when, all at once, I thought it would not do; so I rallied my feelings and walked about, and began to think I should soon feel better. This and the medicine the doctor administered soon began to revive me, and I felt a great deal better. The morning was hotter and closer than I ever felt it before, and the wind was awful — fairly piercing our flesh. We had not marched more than two miles upon the road before men began to fall dead in the ranks... Our line of march was strewed with dead, dying, and

sick… Our doctors and apothecaries were all engaged in bleeding; but as the night was very dark, they could not find the vein, and they cut gashes across the arm any way, so as to get blood. The cry for water was past all describing; the mouth and tongue were swollen and parched, the eyes looked wild and ghastly, and ready to start out of the head. How little do the people of England know the hardships of a poor soldier in India. Men lay upon the sand by dozens, gasping for breath… All the skill of a physician could not restore them. I saw our old colonel looking at them, and he exclaimed, 'Oh, my poor men, my fine regiment — what shall I do?' I felt very sorry for him, for he was in great trouble. As one man died he was carried out, and another came in his place. They were well and dead in an hour. The number who fell sick in the day was 175, and 14 dead. The heat in the tents was 130 degrees. All our dead were buried in a hole together, at sunset; and long before morning the wild beasts had torn them up and dragged them to pieces… We made a junction with the army at Multan on the morning of the 25th of August, at about seven o'clock…

General Whish, in command there, decided to await the arrival of his big siege guns before attacking. But during the two months since Edwardes had defeated Mulraj and driven him back into Multan, the opportunity that Edwardes had longed to take had been lost and the entire military situation had moved in favour of the rebel governor. Aided by citizens zealously defending their homeland, Mulraj had lined the walls with an enormous rampart, reinforced his army with more unemployed Sikhs from the Khalsa, and seemingly, had made a secret alliance with the *panchayats* of a Sikh force under Raja Shere Singh — one of the three columns which had failed to arrive earlier to aid Edwardes and was now camped behind him.

Worse still at this time, in focusing Sikh feelings against the English, notwithstanding the better government of Henry Lawrence and his assistants, was the exile of Maharani Jindan. In August 1847, she had at Lawrence's command, been removed from Lahore — 'dragged out by her hair' she alleged — and sent to the fort of Sheikhapur without her young son because she was suspected of conspiring to assassinate members of the Regency Council. It was a mere suspicion, but she was refused either enquiry or trial to clear herself. One of her impassioned letters[13] of protest to Lawrence is worth quoting in full:

> You have been very cruel to me. You have snatched my son from me. For ten months I kept him in my womb. Then I brought him up with great difficulty. Without any fault you have separated my son from me. You could have kept me in prison. You could have dismissed my men. You could have turned out my maid servants. You could have treated me in any other way you liked. But you should not have separated my son from me.
>
> In the name of the God you worship, and in the name of the king whose salt you eat, restore my son to me. I cannot bear the pain of this separation. Instead of this you put me to death.
>
> My son is very young. He is incapable of doing anything. I have left the kingdom. I have no need of kingdom. For God's sake, pay attention to my appeals. At this time I have no one to look to. I raise no objections. I will accept what you say. There is no one with my son. He has no sister, no brother. He has no uncle, senior or junior. His father he has lost. To whose care had he been entrusted? Without any fault why is so much cruelty being done to me...?

---

[13] Translated by Dr Ganda Singh.

> A great deal (of injustice) has been done to me. A great deal of injustice has been done to my son also. You have accepted what other people have said. Put an end to it now. Too much has been done.

But her appeals fell on deaf ears. 'There is no proof, though there is some ground for suspicion, that the Maharani was the instigator of the late violence in Multan,' Currie told the Governor-General on 16 May 1848.

> It is certain that, at this moment, the eyes of Dewan Mulaj, of the whole Sikh army and military population, are directed to the Maharani as the rallying point of their rebellion... Her removal from the Punjab is called for by justice and policy, and there is no time for us to hesitate about doing what may appear necessary to punish state offenders, whatever may be their rank and station, and to vindicate the honour and position of the British Government.

There was 'no proof', but, the Maharani was the 'rallying point'; she was therefore a 'state offender', and must be exiled. Currie had his harsh way and on 15 May the Maharani, without her boy son, Maharajah Dhulip Singh, was forcibly taken out of the Punjab and exiled to Benares. A wave of anger rose among the Sikhs at the news. Currie had succeeded in making her something near to a martyr, for though during the first war and after, many of the Khalsa would willingly have murdered her, barely a month after her exile, they were ready to die for her. 'The Khalsa soldiery,' Currie admitted to the Government on 25 May, 'on hearing of the removal of the maharani were much disturbed: they said that she was the mother of all the Khalsa, and that as she was gone, and the young Dalip Singh in our hands, they had no longer anyone to fight for and uphold...'

Soldiers now flocked in to Mulraj's standard from all over the Sikh country; daily the defences of the city and fort gained in strength. But nevertheless, Mulraj himself, having been thrice beaten, was, as Edwardes said, in a letter to Currie, 'at his wits' end.'

> Sometimes he talks of a night attack, and sits up all night in a Hindu temple near the bridge, cased in his chain armour from head to foot, like Don Quixote watching for his knighthood in the cathedral aisle. But nothing comes of it. Another time he talks of cutting the canal, but is restrained from doing so by fear of destroying the fort ditch. One day he fortifies the city, another day he fortifies the fort. Today he tells all his soldiers to leave him because he has got no money to pay them; and tomorrow keeps up their spirits by assuring them that when iron fails he will fire silver on the besiegers...

Shere Singh was still loyal, but his Sikhs were aching to go over to Mulraj. A plot to poison Shere Singh, after which his troops were to desert to Mulraj, came to light. The ringleader was a Sikh yeoman named Shoojan Singh and papers implicating him were found under his horse's saddle. He was tried and found guilty by Shere Singh, the proceedings being sent to Currie for confirmation and sentence. Currie summoned the Sikh government to give judgement and they sentenced Shoojan to be 'hung by the neck or shot as may be determined by the Rajah and Sirdars commanding the Sikh force, with the concurrence of Lieutenant Edwardes.' Shoojan Singh was blown from the mouth of a gun before the assembled troops he had persuaded to desert and the leader he had tried to poison.

Meantime, the Sikhs in the north, especially in the beautiful district of Hazara, near Kashmir, where Sirdar Chuttur Singh, father of Shere Singh, was Governor, were breaking into open revolt. Main direct cause again, was the exile of the Maharani. Chuttur Singh's daughter was engaged to her son, Dhulip Singh; the father hoped that his daughter would become maharani and thus, his family, the Attariwalas, become the most powerful in the Punjab. Chuttur Singh, formerly a supporter of the British, believed after the Maharani's exile, that they had no intention of restoring the kingdom to Dhulip Singh when he came of age. He therefore began to press his son, Shere Singh, to go over to Mulraj and join in rebellion against the British.

Chuttur Singh and Mulraj were far from allies, though they believed in mutual aid. One was a Sikh and the other a Muslim; one was fighting for freedom and the other for his life. Chuttur Singh had raised the standard of the Khalsa, called for the unity and independence of the Punjab. Mulraj wished to tear away the province of Multan from the Punjab, gained at great cost by Ranjit Singh. Thus their alliance could not have lasted beyond victory over the English, but first they had a common object in defeat of the common enemy.

Chuttur Singh now called on his followers in the name of the Khalsa to rise against the British and march on Lahore. Major George Lawrence, at Attock, was the Resident's personal representative in the north; Major James Abbott, in Hazara, his assistant. Abbott learned at the beginning of August that Chuttur Singh's Sikh followers and a brigade of his regular troops at Haripur, had assembled ready to march on Lahore. He at once called on all the Muslim irregular troops to block the roads leading out of Haripur.

An American soldier of fortune, Colonel Canora, commanded a troop of Chuttur Singh's horse artillery. The Sirdar ordered him to bring his guns out to a strong fort nearby, which he had made his headquarters. Colonel Canora, who had long foreseen his likely involvement in a rebellion, considered that his duty to the Maharajah Dhulip Singh was to support the British administrators of the Punjab during the monarch's minority and not to join the boy's likely father-in-law in trying to expel them. He therefore refused, unless the order was signed by Major Abbott, and informed Abbott accordingly.

Chuttur Singh sent his most confidential officials to persuade the American to yield. If he still refused, two companies of infantry with them were to take the guns by force. Canora would not yield. Chuttur Singh's infantry advanced. Canora loaded with grapeshot and ordered his gunners to fire. They refused, saying that they were the servants of Sirdar Chuttur Singh. When his sergeant also wouldn't fire, Canora drew his sword, cut him down and seized the match to put to the vent. Shot in the act of firing at the approaching infantry, he staggered to his feet and cut down a Sikh infantry officer, but his throat was slashed from behind by a sabre cut and he fell dead. 'Colonel Canora's last act,' Abbott wrote in a moment of emotion, 'was unsurpassed by anything in recorded history. He stood alone against the whole Sikh army…'

Chuttur Singh rewarded the men who had killed Canora, declared himself in rebellion against the British and sent envoys throughout the Punjab to raise all the Sikhs. In particular he invited Gulab Singh in Kashmir and Dost Mahommed, ruler of Afghanistan, to join him. His motive in involving Dost Mahommed was to obtain Muslim support, and thus influence the local Muslim population. He knew that the Afghan ruler longed for revenge, the British having deposed him eight years earlier, waged war throughout the country, put a puppet on the throne, then, when their policy ended in a disastrous retreat, allowed him to return. Chuttur Singh, therefore, counted it worthwhile to offer the return of Peshawur to Afghanistan as a bribe, provided the Dost expelled the British. But Major George Lawrence's influence was strong enough in Peshawur to keep his troops loyal. John Nicholson, another of the able young political agents in the north, occupied the fort of Attock and the pass between Hazara and Rawalpindi with Muslim irregular troops and armed peasantry. Chuttur Singh's efforts to advance south to Lahore were thus checked.

This then was the situation on 4 September 1848, when General Whish's siege guns arrived from Ferozepore. Optimistically he issued a proclamation, calling upon the inhabitants and the garrison of Multan to surrender within twenty-four hours of the firing of a royal salute at sunrise next day in honour both of Her Most Gracious Majesty the Queen of England, and her ally, His Highness Maharajah Duleep Singh. Otherwise, Whish said, he would commence hostilities on a scale that must insure early destruction to the rebel traitor and his followers, 'who having begun their resistance to lawful authority with a most cowardly act of treachery and murder, seek to uphold their unrighteous cause by an appeal to religion, which everyone must know to be sheer hypocrisy.'

The proclamation was read to a glittering parade of British troops, and a royal salute fired from the heavy guns, faintly echoed by Shere Singh's artillery. 'But the only notice taken of it,' says Major Siddons, in his *Journal of the Siege of Multan*, 'was a shot from the citadel, which was fired just as the reading was concluded, and must have been fired at an immense elevation, as it pitched into the earth just behind General Whish and his staff...'

Thus answered, Whish had to find a way of fulfilling his threat of 'early destruction to the rebel traitor'.

15: Dalhousie

Camped within sight of Multan's great fortress, General Whish seems to have been overwhelmed by the problem of how to take it with his inadequate forces. He pondered for some days without success. Finally, in desperation, he called his staff officers to a conference on 4 September 1848 to hear any ideas they might have. Major Napier, chief engineer, put forward the two obvious ones, from which Whish himself had already in his own mind recoiled in alarm. The first was the do-or-die storming and taking the town in a day by a so-called surprise attack from the south, where the enemy held trenches outside the walls. The second was to move round to the north and attack painstakingly by regular approaches. After much argument, Whish turned down the first, because it would cost too many lives and could just as easily fail as succeed; and the second, both because Mulraj would interpret the necessary change of front as a defeat; and because the new position would imperil his own lines of communication with Ferozepore, Bahawalpur and the south-east.

The conference seemed then to run out of steam, and one can see Whish looking anxiously round the circle of battle-tried, bewhiskered senior officers for ideas that none possessed, on how to crush 'those Sikh rascals'. Finally, more in desperation than hope, he turned to the youngest officer present, Lieutenant Edward Lake, one of the engineers. Lake at once suggested digging a forward trench a mile long and placing heavy guns in it to cover the advance of infantry, who would gradually drive the enemy from the outside gardens and houses. The gunners would then establish a forward battery position there, from which they could bombard and shatter the town wall so that the infantry could storm it. Whish and his staff accepted this plan with an eagerness that bespoke bewilderment in the face of the stern task ahead, and at dawn next day the trench was traced out and begun. 'Thus the base of operations has been laid down, and I trust that all will now go on prosperously to a happy issue,' commented Lieutenant Edwardes, seemingly rather unsure and still smarting at being refused the chance of finishing the job himself earlier.

It is worth remembering in passing, that the army was then still a seniority service, and at the age when officers usually became colonels and majors, not one in fifty could stand the strain of Indian campaigning. 'They became,' says Lieutenant Hodson (later the famous Hodson of Hodson's Horse) 'after a fortnight's campaign, a burden to themselves, an annoyance to those under them and a terror to everyone but the enemy.' Hodson wrote of an infantry brigadier 'who could not see his regiment when I led his horse by the bridle until its nose touched the bayonets; even then, he said faintly, "Pray, which way are the men facing, Mr Hodson?"'

Edwardes, who had already shown the 'old men' in India how to deal with a rebellion successfully and at small cost, was another who suffered under their clumsy and hesitant rule. And better informed than anyone else on the true state of things at Multan, he was far from happy about the outcome. 'Mulraj,' he wrote at this time in his journal, 'has, I think, gained more by recruits from the Manjha, during the past fortnight, than he has lost by desertions... No preventive measures which the civil authorities may devise can be effective, if opposed by the whole native executive of the country.'

The first siege of Multan was opened at daylight on 7 September 1848 by working parties of one thousand men from the Irregular camp and one thousand six hundred from the British camp, eight hundred being men from the 10th and 32nd Foot, who took the night duty, when it was cooler. The city was surrounded by strong high walls defended by bastioned towers, ringed by trenches and redoubts; the fort, built on an ancient mound, towered above the city, and commanded everything around it. Outside the walls were numerous houses and gardens, all defended by infantrymen. Several of these outposts the British had seized; the enemy tried to regain them, but were driven back. 'Our sepoys lost a man or two,' noted Corporal Ryder. 'We relieved them at night and began to erect a battery for four long eighteen-pounders, and we ran another battery to the right. We got the guns into play, which did fine execution.' But two small fortified villages ahead, ringed by trenches, held up the work. A night attack against them was driven off with several killed and wounded. Thus repulsing the British, naturally added much to the confidence of Mulraj and his troops, and during the next two days they extended the trenches around the house outside the walls which the attackers had failed to clear.

The two armies were throwing up defences within a few hundred yards of each other, the Sikhs were disputing every inch of ground and the British were faced by stalemate. On 12 September, Whish ordered a strong attack to clear the front once and for all, so that Lake's plan could go ahead. Ryder, of the 32nd Foot, who was in the thick of the fighting throughout, gives an infantryman's vivid account of it. 'We advanced in columns of companies, and as we got clear, we were exposed to the whole of the enemy's fire,' he noted.

We formed the line to the left, which then brought us facing the villages. Our orders were to wait for the signal gun to fire. The musket balls came shower after shower, cutting the grass off close to our heads, or burying themselves in the sand close by, whilst the cannon shot was ploughing the earth up all round. I lay as close to the ground as I could, expecting every moment that a ball would sink into my head.

We had not lain more than five minutes, when my company (*the light company*) was ordered to advance in extended order, to cover the line as it advanced and to engage the enemy's skirmishers. As soon as the bugle sounded the skirmish, we sprang to our feet and extended. I felt the wind of several balls, and quite expected one to go through me every moment. The signal gun from the battery fired, and our bugles sounded the 'advance' for the whole line. Every man sprang to his feet and the line advanced in good order. We had not gone more than two hundred yards before we came to a nullah, or dry watercourse... about five yards across and twelve feet deep... Down it we went, my company leading the way, one pushing another up the opposite side, while others were getting the scaling ladders to cross with. One man was killed in crossing.

Now the poor infantry were left to themselves, for our cavalry and artillery could not cross. As we rose on the bank the enemy's fire became dreadful, and several of our men began to fall; but forward we rushed, and then the fight became general. We scaled the walls of the village after some desperate fighting in getting over. Several of our men were killed at the top. Our colonel was among the foremost, cutting his way sword in hand. My comrade was shot dead beside me. The ball went through his breast. His name was William Hanson, from a village against Bingham in Nottinghamshire.

We soon made ourselves masters of the first village, but the encounter was terrible, as the enemy were no cowards, nor were they afraid of cold steel. Our dear old colonel was killed here, but not till he had done good work. This village in our possession, forward we rushed, driving the enemy before us to the next, when we commenced a fierce attack. Our foes were not idle, for they as fiercely returned it.

This village, like the other, was walled all round, having a large temple in it, which was well manned, and they did us some damage before we got possession. I was among the foremost at the door, and we had something to do before we could force it open, which we did with the butt end of our muskets, while others scaled the walls on the opposite side. They defended every inch of the ground most bravely; but we drove them from house to house, leaving numbers of dead behind them. I believe not one escaped — they did not ask for quarter and none was given.

The fighting here was awful. What with the rolls of musketry, the clash of arms, and the shrieks, cries and groans of the wounded and dying, all was a dreadful scene of confusion. In one place might be seen men in their last death-struggle, grappling each other by the throat, while others were engaged hand to hand with the deadly weapon, the bayonet, thrusting it through each other's bodies, or blowing out each other's brains — blood, brains, skin, skulls and flesh, being all dashed in our faces!

All fear had left me now. I never thought of dying myself, although numbers were falling all around. By ten o'clock the village was fully in our possession... The field all round presented the most awful sight of the wreck of the action. Broken arms lay strewed all round, with dead men and horses. The village was a heap of ruins.

General Whish lost thirty-nine men and eight horses killed, two hundred and sixteen men and thirteen horses wounded in this attack and that of the ninth. Five hundred enemy troops were counted on the ground on the 12th alone. But the attack succeeded, the British besieging army gaining between eight and nine hundred yards, which the next day and night were spent in securing. General Courtlandt now pointed out to the British engineers and gunners a possible battery position within six hundred yards of one of the wall towers. A day's battering with the 18-pounders and the howitzers, and the city would be ready to fall to infantry assault. Victory was in sight.

Then came an event which snatched it away and changed the whole military situation.

On 14 September, Raja Shere Singh, who had taken little part in these initial operations against Multan, deserted the British, marched his three thousand four hundred infantry, nine hundred cavalry and seven guns to the north of the city and joined forces with Mulraj. It was a setback grave enough in itself, but a portent of even graver things, for it was realized, with the departure of these Sikh forces of the Lahore government, that the British were now probably no longer simply at war with a provincial governor, but with the entire Khalsa, supported by all the ex-soldiers in a struggle for independence.

Whish was thus faced with a new situation. With Shere Singh's force, Mulraj now had a total of fifteen thousand men and seventy or eighty guns. Whish had forty-four guns and twenty thousand men, of whom less than two thousand were British, thirteen thousand were the Pathans, Daudputras and a few Sikhs, all commanded by Edwardes; and the remainder were Bengal Native Infantry. Military science at this time held that a besieging army should be at least three times as many as the besieged. Accordingly, Whish's force was below strength even with Shere Singh's force; and alone it was far too small.

The General conferred with his staff and all agreed that the siege could not be continued without reinforcement.

Whish therefore prepared to withdraw a few miles to the scene of Edwardes's victory at Saddoosam, from whence he could ensure his communications with Lahore and Ferozepore. 'On Saturday, the 16th at four o'clock am, everything was ready to move off,' noted Corporal Ryder regretfully:

> All the men were ordered to leave the outposts as still as possible, and to join us when all was reported ready. We commenced our retreat, not knowing where we were going to, leaving a number of shells behind, as some of our camels had died, and some had been captured by the enemy... The morning was fine, and the stars twinkled brightly. All was as still as death as we were waiting for the words 'quick march' to be given. It was an awful moment of time! God knows what each mind was thinking of! — for the very word 'retreat', to a British army, is like poison: it is hurtful to the soldier's mind. *Retreat!* We think of it with disdain. The people of England would read in the papers that the army at Multan were compelled to give up the siege and retreat. I believe there was not a man there but would not have returned and died fighting, rather than leave with the word *retreat!* In a few minutes the words 'quick march' were given, and the whole moved off.

Thus, the first siege of Multan came to an inglorious end.

A few days after moving back, Whish occupied a stronger position nearby on top of a range of sand-hills, but short of water and five miles from the river Chenab. Here, in this uncomfortable spot, he hoped to hold his ground until the Governor-General and the commander-in-chief organized the forces needful for the Punjab War, or Second Sikh War, which seemed inevitable.

It became so in fact a few days later. Shere Singh burnt his boats by issuing a manifesto accusing the English of oppression, tyranny, undue violence against the people and the Maharani — calling on Sikh, Muslim and Hindu to join the camp of the Khalsa under Raja Shere Singh and Dewan Mulraj in a religious war. Shere Singh thus made himself generalissimo of the resurgent Sikhs. The die was cast. As the news spread, troops would flock to his standard and the British would seize the occasion to invade, first, on the pretext of protecting the Lahore Government, secondly, despite their treaty obligations, to overthrow it when their army was ready.

On the Multan front, Edwardes realized the likely effect of Shere Singh's manifesto upon the loyalties of General Courtlandt's Lahore Government troops. Already they were asking each other for whom, or what, they were fighting. Was it a war between the Sikhs and the British, and by helping the British defeat the Sikhs would they not be throwing themselves out of work?

Realizing that there was a real danger of Courtlandt's three regiments and seventeen guns going over to Mulraj as well — which would be a disaster — Edwardes gave them a formal promise that all soldiers who stayed loyal and fought against the rebels would be taken on as regular soldiers for life of the government of India. Lord Dalhousie ratified this promise, which Edwardes took the responsibility of giving, and thus the loyalty of these troops seemed effectively bought.

The resourceful Edwardes now exploited Mulraj's suspicion of his new ally Shere Singh, so as to try to neutralize his increase in strength. Mulraj, he learned, had refused to let the Raja and his troops enter the city, prudently forcing them to stay in a large garden on the north side. Edwardes employed a spy named Bhumboo, who, he knew, sold the news of his camp in return for the news which he brought about Mulraj. Edwardes did not object, so long as he was well informed about the movements of the rebels. Hurriedly one day, he sent for Bhumboo, and ordering everyone else out of his tent, said to him, with an air of mystery: 'I want you to take this little bit of paper to Raja Shere Singh. If you deliver it to him safely, without letting another human being see it, I will make a man of you; but if you let it fall into the hands of Mulraj, I'll slit your nose as sure as your name is Bhumboo! Now go, and here are twenty rupees for you.'

Bhumboo swore solemnly that Mulraj should never get even a smell of the matter, and of course, took the note straight to him. 'There,' he is alleged to have said to Mulraj, 'if there is not something in that, there is not a nose on my face, and Edwardes has not said that he'll cut it off.'

Mulraj opened the little scrap of paper, smoothing its many creases, and, according to another spy, turning yellow as he read: 'My dear Rajah, What you say about falling into the net has pleased me much. In fact, it is the best joke I have met with for some time. I expected no less from your discretion and management. I must mention to you I have been obliged, for the sake of appearances, to issue a proclamation calling you a traitor, which, among friends, I trust will be excused. Let me know how you get on.'

Mulraj called a cabinet council to consider this apparent trick to obtain possession of Multan that Shere Singh was playing upon him. A few of the councillors detected that it was a clever scheme to incriminate the Raja, and so divide Mulraj from him, but the majority believed that it reflected the true state of affairs. Shere Singh was sent for and the letter laid before him. Livid with anger, he denied the imputed treachery and cursed Edwardes roundly, but, in short, Mulraj's suspicions were confirmed, and the Raja offered to march away north to his father, Chuttur Singh, in Hazara, if Mulraj would lend him enough money to pay his troops. This was done, and at dawn on 9 October Shere Singh marched. General Whish intended to pursue him, with a small force of nine hundred cavalry and eight guns, and only an assurance from Edwardes that so small a force would end in disaster stopped him.

The march north was, says Edwardes, 'marked by plundered villages, fined merchants, murdered priests and defiled mosques of the Muslim country through which he passed.' Thus, he provoked more than half of the Punjab people to oppose the Sikh struggle for independence. But strategically his move was sound. It turned the compass of the impending conflict up to the northwest, the hostile Sikh country, whose rear was supported by Dost Mahommed and his Afghans, soon to pour down to seize the coveted Peshawur region. And it would lengthen the lines of communication of any invading British force, with Multan an ever-threatening outpost in the west.

The Sikh freedom struggle — for such it was — now spread across the Punjab. On 23 October 1848 the Lahore government troops at Peshawur rebelled and attacked the Residency with shot, shrapnel and grape. Major George Lawrence escaped and rode south over the mountains to Kohat, where Sultan Muhammed Khan, the Afghan Governor, promised protection, but later handed him over to the Sikhs. The troops in the mountainous Bunnoo district, south of Kohat, between the Indus and Afghanistan, rose on 21 October, shot dead the Muslim Governor and a British soldier of fortune, Colonel John Holmes, and crossing the Indus, marched west to combine with Shere Singh's army near Ramnuggur. The exiled former vizier, Lal Singh, secretly entered the Punjab, raised a force in the west and marched from Wazirabad to within nine miles of Gujranwala, only sixty miles north of Lahore. Two other chiefs, Arjan Singh and Jowahir Singh, moved their troops to the same area. Thousands of Khalsa soldiers, demobilized under the Treaty of Lahore, flocked to Shere Singh's standard at Ramnuggur, bustling round the armourers for swords to be sharpened, parading joyfully for re-enlistment.

The Khalsa was making ready a great blow to free the Punjab from the British yoke. It moved Lord Dalhousie to a belligerent outburst. 'The result of this mad movement to the people and dynasty of the Sikhs can be no longer matter of discussion or of doubt,' he wrote to Currie at Lahore, as the reports of the rebellion streamed into Calcutta, and he made ready to leave next day for the advanced British base of Ferozepore.

> To the last I have sought honestly to give effect to a policy which I approved. I have sought to avoid war or conquest. I now seek no longer to pursue a policy which I am satisfied can never be successful, and I have resolved to prosecute with vigour a war, which on the part of the Government of India I had hoped to have avoided. The Sikhs have forced me, for this Govt., again to draw the sword, and I beg you to interpret my words in their clearest and most emphatic meaning when I say that being compelled to it I *have* drawn the sword, and have thrown away the scabbard…

The policy of persuading a nation of unemployed ex-soldiers that the government of the boy maharajah at Lahore was their government and a worthwhile one, had collapsed like a tumbledown house about the heads of all inside. Partly, it was inevitable; but British bungling was responsible, too, especially the cruel treatment of the Maharani, whose unabashed sexual virility had caused a mixture of hatred and alarm among the reticent and puritanical English. Was war the ultimate in punishment they could apply, a powerful, but unconscious urge to destroy the offender and her race? Dalhousie had potent reasons for not making war, both financial, and those affecting his own health, which he doubted would stand the strain of additional military anxieties. 'I was broken in health when I started and had no business to come. I landed in Calcutta almost a cripple,' he wrote a year later, and during his entire eight years of office he was rarely well and free from pain. A visionary despot who saw a future India with a network of roads, post offices, railways, canals and telegraphs, public works, colleges, institutes and a modern administration, this Scottish nobleman with the luminous expression, thick dark hair and side-whiskers, this dilettante with the implacable will, at first grudged every penny which went to the military budget. Lord Hardinge, as we know, had on the grounds of economy sold or discharged nearly all the army's transport animals and reduced its strength by nearly fifteen thousand men, thus balancing the books before he left for England and hurrah. Lord Gough told Dalhousie that he would need a force of twenty-four thousand men and seventy-eight guns, reinforced by another five thousand troops and more guns from Sind to invade the Punjab. He had only some ten thousand men and forty-eight guns, including the column at Lahore. He had asked for the reengagement at once of the thousands of drilled soldiers 'ready to take service wherever they may get it'.

Grudgingly, Dalhousie gave Gough discretionary powers to move troops towards the Punjab frontier, but would not, at first, on the supposed grounds of economy, let him re-engage the discharged sepoys, lay in provisions or buy transport animals. The reason is clear. When, earlier in July, Currie's move to send reinforcements to Multan forced his hand, he revealed in a letter to him dated 25 July 1848 the extraordinary financial pressure he was under.

> Where I am to find the money to pay for this, God above only knows. The revenue is about £1,400,000 behind the expenditure. The loan produces *nothing*, nothing is advanced on bills here. Nothing can be raised on bills by the Court at home; and for the *2nd* time since I assumed this Govt. 6 months ago, the Directors have sent for a remittance of half a million of money in bullion! These are grave considerations.

A million in bullion for the East India Company directors and shareholders in six months had emptied the treasury for the time being. So Dalhousie could not authorize earlier the twenty-four thousand strong army of the Punjab requested by Gough on 11 May. But at the end of September, when the danger had become greater and the financial pressure a little less, Dalhousie at last agreed to re-enlist workless soldiers up to this new war establishment. Gough at once ordered an invading force to cross the Sutlej under Brigadier-General Charles Cureton, a first-class cavalryman with the most impressive side-whiskers in India, a formidable soldier who had risen from the ranks. On 2 November, Cureton was ordered to advance his force[14] north to the fort of Gujranwala, sixty miles north of Lahore and thirty south-east of Ramnuggur, to counter the advance of Lal Singh to Wazirabad, twenty-five miles to the north.

---

[14] HM's 3rd Dragoons and 14th Light Dragoons; 8th Bengal Native Cavalry, 12th Irregular Cavalry, three troops of Horse Artillery, one light field battery; Brigadier Godby's infantry brigade — 2nd European Regiment, 31st Native Infantry, 70th Native Infantry; Brigadier Eckford's brigade — 29th Foot, 31st and 56th Native Infantry.

Gough arrived in Ferozepore on 6 November 1848, to be greeted by the news that the Sikh troops under Major George Lawrence at Peshawur — six disciplined Sikh infantry regiments, about a thousand cavalry and thirty guns — had all gone over to the rebels; and that Shere Singh had sent an advanced body of his troops across the Chenab to Ramnuggur, keeping the main force on the north side until the right moment came to cross. He was not dismayed. He had already decided his plan of campaign — to entice all the rebels across the river to Ramnuggur, beat them and if possible capture their guns. Then, by a rapid flank movement to Wazirabad, cross the Chenab there to get in the rear of Shere Singh and prevent his crossing the Jehlum to join his father Chuttur Singh and the Bannu troops and the Sikh garrison at Peshawur. Thus, at the beginning of the campaign, he believed he could defeat the Sikhs piecemeal.

The sepoys re-enlisted, the Indian regiments reached fighting strength, some supplies became available, and Gough sent Brigadier-General Colin Campbell with two battalions of Bengal Native Infantry to support Cureton and take command of the initial invading force.

Meantime, Dalhousie, preparing war against the Lahore state, with whom he still had treaty obligations, had placed Currie, alone with a small force in the capital, in a dangerous situation. He had informed him on 3 October 1848 that the State of Lahore was 'considered to be directly at war with the British Government.' Currie was naturally bewildered; the treaty was still in force. He wrote to Gough at Ferozepore a few days later, asking him to come and strengthen the British position in the capital quickly, pointing out that he and the garrison were still there by treaty to aid, advise and protect the Lahore State. 'We cannot continue to protect and maintain a state which we declare to be at war with us,' he protested. 'And we are not in that commanding or strong position here which would enable us to take the steps such a declaration would render necessary.'

He had received scant help on this delicate question from Dalhousie. 'The intentions of the Government, whatever they may be, should not be declared before the preparations of the C-in-C are completed,' Dalhousie decreed on 3 November. 'In the interval the position of yourself and your assistants must necessarily remain anomalous, as indeed it has long been.'

Gough crossed the Sutlej with General Sir Walter Gilbert's division and hurried with it up to Lahore, still without information as to whether he would be fighting for or against the Lahore State, for Dalhousie had not thought it worthwhile taking even his commander-in-chief into his confidence. 'I do not know,' Gough complained on 15 November, at Lahore, 'whether we are at peace or war, or who it is we are fighting for.' And in this mental no-man's-land Dalhousie was pleased to keep him until two days later, when with Generals Thackwell's and Gilbert's divisions he had actually crossed the river Ravi to join Campbell and Cureton. Only then was he told, and could he tell his generals, that they were fighting to defeat the Lahore Government, not to defend it against Shere Singh and the rebel Khalsa, even though the Government had made no warlike move against the British.

Dalhousie had in fact already decided to annexe the Punjab and some weeks earlier had emphatically told the British Government so. 'There remains no longer any alternative for the British Government. The die is cast,' he wrote to Sir John Hobhouse, President of the Board of Control, on 5 October 1848.

> Regard for the preservation of our own power... and the necessity of maintaining its reputation in order to secure our

position in India, compel us to declare war, and to prosecute it to the entire submission of the Sikh Dynasty and the absolute subjection of the whole people. There will be no peace for India, no security for our frontier — no release from anxiety — no guarantee for the tranquillity and improvement of our own provinces till it shall have been done. The Government of India, after anxious and grave deliberation, have without hesitation resolved, that the Punjab can no longer be allowed to exist as a Power and must be destroyed... The extension of our limits by the subjection of the Punjab is no longer a question of expediency, but a matter of necessity and self-preservation...

Finally, as a sop to the Directors of the Company: 'The defection of so many chiefs will be followed by extensive confiscation; and the available revenue of the Punjab greatly increased.'

But some sections of public opinion and the press in England were by no means satisfied. The question of the future was raised. Did England intend to seize and hold the territory of the Sikh boy maharajah, the nobles and the people, when the Khalsa was defeated? In a letter to Hobhouse on 20 November 1848 Dalhousie sharply brushed these objections aside. 'Our acts require no explanation. The army has, with others, taken up arms with the published and proclaimed intention of expelling us from the Punjab. Their attempt must be at once resisted and defeated and when that is accomplished it will be soon enough to proclaim our intentions as to future policy.' As to the Maharajah Dhulip Singh, Dalhousie branded the boy as 'a child notoriously surreptitious — a brat begotten of a Bhistie — and no more the child of old Ranjit than Queen Victoria'.

But even Dalhousie, blind with the passion of empire building, was a little touched by the continued loyalty of the

Sikh Government and some of the Khalsa. 'It is odd,' he confided in this same letter, 'that at the moment a Sikh regiment furnishes my guard and a Sikh is walking sentry at my door.'

He had not yet told the Lahore Government, the Regency Council, that he was at war with them, instead of merely suppressing a rebellion, nor would he do so until the job was done. 'The subsequent destiny of the Sikh dynasty and Sikh nation will be pronounced upon when the objects above mentioned of ("defeating, disarming and crushing all forces" of the Sikhs) are accomplished,' he informed Currie early in November. Whether or not they realized what was in the wind, the Regency Council fulfilled loyally those of their treaty obligations that they could.

Dalhousie was here guilty of something near to fraud. Pretending he was still bound by treaty to protect the Lahore state, he had secretly advised his officials and generals that British India was at war with it, but that there would be no declaration of policy until the Sikh armed forces were defeated. By such means, added to violence, was the independent Punjab to be added to the Indian Empire.

Gough meanwhile had marched northward, learning *en route* that the rebel Bannu troops from the north-west had joined Shere Singh's main force on the north side of the Chenab, opposite Ramnuggur; and that Chuttur Singh's force of rebels, though still blocked up in the north, was likely soon to join as well Nicholson, in the fort of Attock, nearing the end of his power to resist the Sikh leader's pressure. Gough's chances of defeating the Sikh forces piecemeal had thus receded. He joined Campbell and Cureton on 21 November at the small village of Noewallah, about ten miles from the walled town of Ramnuggur. His army[15] was now complete, except for the heavy elephant-drawn 24-pounders — still on the road — and the besieging force outside Multan under General Whish. It consisted of about twelve thousand five hundred infantry, one-fourth British, and three thousand five hundred cavalry.

On the night of the 21st Gough made plans to drive the Sikh outposts back across the river that very night and if possible to capture their guns. It was a bold and ambitious move, but badly thought-out. The price would be high.

---

[15] Cavalry Division (Brigadier Cureton): 1st Brigade, Brigadier Michael White. British, 3rd and 14th Light Dragoons; Indian, 5th and 8th Light Cavalry. 2nd Brigade, Brigadier Pope: British, 9th Lancers; Indian, 1st and 6th Light Cavalry, 3rd Brigade, Brigadier Salter: 11th Light Cavalry and 7th and 11th Irregular Cavalry. INFANTRY: 1st Division, General Whish, at Multan. 2nd Division, Major-General Sir Walter Gilbert. 1st Brigade, Brigadier Mountain: British, 29th Foot; Indian, 30th and 56th Native Infantry. 2nd Brigade, Brigadier Godby: British, 2nd European Light Infantry; Indian, 31st and 70th Native Infantry. 3rd Division, Sir Joseph Thackwell. 1st Brigade, Brigadier Pennicuick: British, 24th or 2nd Warwickshire Foot; Indian, 25th and 45th Native Infantry. 2nd Brigade, Brigadier Hoggan: British, 61st Foot; Indian, 36th and 6th Native Infantry. 3rd Brigade, Brigadier Penny; 15th, 20th and 69th Native Infantry. ARTILLERY: Brigadier Tennant. Horse Artillery, Brigadier Brooke, Colonels Bird and Grant; six troops, or batteries, commanded respectively by Lieut-Colonel Lane, and Majors Christie, Huish, Warner, Duncan and Fordyce. Foot Artillery, Brigadier Hathwaite. 3 Field Batteries, Major Dawes, and Captains Kinleside and Austin. 2 Heavy Batteries, Major Horsford: commanding Majors Shakespear and Ludlow. (Gough's Army of the Punjab contained three British and seven Indian cavalry regiments, besides Hearsey's Irregulars, with four British and eleven Indian infantry regiments.)

16: Failure

By nature, Gough was a fighting Irishman, so filled with courage and confidence that he imparted it to whatever army he commanded. But sometimes these qualities made him reckless and impetuous, which in the field led to tactical mistakes that only the wild bravery of officers and men could correct. On the field of battle, in a state of intense excitement, his plans of attack, his ideas of strategy, the use of the various arms, all fought against a furious determination in him to get at the 'inimy' at all costs and gain an immediate triumph. And sometimes this thirst for combat overcame reason.

Such was the action at Ramnuggur.

Gough ordered Brigadier Colin Campbell with an infantry brigade, the cavalry division, three batteries of horse artillery and one Light Field Battery under Brigadier-General Cureton to move forward on the night of 21 November and drive Shere Singh's outposts back across the river so that he could occupy this strong position himself.

Lord Gough joined this force at 3 am vanishing — according to some of those present — without telling his personal staff where he was going. At sunrise the Quarter-Master General of the Army, Lieutenant-Colonel Garden, rushed from tent to tent looking for him, finally getting the truth from the chaplain, the Reverend Whiting, whom Gough had taken into his confidence.

Day dawned. Gough and this small force reached Ramnuggur, behind its strong brick walls, and from the high mound on which it stood two miles from the river, he saw that most of Shere Singh's force had already crossed to the far, or north bank of the Chenab, but that large parties of cavalry, the rearguard, were still waiting on the south side. Four or five hundred yards wide, the Chenab had shrunk at this time of year to a much narrower channel, exposing several dry watercourses and sandy flats, in the middle of which, high and dry except for some stagnant pools, was a green island. The far bank was high, the sand in the dried-up bed below deep and soft, a most unsuitable place for horses and guns.

Gough climbed to the flat roof of a spacious building, once a summer palace of Ranjit Singh, from which he could see the Sikh gunners arranged beside their weapons on the far bank and the rearguard riding off to the ford. Perhaps this should have been enough, bearing in mind that his main army was behind him, without a leader, and without orders — that the force with him was a small one; and that Shere Singh might have set a trap for *him*. Perhaps he would have been better advised to let the retreating Sikhs — a mere couple of thousand — retreat, and be content that he had gained his objective without firing a shot.

But the 'inimy' were escaping before he could hit them. This fact seems to have infuriated Gough. Thirsting for battle, he ordered two troops of horse artillery, under Majors Lane and Warner, with five regiments of cavalry, to drive them away with 'as much punishment as possible' and 'to advance as rapidly as the nature of the ground would admit, and to punish the enemy in crossing the river.'

The horse artillery dashed forward, unlimbered, lashed the retreating Sikhs with grapeshot, limbered up, pressed on again into the deep sand on the very banks of the river and opened fire again. But here shot and shell from the Sikh heavy guns on the high opposite bank hit them hard, and Sikh cavalry rode across to help their comrades. Brigadier Michael White let these enemy cavalry reach the flat ground, then charged with the 3rd Light Dragoons, driving them back, but avoiding the deep sand, by the river bed. The Sikhs, seeing him withdraw, came forward again, yet Brigadier White prudently refused to be enticed into the sandy bed, under the fire of the Sikh artillery.

But Majors Lane and Warner were not so wise. They now struggled to bring their guns out of the deep sand there and beyond the range of the enemy guns on the far bank. But one of them had got stuck in the sand — nothing could move it and orders were given to abandon. 'The men of Lane's troop obeyed these orders with the greatest reluctance,' observed Captain E. J. Thackwell, aide-de-camp to General Thackwell.

> But the Sikh fire was taking effect, and there was the probability of the reconnaissance being converted into a bloody battle. To cover the retreat of our own artillery, a squadron of the 3rd King's Own Light Dragoons, under the command of Captain Ouvry, was ordered to charge a large body of the enemy near the island. This squadron swept the sandy plain with such extraordinary rapidity... that though the enemy opened fire on them from six pieces, posted on the opposite bank of the river, they suffered little loss.

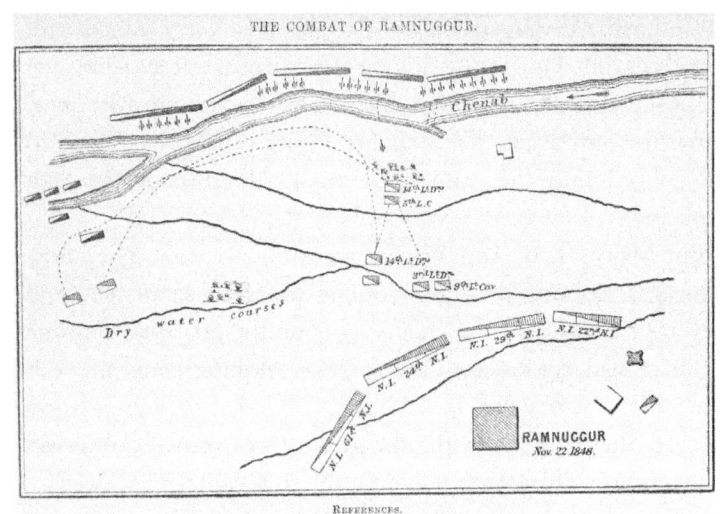

The Combat at Ramnuggur

Despite this no doubt speedy charge, the Sikh infantry refused to budge and when the Dragoons withdrew without having accomplished anything, the Sikhs advanced again to capture and remove the abandoned gun. Gough, now having heard of the situation, left his vantage point and rode forward to where Brigadier Cureton was standing, to take personal command. At this moment, some Sikh light cavalry had ridden across and were now threatening the British flank. Lieutenant-Colonel William Havelock, commanding the 14th Light Dragoons, rode up and asked if he might charge and disperse them. Cureton — and Gough — agreed, and Havelock, intensely excited, led his dragoons in a thundering charge — but, unfortunately, in the wrong direction, straight against some Sikh reserve cavalry in the river-bed. Having dispersed them, Havelock began to charge along the whole face of the Sikh batteries on the opposite side, a most foolhardy move. Here, everything happened at once. The horses floundered about in the deep sand until they were exhausted, while the Sikh infantry, disciplined and in good order, advanced to the kill.

Seeing the danger, Brigadier Cureton, who had been watching the clash with Gough, became frightened of what might happen, and with a grunted, 'This isn't the way to use cavalry!' rode off with a small escort to try to warn Havelock. He was shot through the heart and fell from his horse before he had ridden a short distance. Captain Holmes, who dismounted to pick him up, was badly wounded in the lungs. Gough, alarmed, had before this sent Major Tucker, one of his staff, after Havelock with a similar warning. 'But,' said Gough,

> He went at such a pace that Major Tucker could not overtake him... leaving the body of cavalry he was supposed to be about to attack about halfway between us and where he was. These men, finding themselves free, moved to attack the reserve, a squadron of the 5th Light Cavalry... Seeing the 5th hesitate, I naturally was anxious that the 19th reserve should charge.

The 14th scattered the advancing Sikh horsemen. But Havelock, hero of the Peninsula campaign, was last seen in the thick of the enemy, says Thackwell, who was there, 'his left arm half-severed from his body, and dealing frantic blows with his sword...' His mutilated corpse was found some days later.

Havelock and his 14th Light Dragoons had galloped into the trap the wily Shere Singh had set for them. 'Why Havelock charged where he did no human being can now tell,' Gough uncomprehendingly wrote to his son.

> I myself believe he considered the Guns at this side of the river, and was determined to try to take them. I knew the greater portion were on the other side, because I actually went

within 200 yards of the river, making my staff stay behind, not to draw the Enemy's fire upon me — or on them... I am sure Cureton was as much surprised as I was to have seen the career of the 14th, and it must have puzzled him to guess what object was aimed at.

Thus, the action accomplished nothing, for the mere advance of the British troops had given Gough his objective — the retirement of the Sikhs to the north bank. Twenty-six men were killed or missing and fifty-nine wounded, including the valuable Havelock and the irreplaceable Cureton — 'the best cavalry officer we have seen in India,' said Sir Henry Durand.

By acts of heroism officers and men had tried to retrieve a badly thought-out action. Captain Gall seized a Sikh standard, but his left hand was nearly severed from his arm... Captain Fitzgerald, in a charge to drive away enemy cavalry, received a fatal wound on the back of the head — the Sikh trooper let him pass, then turning his nimble horse, dealt a lightning blow. A cannon ball struck and shattered Colonel Alexander's sword arm as he rallied the 5th Light Cavalry. He fell from his horse and as swordsmen rushed in to cut him up, Sergeant-Major Mallet stepped forward, held them off until troopers came to his rescue. But heroism could do little to influence the course of the action. The British retired, leaving to the Sikhs the gun which the waiting infantry could have covered during the day and removed when night fell.

Gough appointed General Thackwell to command the cavalry division in place of the fallen Cureton, and Brigadier-General Campbell the 3rd Infantry Division in place of Thackwell. The army camped on the plain outside Ramnuggur, awaiting the coming of the heavy elephant-drawn guns. They rattled into camp on 30 November and Gough called a council of war in his magnificent glass-windowed tent. Here, it was decided to cross the Chenab at one of three ferries and to turn the Sikh position by a flank attack on their left. General Thackwell was given command of the attacking column — seven thousand men with thirty-two guns.

Gough directed him to march at 1 am on 1 December and to cross the Chenab either at the ford of Runneekhan, or Wazirabad, which was twenty miles distant, and to march without delay to attack the Sikhs in their trenches facing Ramnuggur. Absolute secrecy and silence were vital, but the camp followers with pots and pans, and the hundreds of bellowing camels raised a din that echoed for miles around and must have alerted the Sikhs. Brigadier-General Campbell and his infantry then became lost in the twenty or thirty square miles maze that was the camp, a mass of infantry stumbling hither and thither in the dark for three hours before finding their way to the rendezvous point three hours late.

Unless he could be sure of marching his troops to the left of the enemy's flank opposite Ramnuggur by 1 pm on 1 December, Thackwell was to wait another day before attacking. 'Night work is to be avoided at all times; if, therefore, you cannot bring all your troops fresh and with ample daylight before them, it is better that the attack should be deferred one day,' Gough wrote.

Just as well, for this small army had to march over rough, broken ground and through heavy sand for most of the way and arrived near the fords, several miles away, not until 11 am the next day. A force of Sikh infantry was then found to be holding the ford of Runneekhan as well as the Chak Ali Sher further up, in positions from which the British guns would find it hard to drive them out. General Thackwell gave orders to march on and cross at Wazirabad, sending on an advance party of Pathans under Captain John Nicholson. The leading troops arrived there at 5 pm exhausted after eighteen hours marching under arms with only meagre haversack rations of a little bread.

The energetic Nicholson had meanwhile commandeered seventeen boats, staked out two fords in the confused waters and sent his Pathans across to hold the other bank against enemy attacks. Three streams, none deeper than four feet, made up the river here, and over them the 24th Foot, two Indian battalions and two guns were at once ferried to establish a footing on the other side. A regiment of irregular cavalry splashed through in the saddle; a brigade of infantry waded, lost its way and spent a bitterly cold night in wet clothes on a sandbank. 'It was now a very dark night,' wrote Captain Lawrence Archer, who was there.

> In the mazes of small channels and pools of water, which chequered the loose sands, many a regiment lost its way, while the increasing darkness added to the general confusion, and the knowledge of abounding quicksands produced a sense of insecurity. It is hard to say what might not have befallen the force, had the enemy only taken the trouble to guard this ford, or to form an ambushcade. The boats were, however, capacious, and the transportation of a portion of the guns was rapidly effected, in reliance on the assurance of the Pathans, that there was no appearance of the enemy on the farther bank.

By noon on 2 December the whole force had crossed the river, and at 2 pm after each sepoy had cooked his individual midday meal, had begun its march down in order of battle, Thackwell having first sent back under escort his heavy cannon with a letter to Gough announcing that he was safely over. Twelve miles were marched through sugar-cane and turnip fields without a sign of the enemy and Thackwell halted his troops for the night at the mud village of Daurawala. Here a fast camel loped in bringing a messenger with a letter from Gough asking Thackwell to attack the left of the Sikh position facing Ramnuggur early next day, 3 December, adding that he hoped to make an attack from his side. He had made a secret agreement with the Sikh boatmen moored beneath the batteries for their boats. 'I shall make,' Gough wrote, 'as great a fuss as possible here today, by a cannonade, to keep their guns here, and... I hope to throw a body to co-operate with your left. Do not hurry your men; bring them and your guns well up in hand, and we are sure of success.'

It was a vain boast. Thackwell marched at 6 am expecting to launch his attack on the Sikh position by 11 am. But when he had gone about five miles he received another letter from Gough, telling him not to move his force on to the attack till reinforced from Ramnuggur by a brigade of infantry and cavalry, which would join him by crossing at the intermediate ford of Ghurriki-Pattan.

The letter may well have saved Thackwell's small force. Forced to change his plan, he now moved up near to three villages of solid mud houses, almost on a line with the ford. To hold the ford for Gough's reinforcements, he sent a battalion of sepoys and some Indian cavalry. Captain Nicholson's Pathans meanwhile went ahead on a patrol to find the Sikh positions. The troops then piled arms and fell out to eat a frugal breakfast of stale bread or a few scraps of meat, or to sleep in the warm sunshine. Soon, Nicholson sent in reports of Sikh cavalry and gun batteries ahead. Captain Archer heard at that moment a peculiar sound above — 'and on looking up, a shell was discovered bursting in mid-air, between the British line and the villages in front... After this came round-shot.'

No one, it seems, expected a Sikh attack then. Captain Thackwell, lying on the grass enjoying a biscuit and a glass of brandy-and-water that Sunday morning, asked a brigadier seated under a tree eating his breakfast, whether he thought an action likely before evening. The brigadier shook his head and in between mouthfuls said mournfully that the Sabbath should not be 'so grievously violated'. At that moment to their mutual surprise, a cannon ball tore up the earth between them. 'The shots rapidly increased,' and, Thackwell noted, 'no doubt could any longer exist that it was the enemy who were showering on us such rough tokens of their attention.'

First impression, it seems, was that these shots came from British guns on the other side of the Chenab, firing none too accurately on the Sikh positions at Ramnuggur, for Gough, both then and the day before, had pounded them. 'The Chief (Gough) came up at ten,' a young subaltern wrote in his diary before Ramnuggur, 'and, after reconnoitring for some time, would stand it no longer, and ordered the batteries to open on the enemy. They commenced an uproar such as I have never heard before; the twenty-fours went off with a roar that shook the very earth; and the shot rushed through the air with a noise like a mighty winged spirit, till the very atmosphere was stunned.'

Unfortunately, Shere Singh had marched off to confront Thackwell with all his army except six guns, which he left to fire from hidden positions, to suggest he was still there in force. So Gough pounded empty trenches. Thackwell, meantime, under heavy fire from Sikh batteries, and believing Gough's order not to attack till reinforced still held, had ordered his line back two hundred yards to a better defensive position on open ground clear of sugar-cane, just in front of the village of Sadullapur. The Sikhs, led by Shere Singh himself, then advanced rapidly, in the belief that the English were running away. Shouts of '*Feringhee baghjaten*,' 'the English are running', were heard with the blare of cow-horns, and soon the green sugar-cane plantation swarmed with red-coated Sikh infantry and yellow-turbaned gunners, above whom the great yellow and blue silk standards waved.

Thackwell had made a serious tactical error.

In retreating, instead of — with a sudden dash forward — occupying the three villages as a defensive position, he had made his force, now on open ground, a target for the twenty Sikh guns hidden in the sugar cane, which now began to bounce round-shot at them. He ordered the men to lie down, deployed in line, so that these ricochet shots, at which the Sikhs were expert, would hit fewer men, and thus, the British force stubbornly received the Sikh fire for four hours without their artillery replying or their infantry attacking. Only when enemy cavalry threatened his flanks did Thackwell take positive action, driving them off with his own cavalry and two batteries of horse artillery.

Finally, at 4 pm the British gunners at last opened on the enemy artillery, with accurate shooting knocked out several guns, and hit the infantry hard. In two hours they stopped the Sikh fire. Thackwell then received still another letter from the commander-in-chief, authorizing him to act as he thought best and advance against the enemy whether or not the promised reinforcements had arrived. Owing to the ford being deeper than was expected Brigadier Godby and his reinforcements were not able to cross on foot. 'Though we worked like horses, the boats were not ready until five,' Lieutenant Sandford wrote in his diary.

> All the officers were up to their waists in water until seven o'clock, keeping the men back from crowding into the boats; and such a scene of shouting, struggling and confusion you never saw. It was all we could do to restrain the men from

overloading the boats; but at last we succeeded in crossing the whole regiment over... Drew up on the other side, piled arms and prepared to bivouac for the night...

Lacking these reinforcements, and with daylight failing, Thackwell consulted with his staff: to advance at once on Shere Singh's position, or wait till daylight? The three villages gave the enemy a fine defensive position. They were also much stronger, Shere Singh's entire army now probably facing Thackwell's much weaker force, almost without rest or food for two days. Thackwell, who despite all the provocations and the chances, had clung to the very letter of Gough's instructions, now wisely put it off until daylight next day.

By sunset deep silence reigned on both sides, and after a scanty meal the British lay down to rest. During the night they were awoken by the loud and persistent barking of dogs. It was the animals following Raja Shere Singh's army, excited by its nocturnal flight to a new position on the River Jhelum, in the middle of a dense jungle, about twenty-five miles north-west — just about the time Gough's army had at last crossed the Chenab, to support Thackwell in his supposed position at Sadullapur.

Thackwell lost twenty-one men killed and fifty-one wounded. Sikh casualties were estimated to be several hundred; the sugarcane plantations and the wells — much to the anger of the villagers — were filled with bodies. The 3rd Dragoons and other cavalry set off in pursuit of this wonderfully mobile army, but failed to catch even a sight of them that day.

So far, Thackwell's force had crossed the Chenab and had lost valuable lives, but not a blow of any importance had been struck against the enemy, who had again withdrawn intact to a strong position of their own choosing. Gough was, to say the least, a little angry. He remarked that he had 'placed the ball at

Thackwell's foot and Thackwell had declined to kick it'. He was certain that he had given Thackwell full authority to attack whether or not he received the expected reinforcements. But since his staff failed to keep copies of the orders sent, he didn't know what he had ordered. All he did know was that in Thackwell's place he would have attacked, and that a chance had been thrown away. He forgot that in the earlier part of the day, when Thackwell was ready to attack, his hands were tied.

Thackwell camped on 6 December at Heylah, ten miles from the swift-flowing Jhelum and the next day spies brought the news that Shere Singh had dug defences between Mong and Russool, near the field where two thousand years earlier Alexander the Great had defeated King Porus. Four regiments and twelve guns from Peshawur had arrived to reinforce him.

It was a challenge to Gough, but for two reasons he was then unable to pursue Shere Singh. First, the commissariat department had so far failed to bring up enough provisions to feed the army properly because Dalhousie, hard-pressed for money, had refused Gough's request to lay in stocks in the summer. Secondly, worried about the worsening of this danger as the distance increased, Dalhousie had written Gough earlier, on 27 November, forbidding him to

> advance into the Doab beyond the Chenab, except for the purpose of attacking Shere Singh in his present position, without further communication with me and my consent obtained. The arrival of reinforcements at Multan, and the surrender of that fortress, will shortly place such an additional force at your disposal as will admit of the army advancing without exposing our present position to the imminent risk in which it would otherwise be placed.

Dalhousie was, of course, far from content with the progress of the campaign in the Punjab. He was displeased too with the tone of Gough's dispatch about the crossing of the Chenab and the commander-in-chief's request that he should fire a royal salute to celebrate it as a great victory, which he refused to do. Dalhousie also pointed out that Gough's communications were open to attack and that he had no reserves. Gough himself doubted whether he was strong enough then for an encounter with Shere Singh. 'Could I on the 8th,' he wrote on 22 December to Dalhousie, 'have attacked the rebel force, I would either have taken all their guns or drove them across the river (the Jhelum). This latter I by no means wished. I felt I was too far from any support, and my communications much too extended, and my supplies too uncertain to justify a forward movement...'

Gough therefore decided to take up a position astride the Chenab stretching from Wazirabad to Gujerat. The advantages were that he would hold the richest parts of the two Doabs, for supplies; he could intercept any advance on Lahore from his mountain kingdom by Golab Singh — who was still an unknown factor — and he would be ready to advance against Shere Singh directly he received reinforcements after the fall of Multan. Meanwhile he would wait.

Dalhousie suggested that while waiting Gough should occupy his forces in destroying the various Sikh forts and strongholds in the Rechna Doab — 'pestilent nests of mischief'. But in no mood to hand over control of his army to a civilian Governor-General, Gough refused on the ground that his forces, already too small compared with those of Shere Singh, would be still more weakened and scattered in such 'small wars', which he had all along opposed. He also on 22 December told the Governor-General that he could not regard the prohibition of an advance as restricting him from 'promptly acting at a moment when prompt measures might be beneficial' and that he would keep his force in hand, ready to take advantage of any opportunity the Sikhs might give. He trusted that the Governor-General was willing to allow something for the prudence and judgement of the commander-in-chief. At the worst, his duty to his country came first. Gough, who had let Lord Hardinge more or less push him around and dictate as to how his army should be employed, had learnt his lesson. For better or worse, only he now would control its fortunes.

Two hundred and thirty miles south-west down the Chenab at Multan, the rebel governor Mulraj had gone over to the offensive, establishing himself on the raised banks of a dry canal which crossed the British lines. For some days he had kept up a more or less constant artillery fire on the British camp, completely raking the lines of the Irregular troops. Powerful counter-battery fire from two 18-pounders, two howitzers and four mortars failed to silence Mulraj's guns, twelve hundred yards away on the canal banks, and General Whish decided to drive them out by an infantry attack on 7 November. But disloyalty now weakened Edwardes's allied force.

Edwardes (promoted to Major) had slept in the advanced and exposed British gun battery during the first few nights of November, to encourage the gunners there. Cold and stiff, he was awoken about 3 am on 7 November by General Courtlandt, who said that one of his three infantry regiments — those whose loyalty Edwardes had hoped he had bought by offering them service in the Indian Army — had deserted and gone over to Mulraj. Courtlandt, who thought this regiment loyal, admitted that he could now no longer fully rely on the two others. General Whish therefore decided that an immediate victory was vital — that it must be won by the British and Indian troops of the regular army — and that it would be fought that morning at 10 am.

It began, however, at seven. Mulraj was bold enough now to take the offensive with an attack on the advanced British battery, held by five hundred Pathans. The gunners reacted quickly, drawing their guns from the embrasures and lashing the enemy with grape so rapidly as to check the attack. Soon it became clear that Mulraj had deployed almost his entire army. Brigadier Markham, who led the British, sent his cavalry under Major Wheeler to charge the Sikh right, which he did with precision and speed, scattering the enemy cavalry, cutting down many of their gunners, preventing them enfilading the British infantry. The horse artillery then opened fire and the infantry — 10th Foot, 32nd Foot and four regiments of Native Infantry, some three thousand men in all — swung into a confident charge. 'We gave three cheers, and with levelled bayonets into them we rushed,' Ryder, of the 32nd Foot, observed.

> We drove them before us upon their own guns and works, bayoneting the artillerymen at their posts. They were as good soldiers as ever took to the field. They would not leave their guns; and when the bayonet was through them they threw their arms round the guns and kissed them, and died. We spiked their pieces as we got possession of them. We drove their infantry into the dry canal, which led to the fort. We stood upon the bank and shot them like ducks; for they had got into such confusion, in trying to make their escape, that they could not move along — they were in one another's road; and the best of it was they could neither return us a shot, nor could they escape out of the canal, the banks on both sides being so steep. It was fairly choked with dead... All

the horses and ammunition, bullocks and camels, fell into our hands, and all kinds of other stores.

The British lost a mere three killed and fifty-eight wounded, the allied troops thirty-nine killed and one hundred and seventy-two wounded. To the bored troops it was an encouraging encounter. Then on 22 December Brigadier Dundas led the long-awaited reinforcements[16] from Bombay into Whish's siege positions. They brought his strength to 15,648, besides Edwardes's seventeen thousand Irregulars. The General now began once more to try to overwhelm this impregnable city and fort.

---

[16] One troop of Horse Artillery, two companies of Foot Artillery, two light field batteries, two companies of sappers, HM's 60th Foot, The 1st Bombay Fusiliers, The 1st Bombay Light Cavalry, four regiments of Bombay Infantry, The Sind Horse.

17: Multan

Eighty thousand people lived in Multan City, beside the wide brown belt of the river Chenab, in the fertile Bari Doab. Among mellowed burnt brick houses and fine mansions six or seven floors high, winding in narrow lanes, merchants traded profitably with the Punjab, India, Afghanistan and Persia. 'Never perhaps in India,' a wide-eyed *Bombay Times* correspondent reported, 'have such depots existed of merchandise and arms... Here opium, indigo, salt, sulphur, every known drug are heaped in endless profusion — ancient granaries in the bowels of the earth disclose huge hoards of wheat and rice...; here bale on bale of silks and shawls; there some mammoth chest discovering glittering scabbards and gold gems, there tiers of copper cannisters crammed with gold mohurs[17]...'

Built on a low hill, Multan was also the gateway from Central Asia to the Punjab and to India. Hence the powerful fort, surrounded by a hexagonal wall up to seventy feet high and a moat forty-five feet wide and twenty-five feet deep, that on the highest part of the hill, to the north-east, dominated the city and its approaches.

Thirty strong towers rose from the fort walls; eighty guns of varying calibre poked their black muzzles out through the embrasures. A high and ancient wall, built on lofty ramparts from which many trees grew, also surrounded the town; immediately above this rose another wall, strengthened with corner towers and battlements. In and around the walls

---

[17] Then about thirty shillings.

towered the high domes and minarets of mosques, temples and a Khan's palace.

Multan, for those with the eye to see, was an ancient, fascinating and in parts beautiful city. To the English politicians, merchants and soldiers — the empire builders — it was at once immensely wealthy and strategically important. Multan must fall.

The plan at first adopted by that seasoned but cautious soldier General Whish was not to take the city as a preliminary, but to attack the north-east angle of the fort, expelling the enemy only from as much of the surrounding suburbs as were needed for his operations. He would, with his artillery in the fort, be able then to dominate its entire surroundings. Mulraj's own garden-house, the Am Khas; his father's tomb and surrounding garden, and some high brick-kilns were Whish's suburban objectives. He launched the attack in four columns, each about a thousand strong and after five or six hours' sharp fighting, the objectives, as well as the famed blue mosque of the Saint of Tubrez, full of priests, women and children, were gained at the cost of some two hundred killed and wounded.

Pursuing his objective of razing the fort, Whish now set up within five hundred yards of the walls, three batteries containing thirteen mortars, adding during the next three days, five more large calibre mortars, two 24-pounders, six 18-pounders and four heavy howitzers, 'but the enemy kept up a troublesome fire and several artillerymen were shot,' noted Corporal Ryder in his never-forgotten diary.

> As soon as day dawned... our batteries opened fire: salvo after salvo went thundering into the town, both shot and shell, and must have committed awful destruction. We had possession of some buildings within one hundred yards of Delhi Gate, where our men and the enemy's kept a regular

fire at each other. Shot and shell were thundering into the town, killing men, women and children. We got more guns into play during the night, and approached much nearer to the walls. Two breaches were commenced in them, one at the Delhi Gate and the other more to the left. A great many prisoners were taken in trying to make their escape from the town; but numbers were women and children. They were treated well.

Changing his tactics, Whish now determined to make breaches in the wall through which the infantry could thrust into the city first. Salvo after salvo crashed into walls and town in the heaviest bombardment yet. Reports came through that it had done much damage — parts of the walls looked shattered, but it was nothing to what followed. At eight o'clock on 30 December 1848, Lieutenant Newall of the Bengal Artillery sited one of his mortars in the direction of Mulraj's main powder magazine, believed to hold no less than eight hundred thousand pounds of gunpowder.

It was an unbelievably lucky shot. The earth trembled and shook, there was a cloud of black smoke, a shock and crash like an earthquake, an ear-splitting detonation which knocked bottles off tables four miles away. Then what to one observer looked like 'an immense solid brown tree rose up to the skies, rolling and belching up, mass over mass, gradually expanding into a thick dark cloud. At a vast height the heavy cloud stood still, like some great tree, and its shadow fell as night over the camps below.'

The devastation was vast. More than eight hundred people were killed and thousands wounded, while mosques, temples, palaces, houses tumbled down in masses of masonry. For some minutes after the last stone had crashed back to earth from the sky there was an eerie silence. Not a gun was fired. It was broken by Mulraj in the fort, whose guns began firing with redoubled fury, for the walls of the solid fort were largely intact, only the lightly-built town houses were smashed.

The British responded, and the bombardment went on steadily into 31 December. About noon, a cloud of smoke and great gusts of flame shot up from within the fort as fire swept through stores of oil, wheat and ghee, which burned day and night so brightly that the countryside was lit up and the gunners aimed without the aid of fireballs. At midnight they were ordered to fire their hardest to celebrate the New Year and salvo after salvo thudded over the walls. Blithely, General Whish now let it be known that if a practicable breach had been made they would storm the city on New Year's Day. In the morning, Mulraj sent word that he still had enough powder and shot to hold out a year — he would remain staunch while one single stone still stood on another; he dared the British to do their worst. Despite this defiance, before the storming parties formed up, Whish sent him a formal request to surrender. According to a *Times* correspondent he rammed the letter down his longest gun and fired it back.

The Engineers were uncertain that the breach was quite ready for storming on New Year's Day, so it was postponed and the cannonade continued purposefully throughout that day and night, Corporal Ryder noting twenty shells in the air at once. Two breaches were at last pronounced ready, one at the Delhi Gate, the other at a tower named the Khoonee Boorj, or Bloody Bastion. Early on 2 January 1849 orders were issued for storming to two columns, one, the right, or Bengal column, under Brigadier Markham, composed of the 32nd Foot, and the 49th and 72nd Native Infantry; the other, under Brigadier Dundas, being the 1st Fusiliers, or 'Bombay Toughs', 4th Bombay Rifles and the 19th Foot. Led by two companies of the 32nd under Captain Smyth, the Bengal column was to storm the breach at the Delhi Gate; and in the early afternoon they took up positions under a hot fire from the walls about three hundred yards off.

The bugles piercingly sounded the *advance* at three o'clock. The three storming companies closely followed by three companies of sappers with scaling ladders and the rifle companies pouring a hot fire at the defenders, rushed forward, Smyth leading with drawn sword. They were met by a blaze of gunfire from the walls, through which they went on, cheering so loudly, observed Corporal Ryder, 'that not even the roaring of the guns could be heard, nor the whizzing of the balls.'

But when the storming party reached the walls, there was no place big enough for even two men to squeeze through.

Confusion followed. The defenders — men, women and boys — launched a hail of boulders, wooden beams, masonry and gunshot at the attackers. Smyth called out 'Retreat!' The bugles echoed it, but this was easier said than done. The rear companies, eager to get out of the hail of shot and into the fray, pressed on from behind. 'Get under cover! There is no breach!' Smyth shouted repeatedly, and at last the rear ranks went about and ran. 'I saw one of our buglers shot dead, close by me, a little to my left,' Ryder noted. 'The ball struck him in the back, and he reeled round and fell; he was but a youth, not more than eighteen years of age. I saw Captain Smyth with blood streaming from his head...'

Twenty-seven were killed or wounded, including three officers, during this untimely episode, but Smyth reacted like the good soldier he was and at once led his men (swearing revenge on the engineer officer who had said the breach was ready), at full speed to the left towards the Bloody Bastion, which the Bombay column had just entered, headed by three companies of the 1st Bombay Fusiliers under Captain Leith. 'When we came to the very foot of the breach,' noted one of the Fusiliers' Officers, 'Captain Leith thundered out "Charge!" (he is six feet five inches high and stout in proportion...)'

> Up we charged and the moment we arrived at the top we were saluted with a volley of Sikh matchlock balls, which, wonderful to relate, all went clear over our heads, except one which struck poor Leith on the shoulder. The enemy had made a large stockade, which we scrambled over somehow (I am sure I cannot recollect how, for it looked a horrible place afterwards), and there stood about a thousand of the enemy with their swords drawn. We gave a volley and a thundering cheer, and charged them with the bayonet. Poor Leith had his left hand cut off through the wrist by a sword. The enemy could not stand a charge with British steel, and fell back; we followed them closely.

Colour-sergeant John Bennet, another six-footer, carried the Union Jack with the storming party, and planted it high on the breach. During the thickest of the firing he stood waving it, cheering on his comrades and firing when he could, regardless of the shower of bullets that rattled around him and riddled the colour. Nor did he quit his post after his comrades had rushed up the breach, and every man of both brigades had mounted it.

Meanwhile, at the heels of the Bombay column, the Bengal storming party led by Smyth had entered and fanned out through the narrow streets and along the irregular walls of the city, shot at by well-armed Sikhs. 'They poured a heavy fire from the windows and down from the housetops,' noted Ryder, in an account that reveals all the horrors of the taking of the city of Multan.

> We broke open the doors with the butt ends of our muskets, and blew off the locks, when not one of those within was left

alive: every one being killed on the spot. They were despatched wholesale. One place was fought very hard for by the enemy. This was a Hindu mosque (sic), occupied by a brave officer and a number of determined men. They had a colour, a very handsome one. They were attacked by a party of our men, who took the colour and killed nearly all the men. The chief part of the struggle took part in the mosque and we were confined for room: our muskets with bayonets fixed we found rather awkward, as we had not room to turn them about. A man by the name of McGuire, a corporal, was attacked by the officer bearing the colour: he came sword in hand, and the corporal not being loaded at the time (for he had just fired) had quite as much as he could do to defend himself. However, he parried off the cuts of the swords until he had a chance, when he made a thrust and gave the officer the bayonet, and at the same time, received a cut from the sword upon the left arm. They closed upon each other, and grappled each other by the throat; when the corporal gave him the foot and threw him upon the floor. The corporal then took his opponent's sword and cut off his head, and brought the colour away as his prize; but he had received a very large wound upon his arm, from the wrist to the inside of the elbow.

Screams, gunshots and the clash of steel, echoed in the tall winding streets, acrid with sulphurous black smoke and the sharp smell of blood. The Sikhs fell back step by step towards the fort, under pressure from the implacable redcoats. Women and children were inseparably involved, for the British were driven on by a mindless passion to crush everything and everyone opposing them, a state of mind not far from madness. 'As our fire was poured down the street into the enemy… intermingled with the men might be seen women and children,' noted Ryder.

> Their wild terrified screams were awful, the cries of the affrighted children, as they clung round their mothers... Grey-headed old men with venerable beards white with age... overwhelmed by grief and age, were weeping for the ruin of their country, and lay down to die near the houses where they were born. The streets, the public squares, and especially the mosques, were crowded with these unhappy persons, mourning as they lay on the remains of their property. In some instances women and children were shot down amongst the men and every one was plundered whom our men could lay their hands upon, regardless of their pitiful cry. Our men now appeared to be brutish beyond everything...

By the hour of darkness the town was entirely in possession of the British, the aged, women and children and the dead, a dark, smoky, eerily silent charnel house. 'We marched over heaps of dead bodies as we began to collect ourselves together, for regiment had become mixed with regiment and brigade with brigade,' Ryder observed. Whish now mercilessly ordered all the inhabitants to be collected together into the main square, apparently to prevent them giving aid to the defenders, and for this purpose the troops, British and sepoy, smashed down doors, and at best herded the occupants out into the street. 'Some of this work was attended with horrible brutality by our men,' the honest Ryder lamented.

> Englishmen! blush at your cruelty, and be ashamed of the unmanly actions perpetrated upon old men... and still worse, upon the poor helpless women. In several instances, on breaking into the retreats of these unfortunate creatures, a volley of shots was fired amongst them as they were huddled together in a corner... All shared the same fate. One of my fellow-corporals, who never was worthy of the jacket he wore, was guilty of cold-blooded murder. He shot a poor, grey-headed old man while he was begging that he would spare and

not hurt his wife and daughters; nor take away the little property they possessed, consisting of a few paltry rings upon their fingers and in their ears. The fellow pulled the rings off in the most brutal manner. He did not wear his stripes long after... I learned that several of our men were guilty of murder... Our native soldiers were much worse, and more brutish; but they were more to be excused, as they were natives.

Another crime, more horrible perhaps than murder, tarnishes the glory of British arms — I mean the ravishments committed by some of the soldiers. A man of the 3rd Company of my regiment... went into a room, and took a young girl from her mother's side and perpetrated the offence, for which he has to answer before the God who heard that poor girl's cries and petitions. Had I been upon the spot at the time I would have shot him dead...

Ryder's account contrasts with those of the officers. 'The soldiery,' observed Dr John Dunlop, surgeon to the 32nd Foot, 'were glad to extract from the town whatever enjoyment it afforded. Few excesses, were, however, committed.' Brigadier Stalker, in charge of the Bombay column, went even further. 'I have the greatest pleasure,' he reported to the commander-in-chief, 'in bearing testimony to the humanity and forbearance of the troops under my command. Not a single instance of wanton cruelty, or ill-treatment of the peaceable inhabitants of the town, has been brought to my notice.' This reassurance was no doubt especially for Gough's benefit, for the difficulty of controlling troops storming a city was widely known.

Strategic parts of Multan had meantime been occupied by the British, ready to repulse any sudden sortie to regain it Mulraj might launch from the fort. The dead were removed from the main squares, and there the troops slaughtered, cooked and ate hunks of bullock meat, then placed sentries and slept, too exhausted after the nervous excitement and bodily exertion of the battle to care much about the steady rain of shot and shell from the fort. In taking the city, British losses in killed and wounded were just below four hundred.

During the night thousands of Multanese fled and next day a death-like silence reigned. 'Never did broken vessel, left high and dry on some inhospitable shore after a storm, exhibit a more perfect wreck than the city of Multan,' Major Edwardes eloquently remarked.

> Its streets were strewn with slain, chiefly Sikhs, whose long religious locks, spread wildly out on the bloody ground, gave their dead a demoniac look which no one who has walked over a Sikh battlefield can forget... There was scarce a roof or wall in the city which had not been penetrated by the English shells; and whole houses, scorched and blackened by the bombardment seemed about to fall over the corpses of their defenders.

As daylight dawned the next day, 3 January 1849, British and sepoy alike stole off to loot before the city's treasures were seized by the prize agents for sale and distribution according to regulations. Ryder noted fine mansions with beautifully carved doors and woodwork, cool patios and rooms with walls covered with brocaded paper. 'What a thousand shames that such splendour should be destroyed!' he lamented. All these places were ransacked, and what could not be carried off was destroyed by the ruthless barbarian troops. Statuary, silks, jewels, gold, silver, fine swords, matchlocks, flintlocks, pistols inlaid with precious metals were fought over and seized. From the dead, rings, necklaces and bracelets were torn away. The prize agents seized stables full of horses and harness, yards full of cattle, camels and elephants. The city was a veritable treasure house, but much was lost. Most of the houses were nothing but heaps of ruins, beneath which were the bodies of those left to die after the shells struck. 'Heaven only can tell what were the sufferings of those poor creatures after the siege commenced,' observed Ryder, the Army of the Punjab's conscience speaking from the ranks.

> And no one can tell how many were killed. No respect was paid to nobility of blood, innocency of youth or to the tears of beauty. Mountains of dead lay in every part of the town, and heaps of human ashes in every square, where the bodies had been burnt as they were killed. Some were only half consumed… Many had been gnawed and pulled to pieces by dogs; and arms, legs, heads and other parts lay in every place… The town swarmed with millions of flies.

General Whish clearly lost all control over his men for nearly twenty-four hours. Orders against looting and destruction were not effective until late on 3 January, after, says Ryder, the city's chief merchants had offered the equivalent of £30,000 to prevent any further plundering.

Thus ended the taking of the city of Multan, named City of the Dead by many who were there. General Whish now began measures to take the fort, separated from the city, to the north, by five hundred yards of flat and dusty parade ground surrounded by stables and cattle sheds. On 4 January 1849 the fort of Multan was entirely surrounded. Fresh artillery positions were completed and by daylight on the 4th the besiegers began bombarding the walls and the defenders' positions as fast as the guns could be loaded. 'We were hard at work all day at our entrenchments, and the fire was most deafening,' Ryder wrote in his journal. 'My head felt quite bewildered from the continual roaring of our guns.'

The trenches crept closer and closer towards the intended breaches. All the time, Mulraj's gunners as well kept up a regular fire of artillery and musketry, killing or wounding the occasional unwary soldier. The British gunnery was shared, oddly enough, by British seamen, Jack Tars led by Commander Powell, of the East India Company's navy, forerunner of the Indian Navy, from the steamboats of the Indus flotilla under his command. Powell had offered to help in the siege, bringing ashore a party of naval gunners to man one of the heavy batteries. 'They looked on their battery as a ship; their 18-pounders as so many sweethearts and the embrasures as port holes,' Major Edwardes observed. 'Now, Jack, shove your head out of that port, and just hear what my little girl says to that 'ere pirate Moll Rag!' was the kind of remark he heard at the sailor-battery as he passed. Their gunnery was so extraordinarily accurate that the 'pirates' in that fort angrily turned such a storm of shells on their battery on 9 January that it caught fire and burnt to the ground.

Ryder's regiment, the 32nd, were digging the trenches across the parade ground and by the night of Tuesday, 9 January, they had got to within twenty yards of the fort walls. 'We had lost several more men killed and wounded,' he noted.

> I have not the least doubt that we should have lost a great many more, had it not been for our mortar batteries, which threw the shell with such skill as to fall just within the fort. This kept them in check. Some of the pieces from our own shells flew amongst us, and over us, as they exploded within the walls. We could now plainly hear the cries of the wounded and dying, but the besieged appeared determined to hold out. We could hear their reveille beat in the morning and their

bugles sounding... The town smelt very badly from the number of dead lying about, gnawed and dragged about the streets. Some I saw half buried and half above ground. What a sight for the inhabitants to see their fellow-townsmen lie scattered about in all parts of the town, and most likely their sons, brothers or fathers... I thought of my own dear country and hoped that such a sight would never be seen there.

Life in the beleagured fort must by now have become nasty, brutish and short, for Mulraj sent a letter to Major Edwardes, in his capacity as the Governor-General's agent, asking if surrender terms could be discussed. 'This I cannot assent to,' Edwardes replied. 'It is quite impossible. The time for that was April last. You then preferred war — now go through with it; or, if you are unable, surrender yourself to General Whish. After that you can represent anything you like.' Mulraj sent another similar petition to General Whish, asking also if he could send an envoy to make 'certain representations', but was told he could do so only if the purpose was to state precisely when and where he would unconditionally surrender. An envoy, one of Mulraj's confidential advisers, resplendent in red silk robes and yellow turban, arrived, proclaimed dramatically — 'The Dewan submits!' then began an oration charged with a budget of issues regarding Mulraj's future. He was ordered to return and tell his master that nothing but unconditional surrender would be heard. To give point to this, a new battery of seven 18-pounders blasted the fort with an earth-shaking roar. Whish hoped at all costs to avoid the final bloodbath of storming and thus save many lives, but the decision had to come soon. On the 19th January he took a walk through the trenches towards the walls and examined the gaps torn in them by the hail of heavy round-shot. They were very nearly wide enough for storming. His force being needed urgently to aid

Gough in the final battle with Shere Singh, Whish decided soon to attempt it.

That evening, desperately trying to save himself, Mulraj once more asked if he might send a confidential agent to the General. He was told, says Edwardes, that if his object was to surrender, he had better do so at 8 am next day, and that messengers sent in with any other communication would be made prisoners. No answer being received to this, Whish gave orders for storming two days later, at 6 am 22 January. 'We were not more than fifteen or twenty yards from each other,' Ryder noted.

> As our officers began to suspect that they were running a mine under us from the ditch of the fort, we were ordered to throw in hand grenades — small shells about the size of cricket balls... The wall looked very much beaten, and large pieces of masonry had begun to fall; but there were three walls, one higher than the other. The first wall was all we wanted to make a breach through. Our men looked very bad; we were nothing more than like bags of bones. On the next day the enemy got several guns into play, but they were speedily dismounted by the superior skill of our artillery. The enemy threw a number of inferior shells, which were not very destructive. While two of our companies were out relieving outposts in the morning, the enemy opened fire of musketry upon them and Captain Bryan fell, very severely wounded by a musket ball through the back. He was a fine-looking brave officer, but he will always be a cripple. There was great sorrow at this misfortune, through the whole regiment, for he was much respected by the men.

Horrifying now was the situation in and around the fort. The smell from the dead penetrated everything, even the men's uniforms. Troops of jackals growled and fought their way into the fort for their nightly feast, great flocks of vultures and ravens lazily flew in. Whish, mindful of the dangers of plague, ordered his gunners to fire unceasingly in an effort at once to force surrender on Mulraj and to wreck the walls, and, noted Ryder: 'The place now looked an entire heap of ruins. The walls were crumbling fast before the weight of our heavy shot. We heard that we were to storm next day, and I hoped that the news was true; we had been long enough at it to wear out the strongest man, and our men were all anxious to be at them!'

Many of the defenders had by now deserted and surrendered, or had been foolishly shot down as they fled, thus probably persuading the remainder that they had nothing to lose by holding out. But flesh and blood could no longer stand the hail of shot and shell. Mulraj's advisers, it turned out later, told him plainly that he must either sally out at the head of his troops and cut his way through the besiegers, or surrender at once. In this hopeless situation, in which to fight any longer was to die, Mulraj made up his mind to surrender, even though it meant certain imprisonment, possible death. To General Whish he wrote on the 21st:

> I am now ready to come in, and for this purpose have sent my vakeel to arrange with you; your slave desires only protection for his own fife, and the honour of his women. The whole of this disturbance was set on foot by my soldiers, and all my endeavours failed to quell it; now, however, I surrender myself. I ask only for my own life, and the honour of my women. You are an ocean of mercy — what more need be said? You are a sea of compassion; if you forgive me, I am fortunate; if you do not, I meet my fate with contentment.

General Whish answered:

> You write that you only ask for your own life, and the honour of your women. This is my answer: that I have neither authority to give your life, nor to take it, except in open war. The Governor-General only can do this: and as to your women, the British Government wars with men — not with women. I will protect your women and children, to the best of my ability. Take notice, however, if you intend to come in at all, you had better do so before sunrise tomorrow, and come out by the Dowlut Gate. After sunrise you must take the fortune of war.

All night the guns thundered at the walls and the shells still burst over the defiant garrison. At daybreak Whish ordered his army to take up final positions to storm the broken fortress. 'We left a strong guard in camp,' Ryder remembered.

> Before we had been assembled five minutes, we had not a dry thread upon us, the rain falling in torrents, and the ground being a regular sheet of water. We were obliged to reverse our arms to keep them dry, and the water from going down the barrels. We were stationed in the entrenchments, as near to the fort as we could get. My regiment was to storm, and we were as near to the breach as possible, and in front of our batteries, which were playing over us. The trenches were up to our knees in water and slough, and the rain still fell heavily. We waited for the appointed time to surrender or the signal to storm.

For an hour the ten thousand men waited, wondering perhaps, whether they were to go in and kill, and be killed, or whether this eastern potentate would mount his horse, ride out and bring it to an end. The mortars, the 18 and 24-pounders, still shook the ground with persistent salvos. The troops clamoured to be allowed to storm, swore vengeance against everyone in the fort, said they wouldn't spare a soul.

Then suddenly the Sikh and the Multanese soldiers streamed out by the Dowlut gate. Orders were sent to the batteries to cease fire. One of them had just fired a salvo and the officer commanding mounted a gun trail to watch the effect. Just as the messenger arrived with the order, he was struck by a ball from one of the fort guns. The last man killed at Multan, he also fired the last shot. He was buried under the flagstaff in the fort.

The army now quickly formed a square at the Dowlut gate and as the enemy came out, wretched and dirty but savage, determined and proud, with heads high, they laid down their arms and were received as prisoners. Mulraj himself followed on a white horse, and the grenadier company of the 32nd Foot, Ryder's company, were ordered to receive him and escort him to the General's tent.

> One man took hold of his horse's head, while the company formed on either side of him. He was accompanied by seven of his officers. He was dressed all in red, or a crimson silk; his cloak, very richly embroidered, was of the same kind. He had a gold chain round his neck and gold bracelets on his wrists, richly set with stones, and upon his finger he had a diamond ring. He was a good-looking man, of the middle stature, having fine features and a mild countenance, yet a keen piercing eye, and a determined expression. I could not help but feel for him; indeed, I felt sorry for him. When we had got about halfway to the camp, he turned round upon his horse and viewed the fort, and tears started from his eyes, and he wept much; and well he might, to see it then! — battered to a heap of ruins, while only months before it bade defiance to the British force and the world, and was proud of its strength and beauty.

Thus ended the twenty-seven day siege of Multan, during

which British losses were the surprisingly low figure of two hundred and ten killed and nine hundred and eighty-two wounded. Some fifteen thousand heavy shot and twenty thousand shells were poured into the city and fort, after being transported in horse, bullock and elephant-drawn ammunition wagons over some four hundred miles of rough country from the arsenals at Delhi. About four thousand of Mulraj's troops surrendered; fifty-four guns and four mortars, all of brass, and in working order, were removed from the ruins. The defenders' loss in killed, wounded and sick must have been enormous.

Mulraj's rule as governor of the province of Multan was said to have been tyrannical, but it must, somehow, have inspired in the people some love or affection, for even allowing for the part played by religious and patriotic feeling in this historic stand how else would they have been ready and willing to throw their lives away and fight to the last? They fought for their homeland, and they fought for their faith, but they also fought for Dewan Mulraj.

With hopes of loot, Whish's troops next day clambered over the heaps of fallen stonework into the enormous tomb that was now the fort. Dead men, horses, camels and bullocks lay in heaps on every square foot of ground. Burial parties of Multanese were pressed into service to burn or bury them. Not one single building stood whole and more than half were battered to the ground. Below, in vast cellars however, were huge quantities of every kind of provision, though the corn stores were after three weeks' burning, still aflame, thousands of sacks having been burnt to ashes. But the soldiers were in search of money and soon they found the treasury, near to Mulraj's house, says Ryder, who was there.

All the gold and silver, precious stones and money were kept there, in a kind of cave, under the ground. There must have been a large quantity of gold and silver, for it occupied the greater part of three days to weigh and count and take it away in ammunition wagons. It did not all consist of coin: there were gold and silver bars, and the coin was all of different countries — of Europe, Asia and America. Some of our men on duty in the fort all night, came out in the morning loaded with gold. It is said that some of them had as much as £6,000 worth. However, it never did them any good; for they would give the weight of gold for the weight of grog, which caused a great deal of drunkenness; and as one man got drunk and could not help himself, another would rob him, and he would have it until he got drunk, and then came his turn to be robbed; and so it went on, until the black men got it all for drink. The money was so plentiful that the men would not carry copper; and some of the men who had got the most would not carry silver!

Thus, through the grog shops streamed the gold from one of the great fortunes of ancient India, for Mulraj's family had garnered wealth for generations. The prize agents alone seized treasure worth nearly three million pounds sterling. One would have thought this a big enough fine for anyone to pay to purge his guilt, especially if it was only presumed. Not so. Dewan Mulraj was taken to Lahore and tried for his life before 'three distinguished British officers', two civilians, and one soldier. No one appears to have defended him. He applied for Major Edwardes to do so, but, said Edwardes: 'I believed him guilty, and would not defend him; I had hunted him with an army in the field and had no wish to follow him into the dock.' He was found guilty and sentenced to be hanged, but recommended to mercy as 'the victim of circumstances'. Lord Dalhousie who felt that to hang him would cause more unrest in India, accepted the recommendation. Mulraj was ordered to be banished across the seas, probably to Penang. No mention was made of the millions which the army had stolen from his treasury. This was 'prize money', legitimate booty according to the uses of war.

On 27 January, General Whish began forced marches to link up and reinforce Lord Gough's army in what were to be the decisive battles for the Punjab against Shere Singh.

18: Chillianwalla

During December Gough had crossed the upper Chenab to reconnoitre the approaches to the Sikh positions in the wild and gloomy region in front of the Jhelum, from Mung to Russool, dominated by the rugged red peaks of the Salt Range. As we shall soon see, it could not have been a very thorough reconnaissance. On 18 December 1848, he brought the rest of the army and his headquarters across the Chenab on the bridge of boats built by Lieutenant Young of the Engineers and camped within three miles of Thackwell's force at Heylah. Shere Singh now made a feint back towards Wazirabad, the gateway to Lahore, as if to threaten the capital. Gough, whose army was still too small for the tasks ahead — Multan not yet having fallen — sent a holding force of three guns and two light cavalry regiments there, more to stop reinforcements for Shere Singh than to hold the ford against any strong attack the Sikh general might try with a lightning move. He believed his own army equal to the task of preventing the Sikh force escaping to the south.

Meanwhile, with the impending approach of the hot season — then the Indian scourge of British armies in the field — Dalhousie had grown less opposed to Gough attacking Shere Singh before Multan fell and thus enabled Whish's army to reinforce him. The probability that Dost Mahommed of Afghanistan would add his strength to that of the Sikhs — the knowledge that Gough now had ample provisions — his own impatience for victory — the over-shadowing danger that the fort at Attock, in the north, fifty miles east of Peshawur, would fall from British into Sikh hands, enabling Chuttur Singh to join forces with his son Shere Singh — all these factors now inclined Dalhousie to hurry the war to an end.

Gough received notice of this change of heart on 9 January 1849 in a letter in which Dalhousie told him of the capture of the city of Multan, and his hope of news, at any time, that the fort there had fallen too, and that Mulraj had surrendered. 'It would give me no less pleasure to announce a similar blow struck by you on the Jhelum,' he told Gough. 'I shall be heartily glad to hear of your having felt yourself in a condition to attack Shere Singh with success.'

Not just permission, but in reality an order to go on and win lay behind Dalhousie's oblique phraseology. Next day, Gough received news of the fall of Attock, and of the advance of Chuttur Singh, now released to reinforce Shere Singh's army, which was already thirty thousand strong, with sixty-two guns. In reply, Gough assured Dalhousie that he felt himself 'perfectly competent effectually to overthrow Shere Singh's army' with the twelve thousand men and sixty-six guns he commanded, and that it was imperative to attack before the Sikhs received Chuttur Singh's reinforcements.

Aware now that even a day's delay was dangerous, on 10 January 1849 Gough marched his army forward twelve miles to Dinghi. Here spies brought him details of Shere Singh's army and the approximate terrain which it occupied — an entrenched position stretching from the village of Lucknawalla, on their right, to the hills of Russool, on which their left flank rested. This range of hills sloped down to the plain, but ravines and fissures crossed it towards the Jhelum, where it ended in sudden precipices above sandy flats and channels. A broad and dense jungle of thorny bushes up to two thousand yards wide and eight feet high ran from a plain at the foot of the hills near the river for several miles in a south-easterly direction.

In this formidable position, behind the jungle and in front of the river, Shere Singh had stationed his army ready for battle. The details of his troops' positions are necessary to understand Gough's intended plan of attack. At Lucknawalla, were the Bannu troops (one regiment of cavalry, four of infantry and eleven guns); at Futteh Shah Kuchuk two regiments of cavalry, six old and four new infantry corps, with seventeen guns of the Peshawur force; at Kot Baloch, Shere Singh himself, with one regiment of cavalry, five old and four new regiments of infantry, and twenty guns, with the main body of Ghorcharras, or irregular cavalry; at Mung, three guns, and at Russool on their far left, two new infantry corps and seven guns.

'I move tomorrow to a position a mile and a half in front of Dinghee,' Gough wrote to Dalhousie on 11 January.

> With God's blessing, I propose to attack the enemy on the following day… It is my intention to penetrate the centre of their line, cutting off the regular from the irregular portion of their army. The only fear I have is that the former, when routed, will throw themselves into the jungle close to which they are stationed, but I hope they will fight for their salt, and if so, and I can get close to them, it will be hard if I cannot take their guns, twenty-two in number. Kotlia and Mong I shall easily dispose of, with about thirty more guns. In all, they have sixty-two guns and about forty thousand men. I shall, I hope, take into action sixty guns and from eleven thousand to twelve thousand men.

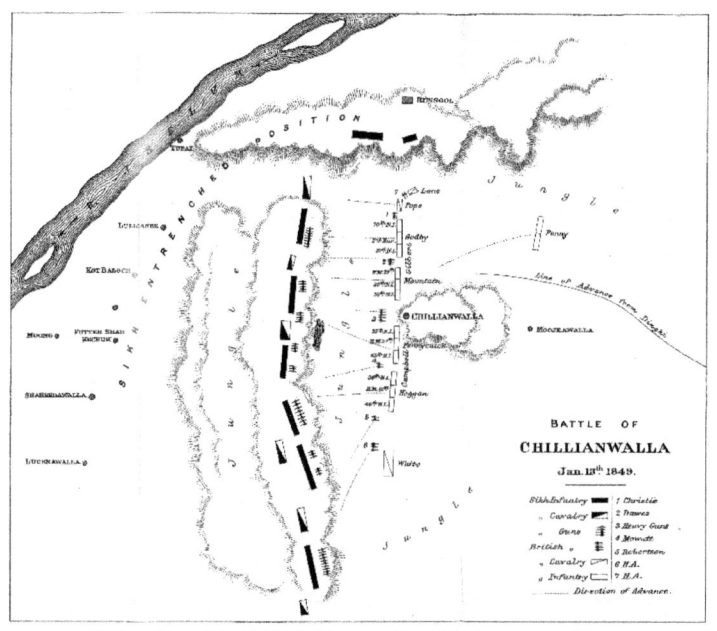

The Battle of Chillianwalla, 13 January 1846

Despite being out-gunned and out-numbered by nearly four to one, Gough, as this letter shows, approached the battle with complete confidence, expecting to finish the war finally. He realized that there were in fact two Sikh lines, one, the regulars, running from Lucknawalla, by Futteh Shah Kachek to Kotlia (Kot Baloch); the other, the irregular troops, stationed along the line of the river from Mung to the entrenched position in the hills at Russool. He planned to attack their centre at the weak point of the link between the regular and irregular forces, break through, turn the left flank of the regular forces and scatter them. All this, he explained to his generals commanding divisions and brigades on 12 January in his roomy tent, with rays of bright light filtering through the windows.

Bugles shrilled, drums reverberated in the chilly dawn on 13 January and tents were struck. The officers of the 2nd Bengal Europeans met together to drink a glass of wine to their survival, the long lines of bellowing camels were loaded, the heavy guns harnessed to the slow-moving elephants and by 7 am when warm sunshine glowed from an almost cloudless sky the army advanced, says General Thackwell, 'in brigade column of cavalry, artillery and infantry towards the Sikh position. Each column formed its own advance guard, and the heads of columns were to be one hundred yards from each other... directed by the heavy battery, in front of which was the commander-in-chief.'

Towards noon, tired after marching ten miles over rough and jungly country, the British neared the dense and to them, relatively unknown thorny jungle tract stretching several miles south from the river Jhelum (or Hydaspes). Memorable is this as the battlefield where, more than two thousand years ago, approaching from the north-west, Alexander the Great vanquished the host of King Porus; and a number of the British officers knew of this, though the commander-in-chief makes no mention of it himself. A strong body of Sikh cavalry and infantry were now seen to occupy a low hill, upon which crouched the mud village of Chillianwalla. The commander-in-chief sent the 24th Foot to drive them off; perhaps too readily the Sikhs avoided fighting and retired, enticing the British forward. Gough and his staff rode up the mound to the village.

From the roof of one of the houses he now saw detachments of Shere Singh's force deployed in battle array on the fringe of the dark jungle, about a mile away.

Gough was faced by two possible courses of action. One, to attack at once while there was still daylight, forcing the jungle without finding out more about the terrain; second, to camp and reconnoitre before giving battle tomorrow, when he would know much better what he was doing. And this is what he decided to do. 'As it was one o'clock before I satisfied myself of his position, I determined to postpone the attack until the following morning,' he wrote in his private diary on 13 January. He gave the necessary orders and staff of the Quarter-Master-General, Colonel Garden, began marking out the ground for a camp on a line with Chillianwalla, where there were wells with plenty of water. Bugles sounded, the regiments piled arms and the men fell out with some relief after their long march. Then came a series of flashes from the Sikh lines — sharp reports — round-shot whistled past Gough on the Chillianwalla house-top.

Gough had to think quickly. Behind him Colonel Garden's staff were laying out the enormous camp, and still farther away through the trees and scrub as far as the horizon, ambled forward the interminable camel and bullock columns carrying provisions and baggage. Engineer officers had already gone out ahead to reconnoitre the roads and jungle fronting the Sikh positions ahead. Retreat was unthinkable, impossible, but there was another possibility, apart from fighting at once. Gough ordered the heavy elephant-drawn 24-pounders to an open space in front of Chillianwalla to hit the Sikh guns to try to frighten Shere Singh into silence. The guns rent the air, but instead, the Sikhs answered this thunderous salvo with the whole of their field artillery. 'Bang, bang went the guns, one after the other, in one continued stunning roar, and our hearts beat, and our pulses quickened with anticipation,' noted an enthusiastic young officer, Lieutenant Sandford. 'The enemy took it up, and a tremendous fire was kept up for half an hour…'

Shere Singh, it was learned later, had hoped that the British, marching since early morning, would camp in this dangerous situation, so that later, at an inconvenient moment for them — as at Mudki — he could launch an artillery bombardment and a full scale attack. But his hot-headed artillery officers, or gunners, unable to control their eagerness, opened up too soon and half spoilt this plan. For when the British replied and every Sikh gun went into action their battery positions, hitherto masked by the jungle, were seen by Gough and his staff.

If at this moment, Gough was asking himself how his cavalry patrols had failed to discover the Sikh positions and let him advance so dangerously near, we do not know. At all events, this lack of information forced him to fight them in conditions of Shere Singh's own choosing. The Sikh commander had won the first round. The bloody battle of Chillianwalla was about to start.

Gough deployed his army[18] for action, despite the arguments of one or two of his staff against it. Brigadier Hoggan's brigade was to advance on the left of the line, with Brigadier Pennicuick's next, both of them commanded by Brigadier-General Colin Campbell, Brigadier Penny's brigade being in reserve. On the right was General Gilbert's division, of which Brigadier Mountain's brigade was on the left and Brigadier Godby's on the right. The big black 24-pounders were ranged in the centre, between them; attached to Campbell's division on the left were three troops of horse artillery under Lieutenant-Colonel Brind, and Walker and Robertson's field-batteries, both under Major Mowatt; attached to Gilbert's division, three troops of horse artillery under Lane, Christie and Fordyce and Major Dawes's field battery. The two cavalry

---

[18] As in 15: Dalhousie except that Thackwell had succeeded Cureton, and Campbell had succeeded Thackwell.

brigades protected the flanks, Brigadier White's on the left and Brigadier Pope's on the right, strengthened by the blue-coated 14th Light Dragoons.

Gough had thus formed his army into a line three miles long facing the centre of the Sikh line, which was about a mile away, and extended for six miles behind the thick jungle. Both flanks, their right especially, overlapped the British. Front for front therefore, the British army faced only the Sikh centre, whose left and right, extending far beyond the left and right of Gough's force, were free to take advantage of the situation, if events favoured it.

The British cannonade continued for another half an hour, hitting the enemy hard, so far as could be seen, until Gough, impatient of this long-range warfare and feeling that daylight was precious, towards three o'clock ordered the whole line to advance and charge the enemy's batteries with musketry and bayonet. 'I saw the effect of our fire,' he noted, in a letter dated 11 May 1849, seemingly justifying this order. 'I plainly saw that a great portion of the enemy's guns were either disabled or withdrawn. I then ordered the advance after upwards of an hour's cannonade.'

A confused, indecisive but bloody battle, it was nearly hidden in the jungle. It is hard to know the exact relationship of events, for there are no really coherent accounts; all are more or less diffuse and obscured by vague abstract detail. Neither the divisional nor the brigade commanders — nor even Gough himself — knew precisely where the various other brigades were in relation to the rest of the army, or what they were doing. 'That action,' Gough said in his dispatch, which he bluntly reminded Dalhousie of his responsibility for initiating, 'was characterized by peculiar features, which rendered it impossible for the commander-in-chief to witness all the operations of the force…'

He was saying in this vague under-statement that the dense jungle hid the fighting and prevented a bird's eye view. Flickering movements of the redcoats in the green thickets — confusion and uncertainty — the metallic bellow of the guns — the frequent clatter of muskets — the constant clash of bayonets on tulwar — the shouts and screams of men locked in hand-to-hand fighting: these were all that Gough could know of the battle, except for the little news his staff officers, groping their way back through the thorns, were able to bring him. More of a spectator than a general, the jungle had forced him — no doubt against his will — to stay with the heavy guns between it and Chillianwalla, where his commanders knew they would find him, for had he gone forward he would too easily have been lost.

According to his dispatch, his sole act during the fighting was to order Brigadier Penny's reserves forward to support Brigadier Pennicuick's brigade on the left, which the Sikhs had badly cut up and flung back. But these reserves lost their way in the jungle, somehow crossed over the front and attached themselves to the right instead of the left. Frustrating though it was, Gough was experienced enough to see that overall command in this difficult situation in which he had been compelled to fight was impossible; and that having given orders to advance first to Campbell, on the left, and second to Gilbert, on the right, he must leave them to get on with it.

In conditions better suited to jungle-fighters of the twentieth century, both Gough's divisional generals now tried to fight a set-piece pitched battle. Brigadier-General Campbell, on the left, decided at once that he couldn't control both brigades of his division in those dense thickets, so he gave Brigadier

Pennicuick independent command of his brigade, rode up in front of the men, assembled on the open ground before the jungle, and told them: 'There must be no firing, the bayonet must do the work!' — an order based on Gough's command that the Sikh guns must be stormed and taken at the point of the bayonet, too literally interpreted. Campbell then galloped off to the left to direct the advance of the other brigade, Brigadier Hoggan's, on the immediate left of Pennicuick's.

Pennicuick marched his brigade (one British regiment of the 24th Foot; and two Indian, the 25th and 45th Native Infantry), forward into the jungle, but it was so dense that he had now and again to break from line into echelon of companies. The line became less and less regular, the tall shakos of the men of the 24th caught in the bushes, and soon companies broke up into sections, then groups. All the time the Sikh round-shot tore through the branches, mostly above their heads, but sometimes low enough to smash through flesh and bone.

Young, and very strong soldiers, the men of the 24th went on at a fast pace through the jungle for slightly over a mile, outstripping both the two sepoy regiments. They emerged on clear ground with a grassy upwards slope about three hundred yards long before them, ending in a network of deep pools.

There, behind the pools were the yellow turbans, white and black uniforms of the Sikh gunners. Behind them the lines of red-coated Sikh infantry.

It was a tragic encounter for the 24th Foot. There was no time to pause or take breath, for the Sikh guns at once showered them with grapeshot. They rushed blindly forward, unsupported by either of the sepoy regiments, who had fallen behind in the jungle, or by their artillery, which no one had ordered into action — the batteries were to be taken with the bayonet! 'It fell to the lot of this gallant regiment,' says Captain

Thackwell, 'to experience an atmosphere solely compounded of fire, grape and round-shot,' to counteract which, 'there was no artillery and no fire of musketry — for the men were unloaded.' They had, it seems, been ordered not to fire, just to charge with the bayonet.

The Sikh guns mowed them down. Finally, in ragged groups they charged up to the smoking gun muzzles and in a ferocious bloodthirsty struggle still managed to bayonet or drive away the gunners. Brigadier Pennicuick was now shot down. A Sikh swordsman began to cut him up, when his son, an ensign, aged seventeen, plunged his sword through the Sikh and stood over his father to protect him. The son was killed over his father's body.

Leaderless now, because Colonel Brookes, the 24th's commander, and several officers as well as Pennicuick had fallen, the men of the 24th were suddenly counter-attacked by the Sikhs, who advanced with reinforcements, lashed them with volleys of musketry, charged with drawn tulwars, killed many of them and forced them to run for their lives back into the jungle. The two sepoy regiments also gave way and the whole brigade, unnerved for the time being, stumbled back to the safety of Chillianwalla.

The 24th had lost two hundred and thirty-one men killed and two hundred and sixty-six wounded, all within a few minutes, at the hands of an enemy armed with muzzle-loading matchlocks and nine-pounders. It was a crazy blood-soaked encounter. Major Paynter, shot through the lungs, was carried out of danger by his horse, but he died of his wound soon after. Lieutenant Thelwall's horse was shot dead under him and Thelwall was wounded in the thigh. He lay on the ground, where the Sikhs would certainly have killed him, but a horse which two days earlier he had sold to Major Harris, who had just been killed, trotted riderless up to him and stood waiting. Thelwall staggered up, mounted and rode safely to the rear. Captain Williams was hit by a round-shot and fell wounded. The enemy cut him up badly on arms, head and legs, leaving him for dead. Carried to the rear later, he was found to have twenty-three wounds and one of his hands was lopped off. Out of the twenty-nine officers in this regiment of nine hundred and sixty men, thirteen were killed and ten wounded. (The bodies of the thirteen officers were laid out on the polished mess table that night, which as a matter of course had been brought into the field.)

This disaster was unknown to General Campbell and Brigadier Hoggan, at the head of the latter's brigade of Campbell's division the British 61st Foot and the sepoy 36th and 46th Native Infantry. The two brigades of Campbell's division by all the rules should have advanced in one co-ordinated line, but because he had abdicated command of one, and because of the terrain, they were widely separated. Thus, while the Sikhs slaughtered the 24th, Hoggan's brigade still advanced slowly and steadily through rather less dense jungle, supported by twenty-nine guns — Mowatt's battery on the right, Robertson's three guns and Brind's three horse-batteries on the left. Their fire knocked out a Sikh heavy battery which sought to enfilade the brigade. The careful Campbell then led the three regiments of about two thousand eight hundred men in a thin, steady red line out of the jungle to the open ground beyond.

Here a mass of Sikh cavalry and infantry and a battery of guns met them. But it was a better managed encounter. The 61st, well supported by the 36th and 46th Native Infantry, accurately fired volley after volley, then charged and scattered the disordered cavalry and spiked the guns. The Sikh infantry, however, repulsed the 36th in sharp and incessant fighting. Brigadier Godby's son, a teenage ensign, severely sabred, was rescued alive. Ensign Conolly, also a mere boy, showed extraordinary courage in several bitter clashes and escaped with cuts and grazes. General Campbell cut down a Sikh gunner, but was sabred in the act.

When the 36th fell back, Campbell changed front to the left two companies of the 61st. They drove back the Sikhs and stopped the pursuit, captured more Sikh guns and repulsed another cavalry charge. The entire brigade now formed up on the right of the Sikh line and began to roll it back in a flank attack, eventually taking thirteen guns and charging from the left the battery position where a few minutes before the 24th were slaughtered. 'It is but just to observe,' says Captain Thackwell, 'that the 61st and its faithful comrades of the 36th and 46th, mainly contributed, on the left, to re-adjust the trembling scale of victory.'

But not the infantry alone, for when the Sikh cavalry during this savage fighting, galloped forward to turn the British left flank, General Thackwell, cavalry division commander, who was with Brigadier Michael White's brigade, gave the word to Captain Unett's squadron of the 3rd Light Dragoons. Red and white plumes streaming above their dark blue jackets, the Dragoons violently charged and scattered the Sikh horse, then swept on furiously into the heart of a mass of Sikh infantry, who bravely closed on their flanks. Led by Unett, the Dragoons cut their way through at great cost, galloped on for half a mile then charged back, driving the opposing horse and foot out of the field. Out of one hundred and forty in this squadron, but ninety-nine came back. Hearing from the survivors of the advance of Hoggan's brigade, Thackwell sent another troop of horse artillery to help them.

Meantime, over on the British right, General Sir Walter Gilbert's division — Mountain's and Godby's infantry brigades, Pope's cavalry brigade, three troops of horse artillery and Major Dawes's Field Battery — had advanced through much thinner jungle almost due west towards Sikh forces in front of the village of Laliani. All seemed well in hand when — just about the time the Sikhs were driving back the 24th on the left — Brigadier Pope, protecting Gilbert's flank with his cavalry, lost control in an episode that would have been comic had it not been tragic.

Seeing a large body of Sikh horsemen sweeping in towards Godby's flank from the direction of Rasul, Pope detached two squadrons each of the 9th Lancers and the 1st and 6th Bengal Light Cavalry with some nine-pounders under Colonel Lane to protect it, still advancing meantime with the remainder of his brigade. Observing more Sikh cavalry on his front, he formed into line and advanced on the same front as General Gilbert's two infantry brigades. Pope, who in his younger days had been a dashing lieutenant-colonel of Indian cavalry was now an elderly gentleman so stiff and corpulent that he needed the help of two men to mount his horse. Even worse, he knew almost nothing of handling large bodies of cavalry. While bringing his brigade forward for the action he had unsteadied them by contradictory orders that faced them in several different directions, partly owing to the jungle and partly because his eyesight was so bad.

Having got his brigade into line he now moved forward at a slow trot with no scouts out, and in his myopic way led his men at an angle instead of straight ahead, until he masked the fire first, of his own horse artillery batteries, and then of Brigadier Godby's infantry brigade. Comprehending this astounding fact, he slowed his brigade first to a walk then to a halt, while he presumably wondered how on earth he could extricate himself — without too much danger from the approaching Sikh cavalry. It seems he meant to give the order 'Threes right!' to clear the artillery's and the infantry's front, but somehow this came out as 'Threes about!' Taken up, passed on and obeyed, just as the mass of brilliantly garbed Sikh cavalry began their charge, it became first a gallop, then a panic-stricken rout, until the whole brigade of some three thousand men tore from the field, through the horse artillery, upsetting horses, carriages and guns — past the astonished Gough, on until they reached the tents of the field hospital. There they were rallied by the chaplain, Mr Whiting, who, pistol in hand, threatened to shoot anyone who passed him. In the confusion, the Sikh cavalry cut down the artillery's Major Christie and several men, spiked a number of guns, then seized and drove away another four guns with the fifty horses harnessed to them.

This alone was bad enough, but Godby's right flank was now dangerously exposed, for there was a wide gap between his brigade and Lane's artillery far out on the right. To protect it he threw back his right wing. His men had meantime prepared themselves for the shock of combat. 'On swept our brigade, and gaining an open space in the jungle, the whole of the enemy's line burst on our view,' Lieutenant Sandford wrote in an account that shows the infantryman's hazards.

> Charge! rang the word through our ranks, and the men bounded forward like angry bulldogs, pouring in a murderous fire. The enemy's bullets whizzed above our heads; the very air seemed teeming with them; man after man was struck down, and rolled in the dust. But a passing glance was all we could give them. And onward we went, bearing on their line with a steadiness which nothing could resist. They fired a last

volley, and then turned and fled, leaving the ground covered with dead and wounded. Pursuit in a jungle like that was useless, where we could not see twenty yards before us; so we halted and began to collect our wounded — when all of a sudden fire was opened upon us in our rear. A large body of the enemy had turned our flank in the jungle, and got between us and the rest of the troops; another party were on our left; and we found ourselves with one light field-battery, completely surrounded and alone in the field.

Captain Dawes's battery was the saving of us — as the cavalry were bearing down, the brigadier shouted, 'A shower of grape in there!' and every gun was turned on them, the men working as coolly as on parade; and a salvo was poured in that sent horse and man head over heels, in heaps. If it had not been for that battery, we should have been cut up to a man. The fire was fearful; the atmosphere seemed alive with balls. I can only compare it to a storm of hail. They sang above my head and ears so thick that I felt that if I put out my hand it would be taken off... Our firing was beautiful: every man was as steady as a rock, and fired low and well; while the sepoys on our right were blazing away into the air, and taking no aim whatever. All this time the enemy were... banging away at us and then disappearing.

Godby's brigade was now in as dangerous a situation as that in which Pennicuick's lost so many of its men, but Brigadier Godby still lived to lead; and artillery was at hand to give support. 'The word was given, "Right-about face!" and we advanced steadily, loading and firing as we went,' Sandford recalled.

At last General Gilbert rode up, and said to Steel, 'Well, major, how are you? Do you think you are near enough to charge?' 'By all means,' said Steel. 'Well then, let's see how you can do it.' 'Men of the 2nd Europeans, prepare to charge

— Charge!' And on we went with a stunning cheer. Poor Nightingale was shot in the head, and fell at my feet... The Sikhs fought like devils. They charged down on us, singly, sword in hand, and strove to break through our line. But it was no go; and after a short struggle we swept them before us.

After all was over, we did what we could for our wounded and a fearful sight it was, and one to make a man's heart bleed: poor fellows lying on the ground and writhing in agony, and not a drop of water to be got. One poor fellow in my company was mortally wounded in the stomach, and lay bleeding to death; another had his leg struck off, and the quivering of his frame was fearful. The enemy lay in heaps around — some dead, some dying — but fierce and untamed even in their dying struggle; numbers of them were bayoneted by our men in the act of rearing themselves up and taking aim at the officers...

Brigadier Mountain's brigade meantime, had carried a Sikh battery at the point of the bayonet, though with heavy casualties, then wheeled left to link up with Brigadier Hoggan's, whose redcoats they could see advancing in line towards them from the left, through the drifting black smoke. Both brigades now pressed like iron pincers on the mass of desperate Sikhs, who fell back and retreated north towards the hills and ravines of Russool, lashed with grape by Colonel Lane's guns as they passed the spot where that officer's battery still held its ground.

The battle was over, but in the twilight that heralded darkness pursuit into the unknown hill territory of Russool, would, Gough decided, more likely bring bad than good. The Sikh losses were heavy, but their army was still intact and they might, with their accurate knowledge of the terrain, make a desperate counter-attack.

Gough therefore told his generals, Campbell, Gilbert and Thackwell, that he proposed holding the lines of the Sikh positions they had occupied to prevent Shere Singh possibly moving in again in the morning, as well as to remove the abandoned Sikh guns and to bring in the wounded. But Campbell pointed out that all ranks were parched with thirst — they would have to fall back on Chillianwalla, the nearest safe point where there was water enough for all, and where the provisions and baggage could be secured. Other senior officers, tongues as dry as leather, also clamoured for water. Gough's final grudging answer was reported to be, 'I'll be damned if I move till my wounded are safe.' And only when every wounded man that could be found was brought in, did he agree to move back to Chillianwalla, by which he lost all the ground he had gained during the day. 'At sunset we collected as many of our wounded as we could find,' Lieutenant Sandford wrote in a letter to his young sisters at home in Victorian England,

> and moved out of the jungle into open ground, where we piled arms and bivouacked on the ground... It came on a thick drizzling rain, and we were wet to the skin — to sleep was impossible, and we were almost perishing with thirst. In my wanderings about in search of water, I came upon the field hospital, and the sight I saw there I shall remember to my dying day — poor wounded wretches lying on the ground without a thing to cover them. 'Water — water — water!' was their ceaseless cry, and not a drop was there to slake their thirst. All the hospital apparatus was behind, and there was not a single comfort for the poor fellows: even medical assistance was very scarce; many were lying bleeding on the cold earth for hours without having a soul near them...

In those three brief hours of battle Gough had lost more than two thousand three hundred men killed, wounded and missing. Certainly, the Sikhs had retired from the field, but he had failed in his objective of driving them into the river or otherwise destroying them. It was generally regarded — apart from the fairly severe losses inflicted on the Sikhs — as a wasted battle. But the men whose comrades had lost their lives didn't think so. White-haired old Gough rode bareheaded in the rain down the lines next day and congratulated men and officers. Hats went into the air and wild ringing cheers rose from one end to the other of those lines of twelve thousand men.

Dalhousie, fretting and fuming at Ferozepore, on the Sutlej, thought and felt differently. That Gough's senior commanders had failed him — Pope who panicked, Campbell who had failed to direct a co-ordinated attack by his two brigades, Pennicuick who impetuously rushed the 24th Foot unaided at the smoking muzzles of the guns — he cared little. He became convinced that Gough had failed because he had relied too much on the bayonet and not enough on his heavy guns and mortars. 'If he (Lord Gough) disregards in his obstinacy these means again,' he wrote in February to Sir John Hobhouse, President of the Board of Control, 'if he again fights an incomplete action with terrible carnage as before, you must expect to hear of my taking a strong step; he shall not remain in command of that army in the field.'

Dalhousie had decided to sack Gough as commander-in-chief in India if he failed again to destroy Shere Singh's army. But such was the outcry in England when the news arrived that at Chillianwalla a British army had been fought to a draw by 'a wild Indian people', that the Government forced the directors of the East India Company to act at once and appoint General Sir Charles Napier to replace Gough. Even the eighty-year-old Duke of Wellington said he would go out to India and fight the Sikhs if Napier was unwilling. 'If you do not go, I must,' he told Napier.

Ignorant of Dalhousie's agitation to have him sacked, Gough now faced the problem of trying to defeat Shere Singh's elusive army and of crushing the Sikhs as an independent military power. For they were unbeaten. He still had time; the order to go would take between two and three months to reach India.

19: Gujerat and The Seizure

Early on 14 January, the day after Chillianwalla, Gough, with Brigadier Tennant, the artillery commander, Brigadier White, commanding the 1st Cavalry Brigade and Major Mackeson, the Governor-General's representative, rode over the battlefield to view the captured Sikh guns and to reconnoitre the enemy's new position. But by the hasty departure Gough had let himself be talked into last night he had forfeited the guns; the Sikhs had taken them away. Only torn and mutilated bodies, Prince Albert hats, military boots, uniforms, broken weapons and other debris of war strewed the field. Burial parties were out roping the dead to camels, removing them for mass burial.

Gough hoped that Shere Singh's force would have fled across the river Jhelum overnight into the barren Singh Sagur Doab, where he could have starved them out, but as he remarked plaintively in his dispatch, 'it did not please Almighty God to vouchsafe to the British arms the most successful issue to the extensive combinations rendered necessary for the purpose of vanquishing the Sikhs.' He saw them now in the distance, camped among the hills and ravines of Russool, a few miles to the north, huge columns of smoke arising where they burnt their dead. The morning was dull and cloudy; soon a heavy rain fell and continued for three days, turning the fine loamy soil into a smooth deep mud which clung to camels' and horses' feet, making movement for cavalry, let alone guns, impossible. The officers waded over to the mess to a miserable dinner. Everything was so wet that the cooks couldn't light a fire and the meat was raw. 'However, we were thankful to have whole throats to eat with,' said Lieutenant Sandford.

Gough was at first uncertain whether to attack at once or to wait for the Multan reinforcements. Meantime he ordered the Engineers to dig trenches round the camp in case the Sikhs made a sortie from their hill positions. The third or fourth day after the battle a tall Muslim with a red beard and a huge turban, wearing flowing Afghan white robes, rode into the camp and surrendered. He was Elihu Buksh, commander of the artillery with the Sikh forces in Peshawur, who earlier had joined Shere Singh. The information obtained from him confirmed Gough's belief that the Russool position was far too strong to attack, at least until he was reinforced by the troops from Multan. 'I do not,' he wrote to Lord Dalhousie on 19 January 1849, 'feel justified in attacking him in a position, to carry which, however shaken as he undoubtedly is, would cause a loss far greater than we can afford with our present list of wounded.'

He determined he would not attack until Whish's army joined him, whatever Dalhousie or anyone else said; and even more certain of this view did he feel when, two days later the surrounding hills reverberated with a twenty-one gun salute announcing the arrival of Chuttur Singh and a force of six thousand in the Sikh camp. News of the fall of Multan's fort reached him ten days later on 26 January 1849, so that he was assured of reinforcements in about three weeks. Above all, he wanted the four British infantry regiments in Whish's force. The four he had in the field at Chillianwalla had taken most of the brunt of the fighting, for the sepoy's morale was uncertain in this war which the Sikhs had stuck with the label of religion.

Dalhousie, not far away at Ferozepore, lashed himself into a vindictive passion over the delay in bringing the war to an end. He could not condemn Gough for awaiting reinforcements, so he attacked him personally in letters to London. 'I regret to say,' he told Sir John Hobhouse on 22 January,

> that every man in the army — generals of division — officers, Europeans and sepoys — have totally lost confidence in their leader — loudly proclaim it themselves, and report it in their letters to their friends. It is with pain that I state my opinion that I can no longer feel any confidence that the army is safe from disaster in the hands of the present C-in-C, and add that there is not a man in India who does not share that feeling with me.

Careful inquiry, had he cared to make it, would have demonstrated that the contrary was the truth; that the men and all the officers except a few disgruntled senior ones and his own agent, Major Mackeson, were devoted to Gough. But Dalhousie, feeling the absence of a decisive victory so far in the Punjab to be a reflection on his own stewardship, had grown totally irrational. He failed to understand that to wait was the only sure way to win. He wanted instant victory. In the end even the prudent Sir John Hobhouse, President of the Board of Control, pointed out to him the irrational tone of his letters.

To Gough, the situation was crystal clear. At Russool the Sikhs occupied a natural fortress of great strength. There, with perfect artillery positions among the hills and ravines, Shere Singh hoped to make his stand and destroy the flower of the British infantry. But there was one snag, of which Gough was aware. The Sikhs lived off the land and in that barren region there was nothing. Shere Singh must therefore quit his perfect position soon or see his men and his horses grow weak for lack of food. Towards the end of January he made a threatening move to try to entice the British into attacking him, but Gough refused, stood firm on the open plain.

Shere Singh saw that he had failed and quietly two days later, on 2 February, he marched some forty to fifty thousand men and about forty guns out through a pass in the hills at night to Khoree, four miles south, in a jungly plain, leaving up to twelve thousand men and twenty-seven guns to hold the position at Russool. Gough sent cavalry pickets to watch them, and on 7 February reported to the angry and excited Dalhousie:

> I had all their movements closely watched from the mound of Mugnawalla, within a mile of Khoree, having a good view of the Pass and country; but they pushed forward so large a force of infantry and cavalry yesterday, that my pickets were obliged to fall back. I am biding my time, and be assured, I will not lose any opportunity of striking a blow when I can do it with effect.

This letter did little to calm the Governor-General, for his agent, Major Mackeson, began now to put pressure on Gough to attack at once. Various other senior commanders, anxious for Dalhousie's approval, supported the clamour, but Gough, having decided what to do, refused to budge until the time was ripe — until his reinforcements had come up and until Shere Singh had been forced by shortage of provisions to move his entire army to the open and fertile Chenab plain near Gujerat, some twenty-five miles to the east.

Shere Singh began to grow uneasy about these same two problems of food and the danger of having to fight Gough strengthened by the Multan force. He tried again to entice the British general to attack him, intending, if he did, to retire, and lure him on to the strong position at Russool. There, he hoped either to defeat or to weaken the British so that they would need to withdraw, when he could provision on the north bank of the Chenab, while still holding Russool.

First, he moved his army south upon Dinghi, as if to threaten Gough's line of communications. Gough stood firm. Then on 11 February, he advanced with apparently the whole of his force at Khoree to try to draw Gough out of his fortified camp, so that 'a strong force he had concealed amongst the jungle towards Mong might have an opportunity of attacking my camp,' Gough said in a letter next day to Dalhousie.

> My cavalry patrols, consisting of only four squadrons, kept the whole of the enemy's cavalry at bay. This proved that they had no intention of bringing on an action at the point they had advanced to, but to draw me on to attack them in the thick jungle in their rear, in which they were ready to fall back. Although well able to punish them, I felt... that it would be more desirable to do so powerfully (which with God's blessing I trust to do) than partially.

The next day, 13 February, Brigadier-General Cheape, of the Engineers, rode in with a few squadrons of cavalry from Multan with the news that Whish's force was marching twenty miles a day and near at hand. The night after, Shere Singh, knowing now that Gough would not be lured into a battle that he didn't want, quickly moved both his main army and his garrison at Russool into a skilfully chosen position before Gujerat, about twenty-five miles east, on the banks of the Chenab, intending, he proclaimed, to cross the river and march on Lahore. More important, he advanced a force of six thousand cavalry and a few guns to seize the Sudra ford at Wazirabad, occupied then only by two regiments of Indian cavalry and a few guns under Lieutenant Hodson. But Gough had foreseen this danger, and Whish, anticipating Gough's order, had sent Colonel Byrne with the 53rd Foot, the 13th Native Infantry, four guns and two regiments of Irregular Cavalry, to oppose the crossing.

The sun glinting on their drawn sabres, the mass of Sikh cavalry, a sea of white splashed with the red, the gold and green of their great silk banners, rode up to the banks of the rippling Chenab. They saw a mile away over the water, the redcoat ranks of Byrne's force, turned their horses and rode away. Skilled though they were in hit-and-run tactics, they were not hardened enough soldiers to cross a half-mile river under fire, then charge and scatter a disciplined force.

So it was with Shere Singh. The valour of the British infantry at Chillianwalla had seemingly shaken at once his own morale and that of his men. Less than ever was he willing to fight except defensively, from a strong position, at Russool first, and now at Gujerat. Faint-hearted, on the open plain he didn't dare attack, though at the eleventh hour, while Gough had still not yet joined forces with Whish's three thousand British and six thousand Indian troops he did not lack chances. The Multan force was only now nearing Ramnuggur, weary after the hard weeks of the siege and the hard marching at twenty miles a day (many of the troops staggering beneath the weight of gold they had hidden in their equipment). With relief, they saw the British reserve force, under Sir Dudley Hill, in camp between town and river, the white canvas walls shining in the brilliant sun. They camped where Gough had his first fateful clash with Shere Singh in November, but relief turned to disgust. The wells were contaminated with the dead and the very ground reeked with dead camels, bullocks and horses.

The so-called pageantry, the 'glorious military promenades' of nineteenth-century warfare in India were mostly a shambles

— the beautiful places of the earth were changed into a hell with a satanic stench.

Gough, on the 15th, again turning down suggestions from his staff that he should now move direct to confront Shere Singh at Gujerat, marched his army out of his camp and made a lightning move south via Dinghi to Lasoorie without the slightest hindrance from the enemy, to secure his communications with Whish's force, then only twelve miles away, across the Chenab. Gough had sent to the stores depot at Ramnuggur, practically all his non-combatant troops, including the records department, ridding himself by this move alone of some hundreds of men and nine thousand camels, greatly improving his mobility.

Part of the 16th he spent in council in the one great glass-windowed tent he now had for all purposes. Here he finalized plans for linking with Whish's force and confronting Shere Singh, then set his army in motion. He marched in battle order — ready always — nine miles south-east to Sadullapore, near the Chenab, where Shere Singh had lost his chance in December of crushing Thackwell's smaller force; four miles to Ishera, next day, where he was joined by one brigade of Whish's force; three miles to Tricca, on the 18th, where Whish's second brigade joined him, the smoke of the Sikh camp fires darkening the sky only five miles away. On the 20th Brigadier Dundas arrived with Whish's third brigade after a forced march of forty-five miles. Gough now advanced through the rich and fertile farmlands to Shadiwala, only three miles from the Sikh battle line. 'For miles and miles around there is nothing but luxuriant green cornfields,' Lieutenant Sandford remarked in his journal. 'I am pitched right in the centre of one, and have a soft verdant carpet under my feet.

Just imagine the damage an army like this must do to the crops.'

With a force of twenty-four thousand men and no less than one hundred and six guns, Gough felt certain of finally shattering the Sikh army. About four thousand men were needed to guard the provisions, forage and reserve ammunition in the camp, so he was able to put twenty thousand fighting men in the field.[19] Generals Gilbert and Campbell commanded the second and third infantry division, as at Chillianwalla, and General Whish the first division.

The Sikhs were estimated at between forty and fifty thousand, with fifty-nine guns, commanded by Raja Shere Singh and his father Chuttur Singh, one thousand five hundred

---

[19] General Gough's Army — 21 February 1849. Cavalry Division — Lieutenant-General Sir J. Thackwell. 1st Brigade: Colonel Lockwood — 14th Light Dragoons, 1st Bengal Light Cavalry, detachments of 11th and 18th Irregular Cavalry. 2nd Brigade: Colonel Hearsey — 3rd and 9th Irregular Cavalry. 3rd Brigade: Brigadier White — 3rd Light Dragoons and 9th Lancers, 8th Bengal Light Cavalry, Sind Horse, two troops horse-artillery, 1st Infantry Division, Major-General Whish. Brigadier Hervey's brigade: 10th Foot, 8th and 52nd Native Infantry, one company of pioneers one troop of horse artillery. Brigadier Markham's brigade: 32nd Foot, 51st and 72nd Native Infantry, 2 troops horse artillery; Dawes's light field battery, 2 troops of horse artillery in reserve. Brigadier, Reserve: Hoggan: 5th and 6th Native Light Cavalry; 45th and 69th Native Infantry, one Bombay light field battery. 2nd Infantry Division, Major-General W. R. Gilbert. Brigadier Penny — 2nd Bengal Europeans, 31st and 70th Native Infantry. Brigadier Mountain — 29th Foot, 30th and 56th Bengal Native Infantry. 3rd Infantry Division, Brigadier-General Colin Campbell. Brigadier Carnegie — 24th Foot, 25th Bengal Native Infantry. Brigadier Mcleod — 61st Foot, 36th and 46th Bengal Native Infantry, 2 light field batteries. Brigadier Dundas — 60th Rifles, 1st Bombay Fusiliers Europeans, 3rd and 19th Bombay Native Infantry, one Bombay light field battery. Brigadier Tennant's heavy artillery: 12 18-pounders, 10 8-in howitzers.

Afghan cavalry being led by Akram Khan, son of Dost Mahommed Khan, ruler of Afghanistan. (Another force of several thousand Afghans led by the ruler himself had been promised, but had not yet arrived.) Cavalry reconnaissance and trusted spies revealed that the Sikhs' infantry battalions and guns were drawn up behind three fortified villages in an open space six thousand yards wide between the dry bed of the river Dwara on their right and the wide stream on their left of the Katela, which ran into the Chenab about a mile south. The ground between these two protective river beds was flat and without any kind of obstruction, ideal for the rapid movement of both infantry and guns. Most of the Sikh cavalry Shere Singh had placed on the far side of the river Dwara on his right, but he had also protected the left with a strong body of cavalry on the far side of the Katela. Thus the Sikh infantry line ran from the Dwara river bed, in which the right wing was placed, across six thousand yards to the Katela, with guns between regiments and in the fortified villages. In front of the villages lay fields thick with green corn.

The Sikh left seemed least well placed and Gough, in conference with his commanders, decided to attack their left and centre first and thrust them back upon their right while simultaneously thrusting their right wing back too. Accordingly, the heavy artillery was placed in the centre of the British line, Gilbert and Whish's divisions forming the right wing, which, as that part expected to bear the brunt of the attack, was supported by most of the field artillery; and the left wing, composed of Campbell's division, was divided between the brigades of Dundas, on the far left, and Mountain, who was by the Dwara river bed. Expected to come into play later than the British right wing, the left was given the task of finishing the destruction and dispersion of the Sikh troops when their left and centre had been forced back on their right. Oddly enough, the small herd of elephants drawing the ten British 18-pounders and their ammunition wagons in the centre were to regulate the pace of the infantry advance. They were easy to see.

The morning of 21 February dawned clear and bright, the larks sang merrily and to the north, high on the distant horizon, loomed the glittering white chain of the Himalayas, a superb backdrop to an epic scene. 'A little before 4 am the orderly sergeant came to call the corporals to go and see the rations drawn, and get them cooked immediately,' Corporal Ryder noted accurately in his journal.

> We had just made fires, and got our frying pans on, and our baggage was not packed, nor the camp struck, when the well-known sound of the bugle was heard, ringing through the camp for us to stand to arms. All was now confusion: we got a dram of grog served out per man, and a pound of bread for every two comrades. Our accoutrements were soon upon us, and our muskets in our hands. Some might be seen with a slice of raw meat in their grasp, which they had snatched up as they went by; and others were running with their bread in their hands, eating it as they went. I caught hold of some meat out of the frying pan, as it was upon the fire, which had not been on long, so it was raw or nearly so; but I was hungry enough to eat my boot-soles, if it had been possible. I had often heard talk of a hungry army, but none could be more hungry than this... Yet our men were all in high spirits, and appeared eager for the battle.

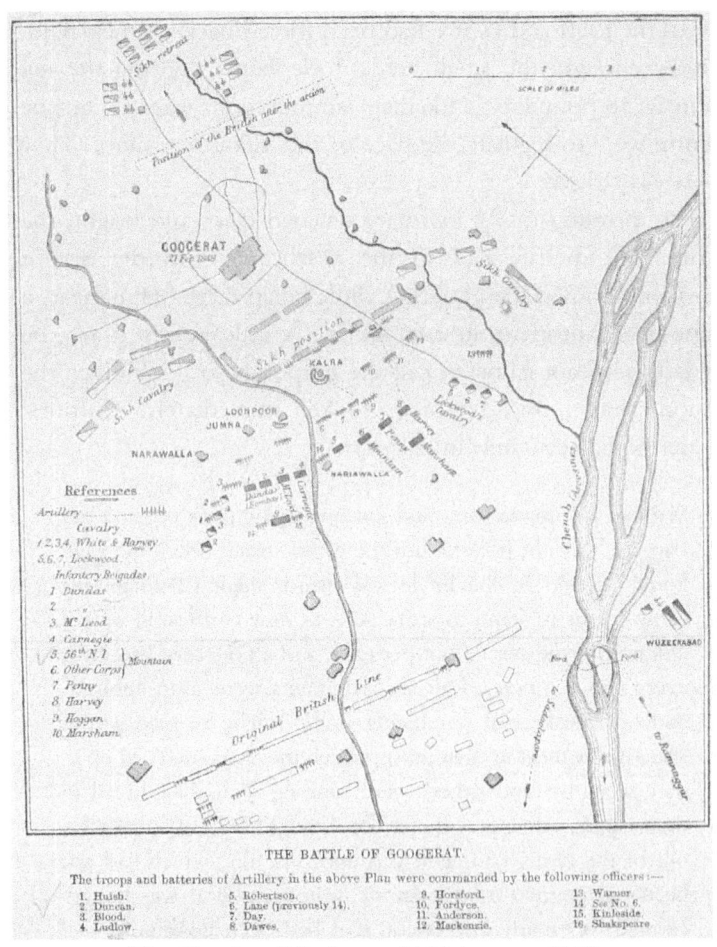

The Battle of Gujerat, 21 February 1849

The whole army was now arrayed in battle order in a line three miles from the Sikhs, behind whom the minarets of Gujerat glittered in the early sunshine. One officer recalled hearing the sudden noise of cheering on the far right of the line. It grew louder and louder, until he saw the men throwing their hats in the air, and out in front of them at the head of his staff,

General Gough, riding with his white hair streaming in the breeze. He passed out of sight and the cheering died away in the distance. 'It was the most fervid demonstration of affection I ever saw in my life,' said this officer.

At seven o'clock, the British bugles sounded the advance and the line strode steadily forward for almost two miles, all the men silent, alone with their thoughts, their hopes, their fears. The Sikh left and centre, about two thousand yards away, now faced the British right wing. Their gunners, just as they did at Chillianwalla, opened fire prematurely, their shot falling short and their battery positions revealed. Continuing to advance until the infantry were just out of range, Gough then halted the line, about nine o'clock, and ordered the artillery to the front to begin a bombardment under cover of skirmishers. The earth shook and the air trembled as every British gun except the twelve of the two reserve batteries opened fire with round-shot and shrapnel shell, the heavier guns at eight hundred to a thousand yards and the lighter ones at six hundred and three hundred. Smoke and dust jumped and whirled above the enemy lines as a deluge of fire lashed them.

The Sikh guns answered with rapidity and precision, advancing, it would seem, to get within range. Two British ammunition wagons were hit and blown up and several guns knocked out during the first half-hour. Lieutenant Sandford, 2nd Bengal Europeans, was in the thick of it:

> The round-shot flew about us, and ploughed up the ground in all directions. Five or six men were knocked down in as many seconds, when we were ordered to lie down... At the end of an hour we were ordered to advance another hundred yards and then lie down again. A company from each regiment in the brigade was sent up to the front to support the troop of horse-artillery attached to us; and, poor fellows, they suffered

dreadfully, being brought in one after another wounded — some with legs shot off, some cut in half, some torn with grape — scarcely half of our rifle company was left. All this time, the fire was very hot on us, carrying off three men at a time, shells bursting over us, or burying themselves in front, scattering the earth in our faces... The troop in front (Fordyce's), suffered dreadfully — every shot pitched right into them; and the gallant manner in which they worked their guns is beyond all praise. Twice had they to retire to the rear for fresh horses and men, and each time as they came up again and passed through our line, we gave them a hearty cheer; and the fine fellows waved their caps and dashed on again as if death was a joke to them.

Gough at this time had taken up his position behind the 24-pounders, clearly determined to continue this violent bombardment until the Sikh artillery was silenced. And in this position he stayed. The story that when he ascended a building for a view of the battle his staff took away the ladder so that, excited by the smell of powder, he could not order in the infantry prematurely, is of course, apocryphal; for one thing, they would not have dared.

The crash of the cannonade split the hot dry air for nearly three hours in its onslaught on the Sikh guns, sweeping away the gunners, dismounting their weapons and silencing battery after battery. The Sikh gunnery too, took its toll, but the outcome was overwhelmingly in favour of the British, who stubbornly fought on. During the cannonade the Sikh cavalry plunged in masses through the Katela stream on the right, intending to scatter the British cavalry and charge the infantry. Brigadier Hearsey, commanding the 3rd and 9th Irregular Cavalry accepted the challenge, warding off the Sikhs mainly by well-aimed blasts of grape from his horse artillery. Move and counter-move of the squadrons eventually separated the

British cavalry from the infantry on their left, dangerously exposing it. Brigadier Lockwood moved in to cover it and the Sikh cavalry retired, Hearsey's Irregulars cutting many of them down as they went.

Gough now decided that the Sikh guns were no longer so dangerous and ordered a general infantry advance along the whole line, at the same time telling General Gilbert to send forward light troops to make the enemy show any hidden gun positions. Gilbert sent forward a troop of horse artillery and Dawes's light field-battery. They had advanced barely two hundred yards when orange flame spurted from two batteries hidden on each side of the brown mud village of Burra Kalra, three hundred yards ahead; and grapeshot whistled among the gunners, who stopped to engage them, while Sikhs manning the mud walls of the village fired a withering volley at the approaching infantry. General Gilbert ordered Brigadier Penny's brigade to storm it, and with Penny at their head, the 2nd Bengal Europeans, mostly Irishmen, followed by the 31st and 70th Native Infantry, began the first infantry move in the battle. 'Our men, who had been held down all the time, started up with a cheer,' reported Lieutenant Sandford.

> It was the last some of them gave, poor fellows! A round-shot took off a man's head close to me, and spattered his brains in my face, the bullets whizzing about like hail, and, as we came nearer, grape was poured into us; but not a man wavered for a second. 'Officers to the front — lead on your men!' shouted the Major; and we sprang forward amidst the shower of balls, dashed across a deep nullah, gave one rattling volley and poured into the village at every point. Many of the Sikhs stood and fought like men; but the greater portion (there must have been at least about a thousand) left the village at one end as we entered at the other. Those who remained were shot or bayoneted on the spot. There was no quarter given. A number

of them shut themselves up in their houses; but our men beat down the doors, and poured in volley after volley, and sullenly and savagely they died, fighting to the last. We captured three of their standards in the village, and then, leaving the left wing to keep possession, we defiled to the right and found ourselves under a hot fire of grape and cannister, totally unsupported, as we had advanced in front of the whole line to storm the village, and the troops of horse artillery had been obliged to retire, being temporarily disabled. This was the most deadly fire we were exposed to during the day, the balls hissing about like winged serpents. A troop of horse artillery dashed past us at a gallop, drew up, unlimbered and returned the enemy's fire. The whole line of infantry was seen advancing; our guns poured in a withering fire; the enemy left theirs and fled.

The first infantry onslaught of the battle, the taking of Burra Kalra, cost Gough six officers and one hundred and forty-three men of the 2nd Europeans, one hundred and twenty-eight men of the 31st Native Infantry and forty-four of the 70th Native Infantry killed or wounded, a total of three hundred and twenty-one — all because of General Gilbert's mistake. He thought that the village 'seemed to be unoccupied,' assumed this to be a fact, failed to ask the heavy artillery to knock it down and sent his best brigade pell-mell to be killed and maimed.

At the same time, the 10th Foot and 8th Native Infantry of Brigadier Hervey's brigade supported by Fordyce's troop of Horse Artillery, had attacked the fortified village of Chota Kalra, about two thousand yards to the right. The Sikhs fired volleys from loop-holes in the village walls, the British horse artillery galloped up, unlimbered and fired at point-blank range; the infantry charged, beat down the doors with musket butts and drove the stubborn Sikhs out in fierce hand-to-hand fighting. The battery of Captain Anderson, an ageing, but good-humoured and likeable Horse Artillery officer, was exposed to a destructive crossfire. Several of his men were wounded and sent to the rear. A round-shot wounded Anderson while he was putting the port-fire to one of his guns himself, and he was told to retire, but he said he would have another shot or two first, when he was hit and killed outright. Nowhere did the Sikhs fight more doggedly, in barely thirty minutes killing or wounding ninety-four soldiers — lives which a few rounds from the heavy guns earlier would have saved. No mention in the dispatches was made of these two fatal errors; great reputations, like buttons and bayonets, were kept bright.

Meanwhile, the enemy cavalry and horse artillery on both left and right surged forward to try to turn the British flanks. Captain Duncan moved his Horse Artillery troop into action at once and at five hundred yards bowled many of them down with grapeshot, but Akram Khan's Afghans came on in a dense fastmoving body. Thackwell ordered the Sind Horse and two squadrons of 9th Lancers to charge them, and, he noted:

> These troops made a most brilliant charge. At the same time I advanced the guns... The fire of the guns soon put the Goorchurras in retreat, and the glorious charge of the troops on their left caused their whole force to seek safety in retreat by the Burradurree (a Sikh 'pleasure-house')... But as we were then considerably in advance of the left of the infantry... and ignorant of the force the enemy might have... it became necessary to proceed with caution. Yet I was soon able to open a fire upon the enemy, both on the right and the left of the former place, which caused them considerable loss, and hastened their retreat.

On the British right, the cavalry and horse artillery under

Brigadier Hearsey also succeeded in repulsing the determined attempts by the Sikh cavalry to turn the British line. At one time a small body of Afghan cavalry charged and swept to the rear of the British heavy guns towards Gough and his staff. They were believed to be Pathans of the Multan force, until Lieutenant Stannus, commanding the 5th Light Cavalry of the personal escort, recognized them, led his men in a charge, and after a short sharp fight in which he was wounded, scattered them.

Now that the Sikhs had been driven out of their strong positions on the left, the British line, keeping level with the heavy elephant-drawn guns (those stately animals stayed calm and patient throughout the battle), moved forward steadily, until the 24th Foot, in and on both sides of the Dwara nulla, were opposed and held up by masses of Shere Singh's infantry, conspicuous in scarlet infantry tunics, with white stripes across the breast. As a result, a dangerous gap widened in the British line between Gilbert's and Whish's divisions in the centre and on the right, and Campbell's on the left. The Sikh commanders opposing Campbell were quick to see this. Speedily, they deployed a body of infantry and cavalry and advanced boldly to penetrate and split the British line.

General Gough was at this time receiving the plaudits of his staff on having by midday overcome practically all opposition. The heroic Sikhs, though facing a terrible crisis, now launched this desperate and courageous bid for victory.

Holding high their great yellow banners, marching in a closely held line with a few surviving guns between regiments, the red-breasted Sikhs, black-bearded and turbaned, strode through the British gap before wheeling to right and left for a massed flank attack. The danger worsened when two troops of Horse Artillery Gough had sent up, at the last moment ran out of shot and shell — they must await a fresh supply from the rear. Forward companies of the Sikhs, shouting their sacred war-cry, began to charge the isolated British gunners.

It looked bad for them, but from his post on the banks of the Dwara that careful commander General Colin Campbell had seen the danger and had quickly given his orders. Captain Ludlow's 18-pounders unlimbered and from five or six hundred yards range blasted the Sikhs, whose officers realized that an advance through this withering flank fire would be suicidal. And as their men began to fall, they turned about and began an orderly retreat covered by cavalry.

Whish's division on the far right had meantime continued to go forward against the stubbornly retreating enemy. This was in one sense desirable, but it tended to widen the gap in the British line and make it vulnerable to another Sikh counter-attack — perhaps this time better supported. Through the smoke that hung heavily over the field, Gough saw the renewed danger, and sent one of his aides galloping a mile to the right to slow down Whish's advance. Corporal Ryder, of the 32nd, was in the thick of the most bitter fighting there and he describes vividly the effect of Gough's order:

> The enemy formed several squares to keep us in check whilst they got their guns away, but our field artillery galloped to the front and opened a most destructive fire of grape and cannister, which swept them down by whole battalions. On we rushed, bearing down all before us, charging and cheering. We took every gun we came up to, but their artillery fought desperately: they stood and defended their guns to the last. They threw their arms round them, kissed them and died. Others would spit at us when the bayonet was through their bodies. An aide-de-camp now rode up with orders from Lord Gough to say that the right of the line was too far forward, and that we were to halt... This was a very trying time for the

right of the line. While we were standing, waiting for orders to advance, the enemy were boldly reforming their line in our front and keeping up a fire on us; although it was nearly harmless, as they (as usual) fired high. Our men were with the greatest difficulty in the world kept in check by the officers. Lord Gough sent a second order for the right to keep back, as the left could not get up; and the Brigadier (Markham) told the aide-de-camp that he could not keep the men back, nor did he, until he rode at all hazard in front of the line, telling the men to cease firing and to halt. The enemy now had brought some guns to bear upon us with grape. The first round they fired fell just in front of us, and as the ground was fresh ploughed, the shots buried themselves in it, but the second round came... slightly wounding one of our men and severely wounding another. They also made a gap in the 51st regiment of Native Infantry...

One of the Sikh cavalry regiments, bearing a black flag, then deliberately formed line in front of us, as if about to charge us, when our men could stand it no longer. We opened fire upon them, and whether any word 'forward' was given or not, I do not know, but forward we went, and when near to them, and just as they were about to spring forward upon us, we opened such a well-directed fire, and poured it into them with such deadly effect, that it fetched down man and horse by scores to the ground, while numbers of saddles were emptied and the horses went off, leaving their lifeless riders behind. On we went, charging and cheering, bearing all down before us and the black flag fell into our hands...

Fortunately, the Sikh right, completely turned now by General Campbell, was in full retreat and, driven in upon the centre, was forced to cross the front and retreat to the east of Gujerat with their left wing. Here and there they made brave attempts to make stands at the villages in their path, but they were overwhelmed in the relentless British onrush and shot or bayoneted.

By one o'clock in the afternoon, Gough had overthrown the Sikh army, and had crowded it in heavy masses upon a line of retreat which offered no hope of support for the disheartened soldiery. By two o'clock, when thousands of riderless horses were careering about the field, Gough's infantry had stormed Gujerat and advanced to the north, while the cavalry and horse artillery pursued the rapidly fleeing Shere Singh and his scattered troops, sabreing and lancing them in repeated assaults. Many Sikh soldiers stripped themselves of their uniforms, quit the ranks and hid to try to save themselves, but no quarter was given, armed and unarmed fell to sword, pistol and grapeshot. As well as the battlefield, the whole countryside was soon littered with untidy heaps of the dead — of abandoned guns, wagons, tents, uniforms, banners, and merchandise dropped by the Sikh camp followers in their flight. (Captain Thackwell rescued a bottle of Maraschino and one of his friends a magnum of champagne.)

Darkness and the Sikh speed in retreat finally stopped the grim chase and General Thackwell, who led it, prepared to camp for the night fourteen miles from the battlefield, but Gough, taking no chances, recalled him to camp. At Gujerat then, Gough ordered an immediate issue of a dram of grog to each and every man and, says Ryder, 'we cheered our aged general as he rode along the ranks. We set fire to the camp and destroyed the gunpowder... Tons upon tons were buried in the ground, which we blew up. Lord Gough came among us and was very full of jokes. He said the enemy's teeth were drawn, and that they were totally defeated.'

Superb mobility had saved what was left of the Sikh army; but it had to be taken, and next day at dawn General Gilbert's entire division, strengthened by the 14th Light Dragoons, a regiment of Irregular Cavalry and two batteries of field artillery, set out in hot pursuit to demand its unconditional surrender. Gilbert and his force covered more than fifty miles in seventy-two hours, then halted for three days, crossed the Jhelum on 28 February and continued the chase. By 8 March, he was within a day's march of Rawalpindi, where Shere Singh had halted with sixteen thousand loyal troops, all that remained of his fifty thousand strong force. Shere Singh and Lal Singh came in to surrender so as to prevent another battle, bringing with them the British prisoners taken at Peshawur and Attock. The next day Shere Singh returned to Rawalpindi to arrange for the unconditional surrender of his army. General Gilbert advanced his forces to the outskirts of the city near Shere Singh's camp, where astride the road he formed a gigantic square. Through this the remnant of Ranjit Singh's proud Khalsa marched and delivered up a total of twenty thousand muskets and forty-one guns. 'The reluctance of some of the old Khalsa veterans to surrender their arms was evident,' noted Captain Thackwell, who was present. 'Some could not restrain their tears; while on the faces of others, rage and hatred was visibly depicted.'

Still high, despite their defeat was the morale of Shere Singh's remarkable men and all would willingly have continued the Sikh traditional guerrilla warfare which their ancestors had waged during their resistance centuries earlier to Muslim repression. But in the north the Muslim peasantry were bitterly opposed to them; they were short of food and after their defeat at Gujerat both the Afghans behind and Gulab Singh's forces in nearby Kashmir might at any time turn against them. So Shere Singh gave in and the power of the Sikhs as an independent nation was finally broken. All that remained was to drive Dost Mahommed's Afghans out of Peshawur and on 21 March 1849, General Gilbert entered the city without firing a shot, the Afghans having fled and retreated through the Khyber Pass two days before.

British losses at Gujerat amounted in the six hours of the battle to the surprisingly low total of ninety-six of all ranks killed and seven hundred wounded, and while no estimate seems to have been made of Sikh casualties, they must have been heavy indeed. Fifty-three guns were captured at Gujerat and three more found afterwards. Extraordinary were the numbers of Sikh guns. Another forty-nine were surrendered to General Gilbert, fifty were taken at Multan and when Colonel McSherry occupied the fort at Govindghur he discovered another hundred buried in the earth. Many more were found by the British at Lahore, Amritsar and Jullander. The Sikhs had a veritable passion for them, turning many of them into works of art, with ivory and polished steel inlaid in the woodwork like fourteenth and fifteenth-century European matchlocks.

They had learned well the lessons of the artillerists Alexander Gardner, Avitabile, and Court, that artillery would decide future battles. Gujerat was decided by artillery. 'The victory was Brigadier Tennant's,' Lord Gough was reported to have said and the precision of the British gunners was superb. Ryder reports seeing all over the field, artillerymen and horses flung one upon another as they had been shot down in whole batteries. Yet in the end, the infantry, as always, turned the havoc done by the guns into victory; what Dr McGregor wondered at and called the extraordinary courage of the ordinary soldiers won the day and amazed the Sikhs, as it usually did. Ryder tells a revealing little story:

> When we asked some of the prisoners if they had had enough of fighting, and if they were tired of it, they said they were not — they should fight yet again; and if we fought fair they should beat us. They asked us what our officers gave us to

make us drunk with; for we must be drunk, they said, when we shouted and ran up to their batteries, in the face of their fire, and to the mouth of their guns. They called us 'beardless boys,' and said we must be mad, or fools, to go up to their fire in the way we did... They were as fine-looking men as ever drew swords. We seemed like children by the side of them. They were well-made and bold-looking, and I wonder how such boys as we were beat them; but it was through having a good heart, steadiness in the field under a heavy fire, and a determined spirit...

Those few words of this country lad sum up, so far as the army is concerned, the whole story of the taking of the Punjab and, indeed, of India.

The Punjab was annexed on 30 March 1849, and proclaimed a British possession. That it was illegal and fraudulent, there is little doubt. By the Agreement made with the Lahore Government on 16 December 1846, the British Government assumed and delegated to its special representative 'full authority to direct and control all matters in every department of the State' until Maharajah Duleep Singh (then nine) was sixteen. The Governor-General was only entitled to end the arrangement before 1854 if he and the Lahore Government were satisfied that 'the interposition of the British Government is no longer necessary for maintaining the Government of His Highness the Maharajah.'

Thus, this agreement, while it made the British Government responsible for law and order in the Punjab, made it as well the protector and guardian of the young Maharajah. Two years and three months later came the rebellion of Mulraj and the rising of the Khalsa against British overlordship. Dalhousie, Lord Gough and the British army defeated the Khalsa and conquered the Punjab. The question which Dalhousie had earlier ignored, then arose again — having regard to the terms of the Agreement, for whom had the British conquered the Punjab? Sir Henry Lawrence, then Resident at Lahore, said firmly that it was on behalf of the Maharajah, whom the British Government recognized as heir to the throne. Having brought troops into the Punjab in 1848 to support the Lahore Government under the terms of the Agreement, 'to put down all opposition to constituted authority', Dalhousie could not declare it null and void, and it still stood. But, a convinced imperialist, Dalhousie nevertheless declared the Punjab conquered on behalf of the British Government. Thus, in the name of this Government, he protected his ward by confiscating his throne, his country and his personal fortune, worth one or two million sterling, apart from the Koh-i-noor diamond. In return the Maharajah was to receive an annual pension throughout his life 'provided he shall remain obedient to the British Government' and reside at whatever place outside the Punjab it might select. He was obliged to sign the document agreeing to this on 29 March 1849, at the age of nine.

The British thus became owners of another fifteen thousand square miles of territory in India, and, most important, extended their boundaries to its natural frontiers, the hills beyond the Indus.

Dalhousie appointed a committee of three to govern the country, Henry Lawrence and his brother John being two of them. Sir Henry Lawrence became Lieutenant-Governor of the Punjab, which became a new province of British India. Fairly and reasonably though the British did then rule, settled and prosperous though the Sikhs did become, they had lost their independence when historically, they seemed to have been destined to occupy and rule all India. For in their religion they possessed a key to ending the ancient hostility between Muslims and Hindus, and a possible enduring unification of the country.

The Sikhs were thenceforward finished as an independent power. They had been brought down by those twin weapons of nineteenth-century imperialism, fraud and violence; which allied though they were with great courage, heroism, humanity, and devotion to the public welfare among individual British, still lay at the heart of the Indian Empire.

Nearly everyone once thought that this Empire throughout the world would last, if not for ever, certainly for generations, yet already it is a memory, a written record — 'an old bitch gone in the teeth... two gross of broken statues'; even the political and civic ideals which we left are now withering away in Africa and Asia. And the feelings of British people about the Empire range from an uneasy sense of guilt to outright disdain. Yet the making of it was the whole of life for the men who fill these pages. They believed in it with all their hearts and minds.

Note on Wounds

Sword-cuts, round-shot from artillery, and the musket-ball caused most of the wounds suffered by nineteenth-century soldiers. In the Punjab, the dangers to life and limb were far greater from any of these than in Europe, owing to the great heat, to flies and to consequent bigger risk of infection. Sikh soldiers fought with sharper and heavier swords than the British. Their technique was also more damaging. They did not simply strike with the sword, but at once struck and drew the weapon back with a cutting motion that made longer and deeper wounds, penetrating bone as well as flesh. If the British soldier, or the sepoy, survived the loss of blood following a deep sword wound, he would probably, by the time the fighting ended, and he received medical attention on the field, or in a field hospital, have contracted gangrene. Almost certainly, he was then too weak to undergo amputation, without anaesthetic or blood transfusion. The chaplain would tell him to make his peace with God. Amputations gave a badly wounded man a slightly better chance of life and were, therefore, extremely common.

A musket ball, fired at short range, say fifty or sixty yards, or less, could be fatal if it struck the head or body, because it made a large wound and caused much damage. But the worst wounds were made by cannon-fire. A surgeon with the British army during the Second Sikh War, Mr J. J. Cole, gives a grim account of the havoc wrought in the human body by the gunfire of the day:

The round-shot, when it fairly impinges on a limb soon after leaving the gun, inevitably destroys it: the member is forever lost! The injury that entails so serious a deprivation must obviously be severe and perilous. Nevertheless, the wound is not so dangerous to life or nearly so difficult to treat as the injury that the same shot produces when it has travelled four or five hundred yards further, or when, perhaps, it has nearly reached its goal: then it is that occur the most serious lesions which can befall the extremities of man.

In the former case the missile cuts completely clean through the tissues without impairing the parts above. Its rapidity is so great, that it has not time, as it were, to do mischief but to the structures with which it actually comes into contact. In the latter (having lost some of its impetus) it tears its way... through the structures and hangs in the wound long enough to impart its destructive influence to the adjacent tissues. The wound, for the most part, has the following aspect, viz, the integuments are extensively lacerated above and below; the muscles dreadfully torn and separated from their attachments, and their interspaces are filled with coagulated blood; vessels, nerves and tendons hang down in shreds; the bones are fearfully comminuted, and, worse still, sometimes fractured a considerable distance from the wound itself.

For example, when the seat of the injury is just above the ankle joint, the tibia may be split up, or broken close to the knee; or when the knee itself, or the thigh immediately above it is destroyed, the femur may be fractured in the middle of the shaft... even as high up as the neck of the bone.

Faced with these terrible wounds all a surgeon could do was amputate or clean, extract the shot or fragments of it and tie up, while supplying, so far as he could, natural conditions such as fresh air, good food, comfort and quiet, in which physical vitality, or what he regarded as the survival reaction, might possibly save a man. And very frequently it did. Chloroform,

Cole detested, because it stopped pain, which, he was convinced, was helpful as a survival agent:

> The practical surgeon views it in the hands of the military medical officer as a highly pernicious agent, which unquestionably it is... In time of war, on the field of battle, on the bloody plain, or in the field hospital, it should not be found, no place should be assigned to it... That it renders the poor patient unconscious cannot be doubted. But what is pain? It is one of the most powerful, one of the most salutary *stimulants* known. It often brings about reaction of the most natural kind... Have we not reason to remember that reaction began to appear with the application of the knife and was fairly brought about before it was laid aside?

But only the British soldier reacted favourably, it seems, to being brought to consciousness as a result of considerable pain; the sepoy frequently died of shock from the initial injury. No account of the battles of the first half of the nineteenth century, and especially those described in this book, should be read without calling to mind the wounds that soldiers then suffered and the surgery they had to undergo, as well as their frequent extraordinary powers of recovery.

Author's Note

The Anglo-Sikh Wars have been ignored by historians for more than fifty years, yet they were the bloodiest the British ever fought in India, and the annexation of the Punjab, which followed them, practically completed British domination of the sub-continent. At the same time, it contributed largely to the Indian mistrust and dislike of the British presence that gave rise to the so-called Mutiny eighteen years later.

I have given a full account of the men and events involved in the causes of the war — on both sides — mainly from hitherto unpublished official reports and from diaries and letters. The violence and ferocity of these battles, fought in jungles and dust-clouds, also emerges.

I should like to record my thanks to Mr S. C. Sutton, CBE, Librarian, and his staff at the India Office Library; to Mr D. W. King, Librarian, and his staff at what used to be called The War Office Library; to the staff of the British Museum Manuscripts Department; and to my wife, who kept a critical eye on the book.

GEORGE BRUCE

If you have enjoyed this enough to leave a review on **Amazon** and **Goodreads**, then we would be truly grateful.

THE ESTATE OF GEORGE BRUCE

Selected Bibliography

UNPUBLISHED

Enclosures to Secret Letters from India, 1835 to 1850 (India Office Records).

Punjab Intelligence Reports, 1837 to 1849 (India Office Records).

Broughton Papers. British Museum. Add. Mss, 36476/77.

Journal Kept During The Siege of Multan, Major G. Pearse, India Office Records.

Diary of The First Sikh War, Robert Cust, British Museum, Add. Mss, 45390-406.

Diary, T. Pierce, British Museum, Add. Mss, 42498-500.

Ellenborough Papers, Public Record Office.

PUBLISHED

The Life & Campaigns of Hugh, Viscount Gough, R. S. Rait, Constable & Co, 1903.

The First & Second Sikh Wars, Lt-Col R. G. Burton, Simla, 1911.

The Sikhs & The Sikh Wars, Gen. Sir Charles Gough, VC, & Innes, Innes & Co, 1897.

The History of the Sikhs, W. L. McGregor, MD, James Madden, 1846.

A History of the Sikhs, Capt J. D. Cunningham, edited by H. L. Garrett, O.U.P. 1918.

A History of the Sikhs, Khushwant Singh, O.U.P., with the Princeton University Press, 1966.

Viscount Hardinge, Charles, Viscount Hardinge, 1891.

Essays Military & Political, Written In India, H. M. Lawrence, Henry Colbourn, 1859.

Leaves From The Journal of a Subaltern, D. A. Sandford,

Blackwood, 1852.

A Journal of the Sutlej Campaign, J. Coley, Smith, Elder & Co, 1856.

The Career of Major George Broadfoot, W. Broadfoot, Murray, 1888.

History of The Reigning Family of Lahore, G. Carmichael Smyth, W. Thacker & Co, 1847.

Despatches of the War In India, Lieutenant-General Viscount Hardinge, General Lord Gough, Major-General Sir Harry Smith, Ackerman, 1846.

Political & Military Events in British India, Major W. Hough, W. Allen & Co, 1853.

Forty-three Years in India, General Sir George Lawrence, John Murray, 1874.

The Bengal Artillery, Capt E. Buckle, W. H. Allen & Co, 1852.

The Second Sikh War, Capt E. J. Thackwell, London, 1851.

The Punjab Campaign, 1848/49, Major J. Lawrence-Archer, W. Allen, 1878.

The Decisive Battles of India, Col G. B. Malleson, W. Allen, 1888.

A Year On The Punjab Frontier, Major Herbert Edwardes, Bentley, 1851.

Autobiography of Sir Harry Smith, John Murray, 1902.

The Military System of The Sikhs, Fauja Singh Bajwa, Banarsidass, Delhi, 1964.

The Journal of a Cavalry Officer, Capt W. Humbley, Longmans, Brown & Green, 1854.

Memoirs of Alexander Gardner, Edited H. Pearse, Blackwood, 1898.

Origin of The Sikh Power, H. T. Prinsep, London, 1897.

Letters From India, Victor Jaquemont, London, 1834.

Mooltan, During & After The Siege, J. Dunlop, MD, 1859.

A Sketch of The Siege of Multan, J. J. Cole, London, 1849.

Four Years' Service In India, Corporal J. Ryder, Leicester, 1853.
The Court & Camp of Ranjit Singh, Capt W. G. Osborne, 1840.
Five Years In India, H. E. Fane, 1842.
Travels In The Punjab, 1845, Baron Hugel, Murray, 1850.
Thirty-five Years In The East, J. M. Honigberger, W. Allen, 1852.
Ranjit Singh, Leppel Griffin, London, 1892.
The Life of Charles Lord Metcalfe, Edward Thompson, Faber, 1937.
History of The British Army, Vol XII, Sir John Fortescue, Macmillan, 1927.
Private Correspondence Relating to The Anglo-Sikh Wars, Edited by Dr Ganda Singh, Sikh History Society, Amritsar, 1955.
A Short History of The Sikhs, Dr Ganda Singh, Sikh History Society, Amritsar.
Maharajah Ranjit Singh, Dr Ganda Singh.
The Army of Ranjit Singh, Sita Ram Kohli, Journal of Indian History, February & September, 1922: May 1923; January, April, 1926.
The Lure of the Indus, Lt-General Sir George McMunn, Jarrolds, 1934.
The Bengal Horse Artillery, Staff Sergeant Bancroft, London, 1885.
Description of a View of the Battle of Sobraon, R. Burford, 1846.
The Night of Feroseshah, Capt J. Cumming, Army Quarterly, 1937.
From Recruit to Staff Sergeant, N. W. Bancroft, London, 1880.
The First Sikh War, Brigadier Ashburton, Army Quarterly.
A History of the 50th or Queen's Own Regt, Colonel A. Fyler.
History of the 31st Foot — The East Surrey Regiment, Colonel Hugh Pearse, 1916.
History of the Bengal European Regiment (Royal Munster Fusiliers), Lieut-Colonel P. R. Innes, Simpkin, Marshall, 1885.

History of the Sixteenth, The Queens, Henry Graham, London, 1912.
History of The Norfolk Regiment, F. Loraine Petre, London, 1905.
Historical Records of the 32nd Foot, F. Swiney.
The Wiltshire Regiment, Colonel N. C. Kenrick, Gale & Polden, 1963.
Field Battery Exercises & The Movements of Artillery, War Office, 1840.
A History of India, Percival Spear, Pelican, 1965.
The Oxford Modern India, Percival Spear, O.U.P., 1967.
The Oxford History of India, Vincent Smith, 1920.
The Dictionary of National Biography.

Acknowledgement

The author and publishers are indebted to the Secretary of State for Foreign and Commonwealth Affairs for his permission to reproduce unpublished Crown-copyright material from the India Office Records.

Sapere Books is an exciting new publisher of brilliant fiction and popular history.

To find out more about our latest releases and our monthly bargain books visit our website: **saperebooks.com**

Printed in Great Britain
by Amazon